实用英汉汉英翻译教程

(医学方向)

主　编　孙俊芳　郭先英
副主编　李晓婧　郑湘瑞

东南大学出版社
SOUTHEAST UNIVERSITY PRESS
·南京·

内 容 提 要

本教材在简要介绍翻译基本概念的基础上,论述了医学翻译的原则、标准及方法,并通过丰富的例证阐述了西医、中医词汇的文化渊源、特点及翻译方法;在此基础上,本教程还介绍了医学文体的句式特征及翻译技巧,其他常用医学文体的特征及翻译方法以及在特定语境下医学文体翻译的注意事项。

本书理论讲解言简意赅,例证典型丰富,术语归纳具有代表性,融时效性、知识性及典型性于一体,可供高等教育普通英语、专门用途英语及相关专业的人士作为教材或参考用书使用。

图书在版编目(CIP)数据

实用英汉汉英翻译教程:医学方向 / 孙俊芳,郭先英主编. — 南京:东南大学出版社,2021.4
 ISBN 978-7-5641-9480-2

Ⅰ. ①实… Ⅱ. ①孙… ②郭… Ⅲ. ①医学—英语—翻译—高等学校—教材 Ⅳ. ①H315.9

中国版本图书馆 CIP 数据核字(2021)第 054540 号

实用英汉汉英翻译教程(医学方向)
SHIYONG YINGHAN HANYING FANYI JIAOCHENG(YIXUE FANGXIANG)

主　编	孙俊芳　郭先英	责任编辑	刘　坚
电　话	(025)83793329/635353748(QQ)	电子邮箱	liu-jian@seu.edu.cn
出版发行	东南大学出版社	出版人	江建中
地　址	南京市四牌楼2号	邮　编	210096
销售电话	83794561/83794174/83794121/83795801/83792174/83795802/57711295(传真)		
网　址	http://www.seupress.com	电子邮箱	press@seupress.com
经　销	全国各地新华书店	印　刷	江苏扬中印刷有限公司
开　本	787 mm×1092 mm　1/16	印　张	12.75　字　数　320千字
版　次	2021年4月第1版	印　次	2021年4月第1次印刷
书　号	ISBN 978-7-5641-9480-2		
定　价	58.00元		

* 未经许可,本书内文字不得以任何方式转载、演绎,违者必究。
* 本社图书若有印装质量问题,请直接与营销部联系。电话:025-83791830。

PREFACE 前言

　　为适应改革开放和经济建设的需要，国家近年来对翻译硕士专业学位的教育给予了大力支持，各地的专业学位建设迎来了欣欣向荣的春天，课程体系的设立、教材建设、师资培养、实践基地拓展等都呈现出勃勃生机。

　　然而笔者在执教"汉英英汉笔译实践"这门课时，发现在众多的翻译教材中，很难找到一种能够满足中医药院校翻译硕士教学需求的教材。因为对于中医药院校的翻译硕士而言，学位获得者不但要具有较强的语言运用能力、熟练的翻译技能和宽广的知识面，还要对医学专业，尤其是中医药专业领域内的翻译有所专长，这也是所有中医药院校翻译硕士培养目标中努力打造的特色。所以在教学中，既要让学生了解翻译的一般规律、原则和技巧，又要熟悉医学领域内的翻译，还要给学生大量操练的机会，提供多样化的翻译样本。针对这一需求，笔者最后决定自编讲义。几年的积累之后，就有了这本教材的雏形。

　　本书共分八章，第一章"翻译概说"阐述了翻译的概念和过程；第二章"医学翻译的'理法方要'"聚焦医学翻译的原则、标准和常用的方法；第三章和第四章分别介绍了"西医词汇及其翻译"和"中医词汇及其翻译"；第五章是"医学翻译中的句式"；第六章和第七章分两章介绍了医学文体的翻译，从一般的学术翻译、正式文体到实用的病历、说明书均有涉及；第八章"翻译与语境"再次回到宏观层面，让学生在翻译时具有语境意识，能根据语境确定语义和用词选择。整体的思路是从宏观到微观再到宏观。每一章内容后面附有练习和参考答案，书后附有中医常用四字术语的中英文对照表。

　　本书具有以下几个鲜明的特点：一是时代性，本书成书之日，正是新冠肺炎在全球肆虐之时，所以文中引入了不同中外媒体对于该病毒的时文，出现了很多与瘟疫相关的表达。希望将来历届学生学习这本教材时，都能回忆起这段难忘的经历；二是实用性，本书提供了大量的翻译语料，除了每一章后面的翻译练习外，文中也提供了多样化的译例，对于翻译硕士专业的学生非常有必要；三是人文性，有人说医学在所有科学当中最人文，在所有人文当中最科学。医学翻译自然也带有丰富的人文色彩。而中医药文本又是最富文学色彩的专业语言，所以无论是译例的选择，还是每章开头引用的中国文化典籍中相关的经典句子，都带有鲜明的人文色彩。作者也希望借着这些文字，让学生感受到翻译不是一件冷冰冰的事，而是有温度有感情的工作，即使是在进行严肃的非文学翻译时，也可以持有丰富的人文情怀："外与物化，而内不失其情。"

本书的编著团队都是翻译硕士专业的一线教师,还有一名是中医药专业的博士,以确保该教材能够符合中医药院校翻译硕士专业人才培养的发展需求。所有涉及医学方面的文献及其翻译,也都经过了专业的审定和筛选。相信在翻译硕士学位教育蓬勃发展的春天里,这本教材一定能够提供一片清新的绿叶。

本书附有课件,PPT 版本可用浏览器扫描二维码下载,PDF 版本可直接扫码播放,也可直接从出版社网站下载。

孙俊芳

2021 年 1 月 10 日

CONTENTS 目录

第一章　翻译概说 ··· 001
　　第一节　翻译的概念 ································· 002
　　第二节　翻译的过程 ································· 007
　　练习 ·· 017

第二章　医学翻译的"理法方要" ·················· 019
　　第一节　医学翻译的原则 ························· 019
　　第二节　医学翻译的标准 ························· 021
　　第三节　医学翻译的方法 ························· 024
　　练习 ·· 033

第三章　西医词汇及其翻译 ·························· 038
　　第一节　西医词汇的特点 ························· 038
　　第二节　西医词汇的翻译 ························· 043
　　练习 ·· 048

第四章　中医词汇及其翻译 ·························· 052
　　第一节　中医词汇的哲学背景 ·················· 052
　　第二节　中医词汇的特点 ························· 054
　　第三节　中医词汇的分类 ························· 055
　　第四节　中医术语的翻译 ························· 059
　　练习 ·· 063

第五章　医学翻译中的句式 ·························· 066
　　第一节　医学学术文体的句式特征 ············ 066

第二节　医学句式翻译的技巧 ··· 073
　　练习 ··· 095

第六章　医学文体翻译（一） ··· 098

　　第一节　记叙文 ·· 100
　　第二节　应用文体 ··· 104
　　第三节　科普文体 ··· 115
　　第四节　政府公文 ··· 117
　　第五节　学术性文体 ·· 119
　　练习 ··· 126

第七章　医学文体翻译（二） ··· 129

　　第一节　病历 ··· 129
　　第二节　医学评估表 ·· 138
　　第三节　药品说明书 ·· 145
　　第四节　口头医学文体 ··· 153
　　练习 ··· 158

第八章　翻译与语境 ··· 159

　　第一节　一般语境和具体语境 ··· 160
　　第二节　语境与文本翻译 ··· 163
　　练习 ··· 172

参考答案 ··· 174

参考文献 ··· 186

附录　中医常用四字术语对照 ··· 188

第一章 翻译概说

惟自古不谋万世者不足谋一时,不谋全局者不足谋一域。

——[清]陈澹然:《迁都建藩议》

Without long-term consideration, short-term strategy is impracticable; Without overall layout, regional planning is unworkable.

By Chen Danran（Qing dynasty）

君子藏器于身,待时而动。

——《周易·系辞下》

The wise conceal their talents and skills, waiting for the opportunities.

尽管这是一本关乎翻译实践的书,但是从事翻译实践的人要对翻译的本质、概念等基本理念有所了解,才不至于陷入盲目状态。

翻译几乎是和书面文献同时出现的,古时候就有专门表达翻译的词。《礼记·王制》中提到:"中国、夷、蛮、戎、狄,皆有安居、和味、宜服、利用、备器,五方之民,言语不通,嗜欲不同。达其志,通其欲,东方曰寄,南方曰象,西方曰狄鞮,北方曰译。""寄""象""狄鞮""译"就是当时负责翻译东、南、西、北四方民族语言的翻译官名,也可作翻译术语用。四者合称"象寄译鞮"、"寄象鞮译"或"鞮译象寄",泛指语言翻译,或简称为"象寄""象鞮""象译""译象""译鞮"等。

纵观我国的语言文化史,不可否认的是中国语言的发展和翻译息息相关。中国历史上曾经出现过四次翻译高潮,每一次翻译高潮都引入了一大批携带异域文化元素的表达法和新词汇。

第一次翻译高潮是从东汉到唐宋时期的佛经翻译。大量的佛教用语涌入,大大丰富了汉语的词汇。许多术语经过转化,成为日常使用频率很高的表达。如:因缘、功德、觉悟、真谛、慧根、作孽、大千世界、一尘不染、五体投地、借花献佛等。

第二次翻译高潮兴盛于明清两代。欧洲传教士和中国的读书人等一些合译了大量的科技著作,如意大利天主教传教士利玛窦曾经和徐光启合译了欧几里得的《几何原本》,此书被梁启超称为"千古不朽之作",其中徐光启厘定的许多科技译名不但至今仍在使用,还传到了韩国和日本,如:点、线、角、直线、曲线、平行线、直角、钝角、锐角、三角形、四边形、平行四边形、平面三角、球面三角等。

第三次翻译高潮出现在"五四"运动前后,主要是文学和社会科学的翻译。严复所译的《天演论》将一大批社会科学术语引入汉语,如:物竞天择（natural selection）、竞争（competition）、学说（theory）、力学（dynamics）、远因（original cause）、近因（proximate cause)、引言(introduction)、图腾(totem)等。此外,"民主"与"科学"这样的术语也在这一时期经过翻译进入汉语中,目前已成为家喻户晓的词语,很难分辨出是译入语了。

第四次翻译高潮为新中国成立后,尤其是改革开放至今的现代翻译,可谓百花齐放,方兴未艾。翻译理论蓬勃发展,翻译研究的视角得到了拓展,翻译的语种也从单一的俄语和英语为主拓展到几乎全部主要语种,翻译的作品也从以文学为主拓展到应用文体、公务文体、领导人文选等,也涌现出了诸多具有代表性的翻译理论研究专家和从事实践工作的翻译家。

实际上,英语之所以具有多源性,原因就在于通过翻译吸纳了大量其他语言的词汇。如:来自汉语的 tuina(推拿)、galingale(良姜)、ginseng(人参)、whangee(紫竹)、loquat(枇杷)、wampee(黄皮)、yin(阴)、yang(阳)、jing(精)、qi(气)、acupoint(穴位)、acupressure(针压法)、acupuncture(针刺)、moxibustion(艾灸)等;来自西班牙语的 mosquito(蚊子)、quinine(奎宁);来自德语的 zinc(锌)、nickel(镍)、bismuth(铋)、aspirin(阿司匹林)、biology(生物学)、chemotherapy(化疗)、chromosome(染色体)、gene(基因)、leukemia(白血病)、neuron(神经细胞)、schizophrenia(精神分裂)等;来自意大利语的 influenza(流感)、malaria(疟疾)、quarantine(隔离)等;来自法语的 massage(按摩)、hormone(激素)、lavage(灌洗)、benign(良性)、grand mal(癫痫大发作)、endocrine(内分泌的)、foie(肝脏)、chancre(下疳)等。

语言文化之间的交流使翻译成为必需,而翻译又促进了各国语言文化的交流与融合,丰富了语言中的词汇。

第一节 翻译的概念

翻译的概念一定程度上揭示了人们对翻译本质的理解。概括起来,人们对翻译概念的认识有以下几种:

1. 翻译即转换

从许多关于翻译的定义中可以看出,"翻译即转换"是人们对翻译最基本的认识:

翻译是许多语言活动中的一种,它是用一种语言形式把另一种语言形式里的内容重新表现出来的语言实践活动。(冯庆华,2010:1)

译,即易,谓换易言语,使相解也。　　　　　　　　——[唐]贾公彦:《周礼注疏》

英语中的 translation 一词来自拉丁语的 translatio(意思相当于"carrying across" or "bringing across")。

翻译就是"把一种语言文字的意义用另一种语言文字表达出来"。　　——《辞海》

翻译是"把已说出或写出的话的意思用另一种语言表达出来的活动"。

——《中国大百科全书·语言》

Translation is the communication of the meaning of a source-language text by means of an equivalent target-language text.(Namit,1992:1051-1054)

上述概念都将翻译界定为一种转换活动,即把源语言的信息用目的语中相应的方式表现出来。这个概念在一定程度上揭示了翻译的本质。虽然人类的语言文化千差万别,多姿多彩,但其基本思维和生活方式是相通的,这使得语际之间的转换成为可能。每种语言的核心词汇对应率是最高的,如英语中的 human、hand、face、mouth、boy、girl、man、woman、dog、desk、house、tree 和汉语的人、手、脸、嘴、男孩、女孩、男人、女人、狗、书桌、房子、树木基本对应。

英汉语言中很多词汇也是这种转换的结果:bottleneck(瓶颈)、honeymoon(蜜月)、hotbed(温床)、crocodile tears(鳄鱼的眼泪)、light year(光年)、side effect(副作用)、ostrich policy(鸵鸟政策)、grass roots culture(草根文化)、jungle law(丛林法则)、golden rule(黄金定律)等。

更加令人惊叹的是,很多民间传说、寓言故事、谚语习语、格言警句居然也惊人地相似,在一定程度上说明了文化的趋同性:

兄弟省市——sister states
空中楼阁——castle in the air
乱七八糟——at sixes and sevens
添油加醋——add spice to...
无风不起浪——There is no smoke without fire.
易如反掌——with a turn of the wrist
不尽举手之劳——not lift a finger to help
喊狼来了——cry wolf
病从口入,祸从口出——A closed mouth catches no flies.
杀鸡取卵——Kill the goose that lays the golden eggs.
颠倒黑白——turn black into white
白纸黑字——in black and white

只要熟悉两种语言的句式和表达习惯,翻译时往往稍加调整即可做到语际转换。如:
Knowledge is power. 知识就是力量。
Strike the iron when it is hot. 趁热打铁。
同病异治:different treatments for the same disease
异病同治:same treatment for different diseases

而且,这种直接转换的翻译方式也将很多外来语补充进来,丰富了汉英的词汇量。如:铁饭碗(iron bowls);white-collar workers(白领工人)。而近几年出现的 road rage(路怒)、zero tolerance(零容忍)、soft landing(软着陆)等,也是这种直接转换翻译的结果。再看下例:

"trans-"本身具有"从 A 转换到 B"或者"横过,贯穿"之意,看下面一组词:
transact 办理;交易;谈判;进行
transceiver 无线电收发器
transcend 超越,胜过
transcode 自动译码系统
transection 横断面;横切

transfection ［生］转染

transfer （使）转移，搬迁

transform *vt.* 转换；改变 *vi.* 变形；变态

transfusion 输液；输血；转移

transit *n.* 运输；运送；载运 *v.* 横越；通过；经过

translocate 改变……的位置

transmit *vt.* 传达；传染；传送 *vi.* 发送信号

transparent 透明的；显然的；明晰的

transpicuous 透明的；（语言等）清晰的；明白易懂的

transplace 改变……的位置；使互换位置

transplant *v.* 移植；移种；移民；使迁移 *n.* 移植；被移器官

transport *n.* 运输；运输机；狂喜 *vt.* 传送，运输，流放，放逐

然而，不同语言的词汇之间并非总存在一一对应的关系，这也是每种语言的魅力和独特所在。叔本华说："翻译如以此种乐器演奏原为他种乐器所谱之曲调。"既然是将一种乐器的曲调改为另一种乐器的曲调，那必然需要很多的调整和适应，这样才不至于在演奏时感到别扭。

意大利传教士利玛窦说："且东西文理，又自绝殊，字义相求，仍多阙略。了然于口，尚可勉图；肆笔为文，便成艰涩矣。"这是说，中西语言结构不同，文章脉络不同，很多术语难以找到对等词，口头解释一下还可以做到，笔译成文，就显得艰涩难懂了。如：

"Only a fool would underestimate you"就不能简单地转换为："只有傻瓜才会低估你。"而应该翻译为更加符合汉语表达习惯的句子："谁要是看轻你，谁就是傻子。"

翻译时还常常需要破句重组。如："In the doorway lay at least twelve umbrellas of all sizes and colors"应译为"门口放着一堆雨伞，少说也有十二把，五颜六色，大小不一。"

语言和文化的独特性和不可取代性有时使得这种语际转换几乎不可能。如下面这几副对联：

宝塔点灯，层层孔明，诸阁亮；

敖光举火，步步照云，照子龙。

山石岩上古木枯，此木为柴；

白水泉边女子好，少女真妙。

放心走吧，此去不论生地熟地远志莫怕路千里；

挥泪去矣，将来但闻藿香木香桂圆时节早当归。

第一副对联是谐音，第二副对联是拆字，第三副对联暗含"生地、熟地、藿香、木香、桂圆、枣（早）、当归"几种中药，很难简单地转换为英语。此外，还有一些文字游戏，如茶壶和茶杯上常见的回文"可以清心也"，"清心明目"可以任何一个字做开头，而意思不变。

所以，翻译不仅仅是简单的、机械的转换，还是艺术。

2. 翻译即艺术

再看下列翻译的定义：

Translating is the art of recomposing a work in another language without losing its original flavor. (Columbia Encyclopedia)

"翻也者,如翻锦绮,背面俱花。但其花有左右不同耳。"(《高僧传三集》)

很多匠心独运的翻译绝非语际转换那么简单,比如左飚教授提到的一个译例:

Ma is as selfless as I am. 妈妈为我,我为妈妈。(左飚,2009)

此例将原本不可译的回文译了出来,且形神兼备,不能不说是一种艺术的再现。

美国当代诗人威廉·伯福德(William Burford)所写的树形诗"A Christmas Tree",被黄杲昕以一种艺术的形式翻译了出来:

Star
If you are
A love compassionate,
You will walk with us this year.
We face a glacial distance, who are here
Huddled
At your feet.

星啊,
如果你那
爱中满含怜悯
来年就和我们同行。
我们面对冰河距离,如今
拥挤
在你脚底。

如果说"翻译即转换"更适用于非文学翻译的话,"翻译即艺术"则更适用于文学翻译。

3. 翻译即创造

"翻译是创造的,因为它赋予作品一个崭新的面貌……,赋予它第二次生命。"(埃斯皮卡,1987:137)

许多品牌的翻译往往要考虑译入语读者的接受程度、文化习惯、欣赏品味、消费倾向等,翻译时不仅仅拘泥于原文的意义甚至读音。经典的脍炙人口的品牌翻译都是创造性劳动的结果。如:Coca-Cola(可口可乐)、Clean&Clear(可伶可俐)、Lock&Lock(乐扣乐扣)、Subway(赛百味)、Best Buy(百思买)、IKEA(宜家)等。

成功的译例还有一汽大众的"家族式名称"——Sagitar(速腾)、Magotan(迈腾)、Phaeton(辉腾)系列,以及别克的 Enclave(昂科雷)、Envision(昂科威)、Encore(昂科拉),本田的 Fit(飞度)、Accord(雅阁)。它们分别将汽车的运动元素、舒适度以及安全特性凸显了出来。Jetta(捷达)、Reiz(锐志)、Veyron(威龙)、Tenna(天籁)、Scirocco(尚酷)基于原名又超越了原名,给产品消费者提供了积极的价值联想,堪称翻译中的成功之作!

一些中医词汇在英译过程中也创造了很多新词,如:acupuncture and moxibustion(针灸)、acupoint(腧穴)等,也是翻译创造性的充分体现。

4. 翻译即叛逆

翻译如以宽颈瓶中水灌注狭颈瓶中,傍倾而流失者必多。

——雨果

翻译即背叛(Tradutorre, traditore)。
　　　　　　　　　　　　　　　　　　　　　　　　　　——意大利谚语

林纾的翻译到底是译文还是"译写"？庞德翻译的汉诗到底是不是翻译？

翻译的不完整性(partiality)即不可能百分百把原文再现到目的语中。由于翻译都经过了译者的处理(manipulation)，同一原文在不同时代、不同译者手里会呈现出完全不同的风格，比如对汉诗的翻译，阿瑟·韦利(Arthur Waley)的处理是舍弃韵脚而保留内容，而许渊冲的翻译则是保留韵脚而舍弃部分内容。

即使是看似对应的翻译，也存在某种程度的"叛逆"，因为很多词表层意义是对应的，但是其构成方式和内涵不一样，给人带来的心理联想也不一样。

表1-1　翻译中的"叛逆"

汉语	英语	汉语	英语
隐形眼镜	contact lens(接触镜片)	鸡冠癣	comb disease(梳子癣)
走钢丝	walking a tightrope(走绷紧的绳子)	鸡皮疙瘩	goose flesh(鹅皮疙瘩)
溜旱冰	roller skating(轮滑)	酒糟鼻	bottle nose(瓶子鼻)
出牙期	ugly-duckling stage(丑小鸭期)	白瞳症	cat's eye reflex(猫眼症)
活字典	walking dictionary(走动的字典)	不冻港	ice-free port(不结冰的港口)
匿名账户	numbered bank account(数字账户)	自来水	running water(流动的水)
母乳喂养	breast feeding(胸脯喂养)	胞衣	afterbirth(出生之后)
人工喂养	bottle feeding(瓶子喂养)	助产士	midwife(中间女人)
葫芦状瘤	hourglass tumor(沙漏状瘤)	鸡胸	pigeon breast(鸽胸)
原发脓肿	mother abscess(母亲脓肿)	白内障	pearl eye(珍珠眼)
结节性声带炎	teacher's node(教师声带)	喉结	Adam's apple(亚当的苹果)
跟风产品	me-too product("我也"产品)	茄子	eggplant(鸡蛋植物)
农民工	migrant workers(迁移的工人)	菠萝	pineapple(松苹果)
假球	fixed game(胜负已定的比赛)	冻疮	frostbite(霜咬)

从表1-1中可以看出，不但文学翻译存在忠实与叛逆的问题，医学翻译也常常面临类似的抉择，比如中医的五脏(心、肝、脾、肺、肾)概念和西医中的heart、liver、spleen、lung、kidney并非一回事。中医认为肾藏精，主生长发育和生殖，反映在骨骼、牙齿、毛发、耳朵和二阴尤其是前阴(排尿及生殖)，而英语的kidney完全无此概念；中医的心除了"主血脉"外，还可以"主神明"，而西医的heart主要是血液循环器官；西医的liver主要是消化器官，而中医的肝除了可以调节胆汁的分泌排泄、促进脾胃对食物的消化外，还调节人体气的运动；西医的bladder仅仅是泌尿系统，而《黄帝内经》将膀胱比作"州都"，能藏"津液"，具有"气化"功能。此外,血与blood,心痛与cardialgia,脑与brain都在内涵和外延上有不同程度的区别。

然而为了迎合目的语读者的需要，降低理解的难度，只能借用英语中现成的解剖术语名称来翻译。这种方法可以追溯至明末清初西方传教士对中医典籍的翻译，他们当时的主要做法是用西医中相似的术语来翻译中医词汇,后来的许多学者也纷纷采用这种方式。李照国(2005)由此提出了"比照西医,求同存异"的翻译原则,如把中医病名"疳积"译为西医术语 infantile malnutrition(小儿营养不良),"肠痈"译作 appendicitis(阑尾炎),"石蛾"译作 chronic tonsillitis(慢性扁桃体炎),"痨瘵"译作 tuberculosis(肺结核),"里急后重"译为 tenesmus(下坠)等。然而对这一译法的争议从未停止过,原因之一就是中西医表面相似的术语在深层含义、内涵和外延上大不相同。澳大利亚的中医翻译家魏迺杰(1995)也是基于中西医术语的相异之处而提出了完全不同的翻译原则,即尽量保留中医的人文精神及中医词汇的多义性。

"忠诚"与"叛逆"似乎构成了翻译的双重性格,愚笨的"忠诚"可能会导向"叛逆",而艺术的"叛逆"可能会显出"忠诚"。(许钧,1989:1-8)

比如"无党派人士"一词,下列三种译法中第一种是最忠实的,但却不能确切地表达该词所要传达的信息。因为"无党派人士"并非指普通百姓中的非党员,而是指没有参加任何党派、对社会有积极贡献和一定影响的知名人士,故而后两种译法看似叛逆,却最忠诚。

People without party affiliation

Personages without party affiliation

Prominent citizens without party affiliation

类似的还有金庸武侠小说中的"江湖"一词,按照字面的意义可以译为 rivers and lakes,但显然无法诠释"江湖"真正的意蕴,更无法再现"江湖"二字所营造出的刀光剑影、名来利往和儿女情长,然而正如《射雕英雄传》的译者郝青玉(Anna Holmwood)所言:"翻译会产生的最大损失,只能是不翻译这本小说。"(The greatest loss that can occur in translation can only come from not translating it at all.)

第二节　翻译的过程

关于翻译的过程,译界有一些不同的提法,奈达等将之分为四步:分析、传译、重组和检验。分析(analysis)是从语法和语义方面对原文的信息进行分析;传译(transfer)是将分析过的信息从源语传译为目的语;重组(restructuring)是把传递过来的信息重组成符合要求的译语;检验(testing)则是对比译文与原文意义是否对等。(Nida & Taber, 1982:33-173)

为方便起见,我们采用大多数国内学者的提法,将翻译过程分为理解、表达、审校三个阶段。

1. 理解

理解即对源文本进行阅读、分析和总体了解。初学者在时间允许的情况下,对原文至少要阅读三遍:

第一遍粗读原文,了解全文大意,对疑难词句做上标记;第二遍细读原文,逐词、逐句、逐段地仔细研究,解决疑难问题;第三遍通读原文,以便"见树见林",将全文精神"融汇于心"。

理解是翻译过程的第一步,也是保证译文质量最关键的一步。

1) 文化背景与上下文

对源语言的文化背景、篇章背景和上下文的理解是准确翻译的关键,因为:

Each word when used in a new context is a new word.(《中国翻译》编辑部,2010:183)

如下例:

A person who apologizes has the moral ball in his court.(《中国翻译》编辑部,2010:72)

了解一点体育规则的人都应该知道,发球权在谁的一边,谁就占主动地位。此句的意思是:一个人如果道歉了,就掌握了道义上的主动权,就如球在他那边的球场上一样。因此这句话可以译为:谁给别人道歉,谁就在道义上掌握了主动。

翻译专业术语则更要在理解知识背景的基础上进行,否则寸步难行,比如中医术语带有古汉语的特征,高度概括:

司外揣内:operating the external to surmise the internal

(相关专业背景:中医学认为,人体是一个有机的整体,内脏与形体诸窍具有特定的联系,所以,通过考察相关的外在征象,即可推测内脏的功能状况。)

滋水涵木法:The method of replenishing water to nourish wood(replenishing the kidney to nourish the liver)

(相关专业背景:中医学应用五行学说,就是用事物属性的五行归类方法及其相生相克的变化规律,解释生理功能、病理现象,并指导临床诊断与治疗。肾有主水藏精的功能,故属水,肝喜条达,故属木。滋水涵木法又称滋肾养肝法。)

不内外因:即既不是内因,也不是外因的致病因素。内因指的是喜怒哀乐悲恐惊七情,外因指的是风寒暑湿燥火六淫。不内外因则指的是饮食、劳倦、外伤、房事、虫兽等致病因素,即 pathogenic factors neither endogenous nor exogenous。但是为了简化术语,将内外因合为 exoendogenous,不内外因则可以译为 non-exoendogenous pathogenic factors。(邹德芳,2016:117)

2) 语法及逻辑关系

理清原文的语法关系及上下文逻辑脉络是把握句子的关键,看下列译例:

(1) Peter hadn't really believed that Dad would be doing it.

误:小彼得实在无法相信爸爸会这么做。

正:小彼得过去一直不太相信爸爸会这么做。

(hadn't really believed 用的是过去完成时态,表示过去不相信。)

(2) But he wished to have only volunteers and to take no one on false pretences.(《中国翻译》编辑部,2010:102)

误:但是,他只要心甘情愿的人,不会接受任何虚情假意的志愿者。

正:但是,他只要志愿者,绝不以虚假的理由骗走任何人。

(on false pretences 不是 one 的后置定语,而是 take 的状语。)

(3) Why nature should conform to theories we find beautiful is far from obvious.

译文:那些打动我们的理论,往往受到自然之母的肯定,其中奥妙不可言宣。
(we find beautiful 是 theories 的后置定语,故译为打动我们的理论。)

(4) She didn't marry him because she loved him.

译文:她并非出于爱才嫁给了他。
(not...because...是比较容易产生歧义的一个句式,除了看语法,还要根据逻辑推断。)

(5) It's simple enough to say that since books have classes—fiction, biography, poetry—we should separate them and take from each what is right that each should give us.(《中国翻译》编辑部,2010:182)

It's simple enough 并非"简而言之"的意思,It 是形式主语,代指后面的整个动词不定式短语。

译文:书既然有小说、传记、诗歌之分,就应区别对待,从各类书中取其应该给予我们的东西。这话说来很简单。

汉语是意合的语言,很大程度上不依赖语法,但是一定要搞清楚逻辑脉络,尤其是古文,看《论语》中的几例:

(6) 君君,臣臣,父父,子子。(《论语·颜渊》)

本句话的意思是:做君主的要像君主的样子,做臣子的要像臣子的样子,做父亲的要像父亲的样子,做儿子的要像儿子的样子。

译文:Let the prince be a prince, the minister be a minister, the father a father and the son a son. (Arthur, 1999:131)

(7) 子曰:"里仁为美。择不处仁,焉得知?"(《论语·里仁》)

此处"里"是动词,意思是"与……为邻",和后面的"处"用法相似,意思是:孔子说:"跟仁德的人做邻居才好,如果居住时不选择住在贤德的人附近,我们又怎么能得到智慧呢?"

译文:The Master said, "Of neighborhoods benevolence is the most beautiful. How can the man be considered wise who, when he has the choice, does not settle in benevolence?"(孔兵,2010:117)

(8) 子夏曰:"贤贤易色,事父母能竭其力,事君能致其身,与朋友交言而有信。虽曰未学,吾必谓之学矣。"(《论语·学而》)

第一个"贤"是动词,第二个"贤"是名词,"贤贤"意思是:尊敬贤德的人。

译文:Tzu-hisa said, "I would grant that a man has received instruction who appreciates men of excellence where other men appreciate beautiful women, who exerts himself to the utmost in the service of his parents and offers his person to the service of his lord, and who, in his dealings with his friends, is trustworthy in what he says, even though he may say that he has never been taught."(孔兵,2010:102)

3) 习语与惯用法

如果不了解语言中的习语和惯用法,很多句子会变得匪夷所思。

(1) A woman without a man is like a fish without a bicycle. 女人不需要男人,就像鱼儿不需要自行车一样。(照样可以活得很潇洒)

此处"a fish without a bicycle"是对习语"a fish without water"的化用。

(2) His new book is strictly for the birds. 他的新书严格意义上讲没有什么意义。

"for the birds"指的是没有意义,为 bird 准备的东西一般被认为是 unacceptable。含有 bird 的习语很多,其中有褒有贬,如:dolly bird(傻美妞),old bird(行家老手),jail bird(犯人),early bird(早起的人),night bird(夜猫子),queer bird(怪人),downy bird(机灵鬼)等。

(3) It's a monster of a dog. 这是一条恶魔般的狗。/这条狗凶得跟恶魔似的。

英语习惯用同位修饰,a monster of a dog 相当于 a dog which is like a monster。

(4) It takes one to know one. 彼此彼此。

这是一个习语,表示什么样的人了解什么样的人,例如:

A:You are a stupid oaf.

B:So are you. It takes one to know one.

(5) John can be relied on. He eats no fish and plays the game. 约翰为人可靠,他既忠诚又正直。

(6) He is so rude and has no class at all. 他太粗鲁了,真是一点风度都没有。

class 可以表示社会等级、类别以及优雅风度。所以,"you have no class"意为"你可真没风度"。类似表达还有:

She has class all right and she looks like an artist. 她还挺风姿典雅的,看上去像一位艺术家。

Jack and Jill:男男女女;

cock and bull story:无稽之谈;bite the thumbs at... 对……嗤之以鼻;Cabbages and Kings 东拉西扯

在翻译过程中,目的语中有现成习惯表达的尽量使用。如:to address the pressing need of... 可以译为"以解燃眉之急"。

4) 词语意义

翻译中的很多错误是由误解词义造成的。"不更衣"并非指不换衣服,而是指"便秘"。"上工治未病"并非指"优秀的工人",而是指"优秀的医生"。再看下列例句:

(1) The stone verticals corresponded, one human-shaped, the other natural.

译文:两道石壁遥相呼应,一边人工打造,一边浑然天成。

U-shaped 译为 U 形,V-shaped 译为 V 形,但是此处 human-shaped 不是指"像人形的",而是指"人工打造的",正如"猪肉松、牛肉松"和"儿童肉松"不可类推一样。

(2) The thirty-two chapters of a novel—if we consider how to read a novel first—are an attempt to make something as formed and controlled as a building. (《中国翻译》编辑部,2010:183)

"controlled"一词一般意为"控制、驾驭",但还有 regulate(使条理化)的意思。

译文:不妨先来谈谈如何读小说吧。一部长篇小说分成三十二章,是作者的苦心经营,想把它建构得如同一座错落有致、布局合理的大厦。

(3) Garlic is a healthy food that may have some antimicrobial properties. However, there is no evidence from the current outbreak that eating garlic has

protected people from the novel coronavirus.

译文：大蒜是一种健康食品，具有一定的抗菌特性。然而，目前的疫情没有证据表明食用大蒜可以保护人们免受新型冠状病毒的侵袭。

此处"novel"显然不是指"小说"，而是指"新型的"。

（4）简其平日所服，寒凉者十六，补肝肾者十三。（《杂病广要》）

古汉语中"十六"可以用来表示十分之六，"十三"表示十分之三。

译文：When daily administration of medicines is examined, six out of ten are those cold in nature, and three out of ten are those for tonifying liver and lung.

（5）奇方者，宜下不宜汗。

译文：A formula with ingredients odd in number is for purgation, and not for diaphoresis.

"奇方"指"药味为单数的方剂"，并非"奇怪的药方"，故根据意思译成"a formula with ingredients odd in number"。

（6）丈夫八岁，肾气实，发长齿更；二八，肾气盛，天癸至，精气溢泻，阴阳和，故能有子；三八，肾气平均，筋骨劲强，故真牙生而长极；四八，筋骨隆盛，肌肉满壮；五八，肾气衰，发堕齿槁；六八，阳气衰竭于上，面焦，发鬓颁白；七八，肝气衰，筋不能动，天癸竭，精少，肾藏衰，形体皆极；八八，则齿发去。（《素问》）

此处"丈夫"不可望文生义译为"husband"，"二八"指的是十六岁。

译文：For a man, at the age of eight, his Shenqi(Kidney-Qi) becomes prosperous and his teeth begin to change…（李照国，2005：5-7）

同样，中医词汇中的女子胞就是子宫的意思，不能译为 female cell，而应译为 womb/uterus。五体在中医中即形体，其广义者，泛指具有一定形态结构的组织，包括头、躯干和脏腑在内；其狭义者，指皮、肉、筋、骨、脉五种组织结构，又称五体，所以五体应译为 five body constituents，而非 five bodies。

对于一些缩略词，更要搞清楚词义再着手翻译。如："三资企业"指的是三类外商投资企业，包括"在中国境内设立的中外合资经营企业、中外合作经营企业、外商独资经营企业"，因此可以译为 Chinese-foreign joint ventures, cooperative enterprises and exclusively foreign-owned enterprises 或 Sino-foreign joint ventures, cooperative businesses and exclusively foreign-owned enterprises in China。

英语中还有很多词加 s 之后发生了变化，要特别注意，如：goods（商品），colors（旗帜），ices（冰激凌），irons（镣铐），greens（蔬菜），spirits（酒精），letters（文学），oils（油画），quarters（住处），futures（期货），waters（海域，水域）等。

5）修辞及歧义

对原文的修辞手法进行分析，可以避免歧义，如下文中和"吃"有关的修辞用法：

饭桶 good-for-nothing

吃不开 be unpopular

吃不了兜着走 land oneself in serious trouble

吃不消 be unable to stand

吃不住 be unable to bear or support

吃老本 live off one's past gains

吃软不吃硬 be open to persuasion but not to coercion

吃闲饭 lead an idle life

吃香 be very popular

他砸了我的饭碗 He has taken the bread out of my mouth.

2. 表达

表达即用目的语转换及重现原文。原文的意思理解了,接下来就是如何用目的语来表达。严复曾感叹"一名之立,旬月踟蹰",表达需要考虑多方面的因素。

1) 译入语的逻辑与习惯:规范性与可接受性

Marriage is the classic betrayal.

译文:婚姻真是一种古典的背叛。(《中国翻译》编辑部,2010:97)

该译文意思表达不够清楚,应改译为:

婚姻啊,从古到今,都意味着背叛。

如果译入语中能用习语表达源语言意义的,即使源语言没有使用习语,也可以尽量使用,以增加译文的亲和力。如:

It(the army) cost roughly a quarter of one percent of today's military juggernaut and looked at it.

译文:当时军费开支仅仅约为今天的庞大开支的千分之二点五上下;果然,一分钱,一分货。(王宗炎译)

该译文将原来的"looked at it"译为汉语的习语"一分钱,一分货"显得非常老到。据王宗炎先生自己说,此处原来的译文是"军容极差",后来他采纳了别人的建议改为"一分钱,一分货",顿时增色不少。(朱明炬等,2010:11)

英译汉中人名的处理往往采用音译,但是字的选择要尊重汉语命名的习惯。如:Lia译为"丽娅"(而非"力呀"),Jimmy译为"吉米"(而非"鸡米")。同样,地名、国名的音译选字也遵照中国人尚美的倾向,如:英国(而非"硬国"),美国(而非"米国"),澳大利亚(而非"饿死他了"),德国(而非"桀国")。

汉语从外来语中借来的词则通过加偏旁部首的方式,很容易就完成了汉化,使中国读者一望而知:

金属:镁、钾、钠、铬、锰、钙、锶、钡、钴、镍、锑、镉、铋、钌、铑、钯、锇

气体:氧、氦、氩、氙、氪、氖、氮

翻译时译者要始终将译入语读者的感受装在心里,考虑他们的接受能力和理解能力。如:"新中国成立以来"如果译为"since the founding of New China",很容易让西方读者产生误解,不如翻译为"since the founding of PRC/since 1949/since the founding of the People's Republic of China in 1949"。

此外翻译带有典故的句子更要考虑读者的接受能力,如:"以韦编三绝、悬梁刺股的毅力,以凿壁偷光、囊萤映雪的劲头……"这句话包含了六个典故、六个人物,其中,"韦编三绝"来自《史记·孔子世家》:"孔子晚而喜易……读易,韦编三绝";"悬梁刺股"的主人

公是孙敬和苏秦,典自《战国策》;"凿壁偷光"指的是匡衡;"囊萤"指的是车胤、"映雪"指的是孙康,均来自《萧淑兰》。翻译时不可能在一句话中将这些典故一一再现,所以采用简化的方式,将其译为"with the strong will of Confucius, Sun Jing and Su Qin, the strength of Kuang Heng, Che Yin and Sun Kang(带脚注)……"。

2) 褒贬和轻重:与源语在信息上的对等

译文应该是原文信息的再现,力戒藻饰。

(1) I smooth out the snapshot and look into his face, and do and do not see my own.(《中国翻译》编辑部,2010:98)

原译:我把其中一张照片轻轻抚平,凝视着祖父的脸,隐隐约约发现自己的影子。(原文表达作者端详祖父照片时,感觉又像自己又不像的心理过程。)

改译:我抚平照片,注视着祖父的脸,依稀看到自己的影子,又似乎没有。

(2) an aerial photograph of the site for a shopping center my father did not build in 1954(《中国翻译》编辑部,2010:98)

原译:一张我父亲没有在1954年建设的购物中心地址的航拍照片

此译文显得别扭、生硬,令人难以理解。

改译:一张从空中拍摄的选址照片,1954年父亲曾打算在那儿建购物中心。

(3) 法律是治国之重器。"重器"不宜译为 great weapon,语气太重,可以译为:

The law is of great value in the governance of a country.

Law matters in the governance of a country.

The law is an indispensable tool in the governance of a country.

(4) 韬光养晦

to hide our capabilities and wait for our time

to hide one's ability and pretend to be weak

to conceal one's fame and ability

to conceal glory and continue strength building

to hide one's light

以上几种译法均显得阴险狡诈,给人带来不好的感受,故宜淡化处理,译为 to keep a low profile 即可。

(5) 中国共产党和八个民主党派

若译为"Communist Party of China and eight democratic parties",给人的感觉是中国共产党是专制不民主的党派,应该改译为"CPC and eight non-Communist parties"或者"CPC and eight other political parties"。

3) 语体风格:严谨与优雅

翻译时要在理解的基础上弄清原文的语体风格:有的是正式语体;有的是非正式语体;有的结构复杂,句式长而严密;有的则以对话为主,句式简短;有的辞藻华丽;有的则平易朴实;有的还有很多俚语。翻译时要尽可能与原文在风格上保持一致。

阅读源语言时要把其中的人物身份和关系搞清楚,这样翻译时才能确保与其语言风格相称。

弗洛伊德·德尔(Floyd Dell)的小说《毛毯》(*The Blanket*)中有这样一句话:"There will be few blankets there the equal of this one",有人将之译为"那里能与之媲美的毯子将寥寥无几"。而将另一处"He'll be feeling young again, with a pretty wife like that"中的"pretty wife"译为"娇妻",均不太恰当。因为这些话是爷爷对孙子说的,所以可将前一句译为"那地方哪有这么好的毛毯啊",后一句译为"有这么个漂亮妻子,他又会觉得年轻了"。改译后更符合人物的身份和口吻。

3. 审校

审校是对译文的行文进行润色加工,点睛出神。审校不仅要检查译文有无遗漏丢失、错译误译、前后矛盾、关系混乱、文体逻辑等方面的问题,还要润色文字,在译文的"传达"上下功夫,力求用词贴切,文从字顺,增强译语的可读性。

审校时要重点检查:在数字、日期、距离、方位以及名称等方面有无漏译,有无误译,有无逻辑不通、行文不顺之处,有无误用标点符号之处。通常要校核两遍。第一遍重点看内容,第二遍重在文字润饰。

具体地,主要从以下几方面对译文进行审校:

1) 是否有信息添加、走样或者缺失的地方

(1) mounted the steps

原译:迈上台阶(未能将原文的复数表现出来,只是一个一次性的动作)

改译:拾级而上

(2) 所谓主色,是指人终生不改变的基本肤色、面色。由于民族、禀赋、体质不同,每个人的肤色不完全一致。中国人属于黄色人种,一般肤色都呈微黄,在此基础上,有些人可有略白、较黑、稍红等差异。

原译:The so-called chief color is a person's basic skin color which does not change in his life. Because of the different races, endowments and constitutions, each person's skin color is not completely consistent. Chinese people belong to the yellow race, so the general color is slightly yellow on the basis of which some people have a slightly white, black, red and other differences.

改译:The so-called chief color is a person's basic skin color which does not change in his life. Because of difference in races, endowments and constitutions, <u>one person's skin color is not identical with another</u>. Chinese people belong to the yellow race, so the general color is slightly yellow on the basis of which some people slightly show white, black, red and other differences.

原文"每个人的肤色不完全一致"并非指一个人的肤色会出现前后不一致的现象,而是指"不完全相同",原译的"each person's skin color is not completely consistent"信息走样,故改译为"one person's skin color is not identical with another"。另外,"有些人可有略白、较黑、稍红等差异"均指程度轻微,故改译为"some people slightly show white, black, red and other differences"。

2) 逻辑是否分明

逻辑是否分明即译文是否如实反映出了原文的逻辑关系,尤其是汉语,往往逻辑关

系是内隐的,英译时需要理顺关系,将隐藏的脉络表现出来。

（1）多渠道灵活就业

原译：multiple channels and flexible employment（从逻辑性来看,"灵活就业"是通过"多渠道"得以实现的。）

改译：flexible employment through multiple channels

（2）环境污染问题严重

原译：In addition, the problem of environmental pollution is also very serious...（environmental pollution本身就是一个problem,无须译出该词,为冗余信息。）

改译：In addition, environmental pollution is also very serious...

（3）促进产业结构优化升级

原译：The promotion of the upgrading and optimization of the industrial structure...（原因同上,the promotion of 为冗余信息。）

改译：The upgrading and optimization of the industrial structure...

（4）掌心皮肤燥裂,疼痛,迭起脱屑,称鹅掌风。

原译：Palm skin cracks due to dryness resulting in pain and frequent desquamation, which is called tinea unguium.

改译：The dry cracked palm skin resulting in pain and frequent desquamation is called tinea unguium.

3）译文是否有歧义

翻译中的歧义有两种情况,一是译文本身容易引起歧义。如：

During the four-year period about 600 years ago, the Black Death killed at least 25 million people in Europe.

原译：大约600年前黑死病在四年中至少使2 500万欧洲人死亡。

改译：在大约600年前一次为期四年的流行期中,黑死病至少使2 500万欧洲人丧生。

原译容易让人理解为600年前,只要发生黑死病,每四年就会有2 500万欧洲人死亡。

二是译文的首字母缩略容易产生歧义。如：

国家互联网信息办公室

原译：Cyberspace Affairs Office of China（CAOC）（缩略词容易令人产生不好的联想）

　　　State Cyberspace Affairs Office（SCAO）（同上）

　　　Cyberspace Affairs Administration of China（CAAC,和中国民航局同）

改译：Cyberspace Administration of China（CAC）

4）语言是否流畅

（1）How often do we reflect on the joy of breathing easily, of swallowing without effort and discomfort, of walking without pain, of a complete and peaceful night's sleep.（《中国翻译》编辑部,2010:165）

原译：我们多么经常思考轻松地呼吸的乐趣,不费劲地自在吞食的乐趣,没有痛苦地行走的乐趣和一个完整的夜晚安静睡眠的乐趣。

改译：平时呼吸轻松,吞食自如,走路毫不费劲,一夜安寝到天明,我们几曾回味过其中的乐趣?

(2) What would doctors say, for example, to a 46-year-old man coming in for a routine physical checkup just before going on vacation with his family who, though he feels in perfect health, is found to have a form of cancer that will cause him to die within six months? (*To Lie or Not to Lie: The Doctor's Dilemmas*)(季佩英,孙庆祥,2012:29)

原译:医生应该说什么呢?例如一个46岁的在和家人去度假之前来做例行身体检查的尽管感觉良好的男人发现得了一种可以六个月内使他死亡的癌。

改译:例如,一个46岁的男子,在和家人去度假之前,进行常规体检,尽管他感觉非常健康,但医生发现他患有某种癌症,只能活六个月。医生应该怎么对他说呢?

(3) I stopped. Something happened.(《中国翻译》编辑部,2010:76)

原译:我停下来,一些事情发生了。(这句话描写作者登山览胜时的经历,紧接着作者开始描述看到的奇观。因此此处的 something 不是一般意义上的"一些事情、某件事情",而应该理解为"奇观、胜景、不同寻常的景观"。)

改译:我停下脚步,奇观出现了。

(4) The Negro lives on a lonely island of poverty in the midst of a vast ocean of material prosperity.

原译:黑人依然生活在物质富裕的汪洋大海中贫乏的孤岛上。

改译:黑人仍生活在贫困的孤岛上,尽管放眼四周,是一片繁华的景象。

(5) 我国多家企业正在临时雇用因为新冠疫情而没有复工或仅部分复工企业的员工。这些员工被称为"共享员工",他们受雇于超市、电商零售店以及其他公司或工厂以缓解用工荒。

原译:Many enterprises in China are temporarily employing employees who have not returned to work or only part of them have returned to work because of the novel coronavirus epidemic. These employees, known as "shared employees," (gongxiang yuangong in Chinese), are employed in supermarkets, e-commerce retail stores, and other companies or factories to alleviate the labor shortage.

改译:Several Chinese companies are temporarily hiring—or "sharing"—employees from businesses that haven't resumed operations or are only partially operating due to concerns over the novel coronavirus epidemic. The so-called shared employees, known as gongxiang yuangong in Chinese, are being hired by supermarkets, e-commerce platforms' retail stores, and other companies or factories to ease the workforce crunch.

原译的"employing employees""who have not returned to work or only part of them have returned to work because of the novel coronavirus epidemic"等处显得不太流畅自然。

练 习

Ⅰ. 翻译下列短语（英译汉）

(1) sophisticated man

(2) sophisticated columnist

(3) sophisticated electronic device

(4) sophisticated weapon

(5) English disease

(6) Irish promotion

(7) bloodthirsty

(8) homesick

(9) hot-tempered

(10) drip-feed

(11) declaration of health information

(12) concentrated observation

(13) curb the cross-border spread of the epidemic

(14) epidemic prevention at borders

(15) sporadic cases

Ⅱ. 翻译下列句子（英汉互译）

(1) Translation is an exchange between two cultures. For a real successful translation, knowing two cultures is more important than grasping two languages, because words become meaningful only in its effective cultural background. (Eugene Nida)

(2) Translation should give a complete transcript of the ideas of the original work. The style and manner of writing should be of the same character as that of the original. A translation should have all the ease of the original composition. (Alexander Fraser Tytler)

(3) It is rendering the meaning of a text into another language in the way that the author intended the text. Common sense tells us that this ought to be simple, as one ought to be able to say something as well in one language as in another. On the other hand, you may see it as complicated, artificial and fraudulent, since by using another language you are pretending to be someone you are not. The translation cannot simply reproduce, or be, the original. And since this is so, the first business of the translator is to translate. (Peter Newmark)

(4) Some professional translators take considerable pride in denying that they have any theory of translation—they just translate. In reality, however, all people engaged in the complex task of translating possess some type of underlying or covert theory,

even though it may be still very embryonic and described only as just being "faithful to what the author was trying to say."(Eugene Nida)

（5）A good translation is one which the merit of the original work is so completely transfused into another language as to be as distinctly apprehended and as strongly felt by a native of the country to which that language belongs as it is by those who speak the language of the original work. (Alexander Fraser Tytler)

（6）许多人喜欢中餐，在中国，烹饪不仅被视为一种技能，而且也被视为一种艺术。由于食物对健康至关重要，好的厨师总是努力在谷物、肉类和蔬菜之间取得平衡，所以中餐既味美又健康。

（7）闻名于世的丝绸之路是一条连接东西方的路线，丝绸之路代表了古代中国的丝绸贸易。如今，茶是世界上最流行的饮料（beverage）之一，茶是中国的瑰宝，也是中国传统和文化的重要组成部分。

Ⅲ．审阅并修改下列译文

（1）这一理论在养生防病方面非常重要，有指导意义。

译文：This theory is very important for the guiding significance for health preserving and disease prevention.

（2）脾与胃的关系，体现为水谷纳运相得、气机升降相因、阴阳燥湿相济三个方面。

译文：The relationship of them manifests in the coordination of containing and transporting foodstuff, ascending and descending qi, yin, yang, dryness, and moisture.

（3）肾中藏的精气，主要有两方面来源：一是来源于父母的生殖之精，就是我们通常说的"先天之精"；二是来源于人出生后，机体从饮食中摄取的营养成分和脏腑代谢所化生的精微物质，就是我们所说的"后天之精"。

译文：The essence stored in the kidney has two main sources: the first one which is from the parental reproductive essence is called the "congenital essence"; the other one, the nutrient acquired from diet after birth and subtle substance metabolized by viscera, is called "acquired essence".

（4）可是我从头到脚淋成了落汤鸡。

译文：But I was drenched from head to foot like a chicken in the soup.

（5）The resounding success of the Cucarao experiment whetted the appetites of Florida livestock raisers for a similar feat that would relieve them of the scourge of screw-worm.

译文：库卡索岛上的实验的巨大成功引起了佛罗里达州牲畜养殖者的兴趣，用相似的办法来缓解螺旋锥蝇的祸害。

第二章 医学翻译的"理法方要"

工欲善其事,必先利其器。　　　　　　　　　　　　　　　　　　　《论语·卫灵公》
A craftsman, if he means to do good work, must first sharpen his tools. (translated by Arthur Waley)

外与物化,而内不失其情。　　　　　　　　　　　　　　　　　　　　　　《淮南子》
Externally we may use materialized methods, yet internally we maintain the spiritual pursuits.
　　　　　　　　　　　　　　　　　　　　　　　　　　　　　　　　　　（编者译）

任何一门学科都有规律可循、有方法可依、有原则可依,医学翻译同样如此。下文将从翻译的原则、标准和方法来探究医学翻译的"理法方要"。

第一节 医学翻译的原则

早在2004年,中医翻译的领军人物李照国就提出中医名词术语的几个翻译原则,虽然几经修改,但至今依然有一定的指导意义。(牛喘月,2004)

1. 自然性原则

自然性原则即考虑到自然科学的共同之处,使用英语中自然的对应语来翻译中医术语,如:带下医译为 gynecologist(妇科医生),牛皮癣译为 psoriasis(银屑病),瘰疬译为 tuberculosis of cervical lymph node(颈部淋巴结核),脱肛译为 prolapse of rectum(直肠脱垂),瘿译为 thyroid enlargement(甲状腺肿大)。虽然这些西医病名和中医术语有不同之处,其相似性依然是显而易见的。

2. 简洁性原则

中医用语的一大特点就是简明扼要,译为英语后要尽量保留这一特点。因此,在科技名词术语的翻译上,既要注重译文意义的准确性,又要注重译文的信息密度,不能太冗长拖沓,否则名词术语就不是术语了,完全成了句子甚至段落。

比如"辨证论治"这一术语,以前比较流行的译法是"differential diagnosis in accordance with the eight principal syndromes" "analyzing and differentiating pathological conditions in accordance with the eight principal syndromes"等。现在常被简化为"syndrome differentiation and treatment"。或者:treatment based on syndrome differentiation.

句子翻译也要遵循简洁性原则。如:"Old people lie down but have difficulty in falling into sleep"可以译为"老人卧而不寐"。

3. 民族性原则

广义上讲,大部分中医术语都处于人类语言的"共核"之中,但也有一部分是汉语或中医所特有的,很难在英语中找到"对应词"。这部分词所占比例较少,却极为重要。因为它反映着中医基本理论的核心及辨证论治的要旨,翻译时一般采用音译来解决。如:yin,yang,qi 等。

还有一部分中医用语在英语中似乎有对应语,如:表里(external,internal),风寒暑湿燥火(wind,cold,summer-heat,dampness,dryness,fire)。但是这些英语的概念却没有中医的特定内涵。再如英语中有 heart 和 fire,却没有 heart-fire 这样一个概念。翻译时一般借用这些英语中固有的词汇,按照中医概念的特定内涵重新组合其结构形式,使其承载中医概念的信息,比如将"肾虚"译为"kidney deficiency"等。这些翻译虽然流于表面,但是相信经过不断的交流磨合,必能达到"形"与"意"的有机结合。

4. 回译性原则

所谓回译性原则,指的是英译的中医名词术语在结构上应与中文形式相近。这样在中医药的国际交流中,就能较好地实现信息的双向传递。如:将"活血化瘀"译为"activating blood to resolve stasis",将"湿热"译为"damp-heat",等等。英译的中医术语与原文相比,在结构上和字面意义上都比较接近,因而具有一定的回译性,这样的翻译称为回译性翻译。

之所以要强调回译性,原因有三:其一是具有回译性的译语有利于翻译人员准确地传递信息,有利于我国中医人员能较快、较好地掌握中医英语;其二是具有回译性的译语能较为准确地再现原文所含信息,减少翻译过程中对信息的损益程度;其三是强调译语的回译性有利于提高翻译质量,限制滥译。当然,对回译性的追求以不影响信息的再现为前提。

但是,因为中医药语言不同于其他科学术语,其词句结构和英文表达方式明显不同,所以很难强调这一点。如:"痹症"在英语里没有一个对应词,有人译为"arthralgia syndrome",回译回去就是"关节痛证",如果按原意翻译,应该是"joint and muscular disorders with pain due to wind, cold or dampness",……简化为"impediment syndrome",依然无法满足回译的要求。

5. 规定性原则

规定性原则指的是对中医名词术语的翻译在内涵上加以限定,使其不能另有解释。提出这样一个原则主要是为了解决中医名词术语翻译上内涵的对等问题。

在翻译中医名词术语时,我们可以对其译语的内涵加以规定。这样既可以保证释义的一致性,又能消除种种误解。如:"辨证"尽管一般多被译作"syndrome differentiation",但对这一译法历来争论不休。有人认为中医的证不同于西医的 syndrome。但是,如果我们从名与实的辨证关系出发来考虑问题,便可以将 syndrome differentiation 加以规定,规定其只能表达中医辨证这个概念,不能作任何其他的解释。在这一规定下,译语的内涵与原语的内涵便趋于相等。在约定俗成的力量作用下,这一规定很快便成为习惯。比如世界卫生组织对针灸经穴名称的国际标准化，实际上就是一种规定。它规定三焦的英语译名为 triple energizer，经脉的译名为 meridian，冲脉的译名为 thoroughfare vessel，等等。如果我们将其英语译名与中文原文加以比较，便会发现诸多不相对应或不相吻合之处。然而由于对它们的内涵作了规定，所以并没有在实际的交流中引起人们想象中的混乱不堪。这就是规定性原则的作用所在。

厘定中医药术语翻译的原则对于术语的统一性起着非常重要的作用。一门术语混乱的学科，是很难登上国际学术舞台的，中医药要走向世界，统一规范的术语是交流的前提，是中医推广的前提。

当然，这些原则随着翻译实践的推进，也在不断得到补充、更新和完善，还有很多尚待解决的问题，比如回译性原则是否一定要坚持，在何种程度上坚持等。

第二节 医学翻译的标准

翻译是语际交流的桥梁，它的任务是把原文信息的思想内容及表现手法，用译语原原本本地重新表达出来，使译文读者能够得到与原文读者大致相同的感受。译文读者和原文读者的感受大致相同或近似，就是好的或比较好的译文；相去甚远或完全不同，则是质量低甚至是不合格的译文。从翻译效果，也就是以译文读者得到的感受如何来衡量一篇译文的好坏，这就是翻译的标准。

关于翻译的标准，无论是严复的信、达、雅（faithfulness, expressiveness and elegance），尤金·奈达（Eugene Nida）的功能对等（functional equivalence），傅雷的神似（spiritual conformity）还是钱钟书的化境（sublimed adaptation），不外乎以下几个方面：

1. 忠于原作

忠于原作即不能任意歪曲、窜改、增删、遗漏，不能加上译者的观点和感情。其中"忠实"是第一位的，指译文要准确表达出原作的思想、内容和语体风格。译者必须把原作的内容完整而准确地表达出来，不得有任何窜改、歪曲、遗漏或者任意增减的现象。要实现译文忠实于原作，首先便要对原文有正确的理解，吃透原文的词义、语法关系和逻辑关系。看以下例句：

（1）Scientists defined the temperature requirements necessary for survival of the black carp.

原译：科学家们规定了青鱼生存的必需温度。

改译：科学家们查明了青鱼生存所需的温度。

（2）目的是要领导干部年轻化。

原译：The aim is to make our leaders younger.

改译：The aim is to ensure that more young people will rise to positions of leadership.

（3）He is physically weak but mentally sound.

原译：他身体虽弱，但思想健康。

改译：他身体虽弱，但精神尚佳。

（4）心是君主之官，五脏六腑之大主，自然不能随便被打扰，一般由心包代其行使功能。

原译：The heart, as the monarch governing five zang-and six fu-organs, could not be disturbed randomly, so its functions are conducted by pericardium.

改译：The heart, as the monarch governing five zang-and six fu-organs, could not be disturbed casually, so its functions are conducted by pericardium.

randomly字面上有"随意"的意思，但重在随机性和无计划性，而casually则有随便的含义，与原文更加接近。

（5）先天之精和后天之精虽然来源不同，但都同归于肾，两者相互依存、相互为用，不可分割。

原译：Although the congenital essence and acquired essence have the different sources, both of them attributing to the kidney are interdependent, mutually used and indivisible.

改译：Although the congenital essence and acquired essence have the different sources, they both pertain to the kidney, and they are interdependent, mutually used and inseparable.

indivisible指的是内部不可再进一步切分，而inseparable指的是两者不可分开，更符合原意。

2. 语言通顺流畅

语言通顺流畅即译文通俗、合乎行文习惯，不生搬死译。看以下例句：

（1）It is now thought that the more work we give our brain, the more work they are able to do.

原译：现在人们认为，我们让脑子工作得越多，它就能干更多的工作。

改译：现在人们认为，脑子越用越好使。

原译有明显的欧化现象，不符合汉语的行文表达习惯。

（2）肺主呼吸是一身之气的主要来源和体现，民间通过观察鼻部的气体出入，以"有气没气"来作为生命活动的重要现象。呼吸微弱，气生成不足，自然少气无力。肺有节律的呼吸（宣发和肃降），调节着全身气的向上、向外、向下、向内等升降出入运动。

原译：The lung governing respiratory qi is the main source and manifestation of qi of the whole body. Chinese people usually through observing gas coming into or out of nasal passage consider "whether there is gas or not" as an important phenomenon of life activities. Weak breathing and lack of gas generation can cause dispirited. Rhythmic breath(dispersing and descending) regulates motion of the whole body's qi to go upward, outward, downward and inward.

改译：The lung governing respiratory qi is the main source and manifestation of qi of the whole body. Through observing air coming into or out of nasal passage Chinese people usually consider "whether there is air or not" as an important sign of life activities. Weak breathing and lack of qi generation <u>result in feebleness</u>. Rhythmic breath (dispersing and descending) regulates motion of the whole body's qi to go upward, outward, downward and inward.

(3) 机体的生、长、壮、老与肾中精气的盛衰密切相关。

原译：The body's birth, growth, <u>being strong</u> and <u>getting old</u> are closely related with the rise and fall of kidney essence.

改译：The body's birth, growth, <u>maturity</u> and <u>aging</u> are closely related with the rise and fall of kidney essence.

(4) 肾精亏虚，髓海失充者，易出现恐惧的情志病变。临床上多从肾论治。

原译：Deficient kidney essence-qi and insufficient Marrow Sea is apt to getting emotional disease, such as fear. Clinically, many of them are treated from the kidney.

改译：<u>People with deficient</u> kidney essence-qi and insufficient Marrow Sea <u>are</u> apt to conducting emotional disease, such as <u>panic</u>. Clinically, many of them are treated from the kidney.

3. 保持原作风格

保持原作风格即尽量保持原作的语体风格、民族风格和个人风格。看以下例句：

(1) 严禁学生提前返校。校园要实行封闭管理，禁止校外人员进入，不组织大型集体活动。

译文：Closed-end management is required and people from outside are not allowed to enter.

(2) 对农贸市场、商场、超市等生活必需类场所及酒店、宾馆等生活服务类场所，在精准有序推动开业的同时，严格落实环境卫生整治、消毒、通风、"进出检"、限流等措施。

译文：Public areas, including markets, shopping malls and hotels, need to restrict the flow of people and strictly conduct disinfection and ventilation while open for business.

由于英汉两种语言在风格上的差异，保持原作风格只是相对而言，汉语中常用的二四八结构很难在英语中表现出来。如：

各地要指定发热门诊、定点收治医院开展发热病人筛查，及时诊断并隔离治疗新冠肺炎病例，做到"应检尽检""应收尽收""应治尽治"。

译文：Fever clinics and hospitals are designated to keep screening fever patients and isolating COVID-19 patients for therapy to make sure all patients are examined, admitted to hospitals and treated.

语体风格方面表现为尽量以诗译诗，以文译文。比如下面这段话有很多不同风格的译文：

My enemies are many, my equals are none. In the shade of olive trees, they said Italy could never be conquered. In the land of Pharoahs and kings, they said Egypt could never be humbled. In the realm of forest and snow, they said Russia could never be tamed. Now they say nothing. They fear me, like a force of nature, a dealer in thunder and death. I say I am Napoleon, I am emperor... Burn it!

译文1：我树敌无数，却从未逢对手。在橄榄树荫下，他们说意大利永远不会被征服。在法老和国王的土地上，他们说埃及永远不会臣服。在森林与暴雪的国度，他们说俄国永远不会被征服。现在他们已无话可说。他们畏惧我，如同畏惧带来雷霆和死亡的自然的力量。我就是拿破仑，我就是皇帝……烧掉它！

译文2：吾敌者众，橄榄荫之意，曾言未可征，法老万丈国，誓书绝不臣。林海雪原深处，俄之不败如神。俱往矣，唯今皆为庙堂之下，俯首叩拜。吾之天命皇者，吾名拿破仑，天之子也，燃尽天下皆为我枕！

译文3：朕之仇寇多矣，然敌手则未之有也。大秦、大食、罗刹，皆自诩不可胜之，而今寂然。彼畏朕，犹若畏天。朕，天之子也……焚！

译文4：朕树敌无数，平生未遇对手。油榄树之荫，或曰意大利不可战胜；法老与诸王之地，或曰埃及永不屈服；莽林白雪之国，或曰俄罗斯誓不低头。今日，人皆词穷无语。尔等惧朕，如天地之力，雷电死神。朕为拿破仑，九五之尊……焚之！

译文5：（古词版：破阵子）数载干戈快意，一生刀剑称雄。闻有榄枝折不易，难渡黄沙却王公。北原尽雪熊。青树摧自铁蹄，诸侯屠于强弓。且看九州谁不惧，划地指天亦从容。（焚）克里姆林宫！

尽管欣赏这些译文是一件很有趣的事，然而不得不承认，有些译文离原作的风格太远，显然不能称其为恰当的翻译。

再如人们常常把"Talk of the devil and he comes"翻译为"说曹操，曹操到"，但是在英语语言文化的背景下出现这样的名字会显得不伦不类。林纾的译作受到诟病的很大原因也在于他把原作的情节完全置于中国文化的语言和背景之下，已经超出翻译的范畴了。在形、意、风格与效果上与原文完全吻合是翻译的理想境界，是翻译工作的努力方向，而最低标准是译文起码应该达到的水平，低于这个水平就是不合格的翻译，失败的翻译。

翻译既是一门科学，又是一门艺术，翻译的复杂性和严肃性对译者素质也提出了较高的要求。一个成功的译者首先需要有较高的语言水平，包括英语水平和汉语水平，能够娴熟地驾驭两种语言；其次需要有一定的专业知识，不至于误读误解原文；最后还需要有一定的现代技术水平，能够使用现代化的翻译技术来提高翻译效率和准确性。

第三节 医学翻译的方法

翻译的方法有很多种，从宏观的角度来看，一般常用的是直译和意译、归化与异化，它们也是在翻译界引起争议最多的。下面分别进行探讨：

1. 直译和意译

翻译中的直译和意译之争和翻译的历史一样久远。对直译的攻击和批评也伴随始终，但是诚如大卫·贝洛斯所言，如果直译真的如此臭名昭著，为什么要动用那么多的翻译家、批评家不遗余力地把它打倒呢？（Bellos, 2011:75）

魏迺杰(Nigel Wiseman)多年来致力于中医翻译,他坚持认为,直译是唯一可以让西方读者清楚看到中医真正面目的方式。他甚至将中医翻译中的直译发展到如此地步,将每一个中医常用字找到一个英语中的对等词,然后用这些词造出英语中的中医术语。在他的《实用英文中医辞典》中,"神"即"spirit","昏"即"cloud","气"即"qi",于是"神昏"就是"clouded spirit","神气"就是"spirit qi",而"神水"则为"spirit water"。(谢竹藩,2005)

直译曾经一直是典籍翻译者的首选,因为他们担心意译会改变原文的意义,哪怕这意味着极细微的改动。中医翻译也是如此,在可能的情况下,尽量使用直译,但是当直译带来了更多的困惑而非交际时,解释意义而非逐字翻译就显得更加重要。

1) 直译

直译就是把原文的意思完整而又正确地表达出来,基本上保留原文的语言形式(词语、句子结构、修辞手法等)。

看下面的例子:

Easy come, easy go. 来得容易,去得快。

Example is better than precept. 身教胜于言传。

All roads lead to Rome. 条条大道通罗马。

雪中送炭:to offer fuel in snowy weather

一人得道,鸡犬升天:Even the dog swaggers when its master wins favor.

瓜田李下/瓜田不纳履,李下不整冠:Neither adjust your sho-s in a melon patch, nor your hat under a plum tree.

直译的优点是能传达原文意义,体现原文风格。但容易使译文冗长啰唆,晦涩难懂,有时不能表达原文的意思。如:

张从正以汗、吐、下为攻去病邪的三个主要方法,后世称他为攻下派。

原译:Zhang Congzheng mainly treated diseases with three therapeutic methods, i.e. sweating(diaphoresis), vomiting(emesis) and purgation. That was why the school represented by him was known as purgation school.

该译文为忠实直译,意思也基本传达,但是在句式上还可以调整,使之更符合英语的行文习惯。

改译:The therapeutic methods of sweating(diaphoresis), vomiting(emesis) and purgation were mainly used by Zhang Congzheng in treating diseases. That was why the school represented by him was known as purgation school.(李照国,2005:245)

事实上,大部分中医术语都采用直译的方法:

表寒里热:superficies cold with interior heat

表热里寒:exterior heat and interior cold

表虚里实:exterior deficiency and interior excess

表实里虚:exterior excess and interior deficiency

表里俱寒:cold in both superficies and interior

里病出表:interior disease moving out to the exterior

甚至一些带有文学色彩的术语也多采用直译,如:"戴阳"指下真寒而上假热的危重病征,因下元虚衰,真阳浮越,两颧淡红如妆,游移不定,名曰"戴阳",译为"upcast yang";"娇脏"是对肺的指称,因其易于遭受外邪侵袭而得名,译为"delicate viscus";"刚脏"是对肝脏的指称,因其易于亢盛横逆(has a tendency to hyperactivity and counterflow of qi)而得名,译为"unyielding viscus"或者"resolute viscus";"贮痰之器"和"水之上源"均指肺脏,因其与痰的生成排泄有关,且位于上焦,而三焦具有通调水道之用,故得此名,分别译为"receptacle that holds phlegm"和"upper source of water"。有些直译来的术语需要做一注解,如"明堂"译为"bright hall(an ancient term for nose, especially the apex of the nose)"。

再看一些其他例子:

奔豚:running pig syndrome

微脉:faint pulse

散脉:scattered pulse

弱脉:weak pulse

牢脉:firm pulse

伏脉:hidden pulse

动脉:stirred pulse

疾脉:racing pulse

怪脉:strange pulse

屋漏脉:roof-leaking pulse

虾泳脉:shrimp-darting pulse

解索脉:rope-untwining pulse

弹石脉:stone-flicking pulse

转豆脉:bean-spinning pulse

鱼翔脉:fish-waving pulse

雀啄脉:sparrow-pecking pulse

釜沸脉:seething cauldron pulse

潮热:tidal fever

但热不寒:fever without chills

但寒不热:chills without fever

半身无汗:half-body absence of sweating

心下急:distress below the heart

心下坚:rigidity below the heart

心下满:fullness below the heart

三部九候:three body parts and nine pulse taking sites

脐下不仁:numbness below the umbilicus

小腹不仁:lower abdominal numbness

保命之主:principals of life preservation

有些句子看似生硬的直译却很好地保留了中医的语言风格、思维方式和表达习惯。

如：

气为血之帅，血为气之母。

译文：Qi is the marshal of the blood and the blood is the mother of qi.

2）意译

胡庚申强调，"交际维的适应性选择转换，要求译者除语言信息的转换和文化内涵的传递之外，把选择转换的侧重点放在交际的层面上，关注原文中的交际意图是否在译文中得以实现。"（胡庚申，2008）

在很多情况下，直译无法实现原文中的交际意图，这时候就需要在正确理解原文意思的基础上，摆脱原文句子结构，重新遣词造句，把原文的意思用通达的目的语表达出来，这种翻译方法就是意译。意译时要注意把握分寸，不得随意增删内容或篡改原意。意译强调的是交际的效果，而非形式上的对应。

在以下情况下可采用意译法：

（1）直译会导致意义上的错误；

（2）出现语义空白；

（3）形式对等引起严重的意义晦涩时；

（4）形式对等引起作者原意所没有的歧义时；

（5）形式对等违反目的语的语法或文体规范时。

中医词汇如"天癸"指调节人体生长、生殖机能、维持妇女月经和胎孕所必需的物质，长期以来以音译译之，近年来常被意译为"reproduction-stimulating essence"；"山根"译为"root of the nose"或"the upper portion of the nose, which is situated between the eyes"；"女劳复"译为"relapse due to sexual intemperance"。

再看其他例子：

五心烦热：vexing heat in the chest, palms and soles

视歧：double vision

鼻不闻香臭：loss of smell

癃闭：difficult urination

项强：stiffness of the neck

盗汗：night sweating

郑声：unconscious murmuring

里急：abdominal urgency

立迟：retarded standing in infants

利胆：normalizing the gallbladder's function

十八反：eighteen antagonisms(the eighteen incompatible medicaments)

十九畏：nineteen incompatibilities(the nineteen medicaments of mutual restraint)

木郁化火：liver depression generating fire

一些带有数字的中医术语往往在后面加一个类别词，使语义更加明确。如：

七恶：seven malign signs

五善：five benign signs

五刺: five needling methods

子盗母气: illness of the child organ may involve the mother organ

有的术语两种译法并存。如:

烧山火法: mountain-burning fire method; heat-producing needling/heat inducing needling

透天凉法: heaven-penetrating cooling method; cool-producing needling

2. 归化与异化

在翻译的过程中,译者要么(1) "disturbs the writer as little as possible and moves the reader in his direction",要么(2) "disturbs the reader as little as possible and moves the writer in his direction"。(Robinson,2006:229)

归化是以译入语读者为中心和归宿,尽量采用译入语文化中的语言表达方式,适应和照顾目的语读者的文化习惯,帮助读者消除障碍,处处为读者着想,向读者靠拢;而异化则恰好相反,以源语文化为中心和归宿,主张尽可能保留源语文化的特有表达方式,直接再现源语的文化特征和风格,把源语文化引进、输入到译入语中去,有意让读者体会"异域风情"。

归化、异化的概念虽是舶来品,然而鲁迅的"硬译"可以算是异化的理念,而傅雷的"神似"和钱钟书的"化境"称得上是归化论的延伸。

异化译法能把一种文化和语言中的信息以近乎保持其本来面目的方式贡献给另一种文化及语言,有利于两种异质文化和语言的相互交流、渗透和融合,极大地丰富了译入语的词汇和文化意象,比如很多外来语中译过来的表达已经为中国人所熟知: Achilles' heel(阿喀琉斯之踵)、Pandora's box(潘多拉之盒)、the last straw(最后一根稻草)、The Trojan Horse(特洛伊木马)。汉语中的很多表达也在丰富着英语的词汇,成为英语中非常形象化的表达。如:

跑得了和尚跑不了庙: The monk may run away but the temple can not run with him.

狗抓老鼠——多管闲事: A dog shouldn't chase mice—that's the cat's job.

也有两种译法并存的。如:

Kill two birds with one stone:一石二鸟;一箭双雕;一举两得

All roads lead to Rome:条条大路通罗马;殊途同归

英语和汉语虽然有很多相异之处,但是由于人类的共性,文化的交融,也有很多表达是相似的,虽然携带着各自的文化色彩,倒也有异曲同工之妙。如:

君子之交淡如水: A hedge between keeps friendship green.

兜揽生意: drum up business

白手起家: start from scratch

天网恢恢,疏而不漏: Justice has long arms.

屋漏又逢连夜雨: It never rains; but pours. (均表示麻烦事不来则已,一来就接踵而至。)

权衡: weigh

嘴嚼：chew on

归化译法把一种文化中的异质成分转化为另一种文化中人们所熟知的内容，使读者领略到不同文化之间不谋而合的妙趣，降低了理解的难度。但在翻译过程中却失去了了解、欣赏和借鉴其他国家和民族文化的机会。

1) 医学翻译中的归化与异化

西医词汇很多来自希腊神话，有很强的文化特点；中医药术语产生于中国传统哲学的土壤，文化负载词更多。所以归化与异化之争，也就一直伴随着医学翻译的始终。然而这两种策略从来都不可分割且互相依存，很难看到一个译者只采用其中一种策略而完全不用另外一种。常见的做法有以下几种情况：

(1) 用归化译法翻译中医的解剖术语和部分病名

尽管西医的解剖术语和中医的五脏概念在内涵和外延上有很大差距，如中医的"心"除了"主血脉"外，还可以"主神明"，而西医的"heart"主要是血液循环机构；西医的"liver"主要是消化器官，而中医的"肝"除了可以调节胆汁的分泌排泄、促进脾胃对食物的消化外，还调节人体气的运动。此外，西医的"bladder"仅仅是泌尿系统，而《黄帝内经》将膀胱比作"州都"，能藏"津液"，具有"气化"功能；"血"与"blood"，"脾"与"spleen"等均有不同程度的区别。然而并未因此全部采用音译或者再造新词出来，采用西方人熟悉的术语更有助于沟通与接受。中医还有一些带有隐喻色彩的术语也可以直接用西医的术语来翻译。如：天柱骨折(fracture of neck)，天柱骨倒(flaccidity of neck)。

还有很多中西医疾病名称相同，所指也一样。如：

- 感冒(common cold)
- 麻疹(measles)
- 痛经(dysmenorrhea)
- 腰痛(lumbago)
- 胃痛(stomachache)
- 牙痛(toothache)
- 水痘(variola)
- 痢疾(dysentery)
- 疟疾(malaria)
- 夜盲(night blindness)
- 脚气病(beriberi)
- 心悸(palpitation)
- 腹痛(abdominal pain)
- 黄疸(jaundice)
- 水肿(edema)
- 白喉(diphtheria)

(2) 用相似的西医术语翻译中医病名

某些疾病的名称在中西医上虽然不尽相同，但其具体所指的疾病在病理上基本一致，也尽量采用归化译法，用相似的术语来翻译。如：

- 流行感冒(influenza;流感)
- 瘰疬(scrofula;tuberculosis of cervical lymph node;颈部淋巴结核)
- 瘿(goitre;thyroid enlargement;甲状腺肿大)
- 噎膈(dysphagia;吞咽困难)
- 疠风(leprosy;麻风)
- 痄腮(mumps;腮腺炎)
- 痉症(convulsion;惊厥)
- 产后痉(puerperal tetanus;产后破伤风)
- 痨瘵(pulmonary tuberculosis;肺结核)
- 缠腰火丹(herpes zoster;带状疱疹)
- 阴蚀(ulcus vulvae;外阴溃疡)
- 鼻渊(sinusitis;鼻窦炎)
- 乳蛾(tonsillitis;扁桃体炎)
- 雪口(thrush/aphtha;口疮,小溃疡)
- 脱肛(prolapse of rectum; proctoptoma; proctoptosia;直肠脱垂)
- 牛皮癣(psoriasis;银屑病)

(3) 淡化西医术语中的神话和修辞色彩

西医中和希腊神话有关的词汇,在翻译时往往采用归化译法,淡化其神话色彩,只保留其医学术语含义。但是有时为了让学生更多地了解这些术语背后的人文内涵,可以适当讲述其术语的渊源。如:

Achilles tendon 跟腱——Achilles(希腊神话英雄)

narcissism 自恋——Narcissus(希腊神话人物)

sphincter 括约肌——Sphinx(狮身人面像)

还有的西医词汇带有浓厚的修辞色彩,翻译时要么淡化其修辞,要么采用中国人熟悉的喻体。如:bridge of the nose 鼻梁(而非鼻桥),frostbite 冻疮(而非霜咬),cat's eye reflex 白瞳症(而非猫眼反射),hourglass tumor 葫芦状瘤(而非沙漏瘤),candle wax bone 肢骨纹状肥大(而非蜡状骨),pearl eye 白内障(而非珍珠眼),ugly-duckling stage 出牙期(而非丑小鸭期),comb disease 鸡冠癣(而非梳子病),bottle nose 酒糟鼻(而非瓶子鼻),drum stick finger 杵状指(而非鼓槌指),hay fever 花粉症(而非干草热)。

还有一些和动物有关的隐喻也根据中国人的习惯对喻体做了调整。如:goose flesh 鸡皮疙瘩(而非鹅皮疙瘩),pigeon breast 鸡胸(而非鸽胸)。

有些医学术语中的人名、职业名、地名也被弱化。如:charley horse(抽筋),German measles(风疹),teacher's node 结节性声带炎。

当然也有异化翻译的。如:elephant leg(象腿,象皮病),butterfly fracture(蝴蝶状骨折),bow leg(弓形腿),lock finger(锁指),spade hand(铲形手),crocodile tears sign(鳄泪综合征)。

(4) 弱化中医术语中的文学色彩

由于中医语言丰富的人文和文学色彩,在翻译成英语时往往要在表层意义和深层意义之间做出取舍,如:中医将"……聚会之处"称作"海",翻译时也常被译为"sea"。

血海:the sea of blood

气海:the sea of vital energy(qi)

髓海:the sea of medulla(marrow)

水谷之海:the sea of grain and water

四海:the four seas

实际上这些术语大多均有实际所指,可以放弃其表层的文化特点而选择易于被译入语读者接受的方式来翻译:

血海:thoroughfare vessels

气海:qi convergence

髓海:brain

水谷之海:stomach

四海:four convergences

另外,中医"……之府"的术语也有很多,常见的译法有:

血之府:the residence of blood; house of blood

筋之府:the residence of tendons; house of tendons

肾之府:the residence of kidney; house of kidney

髓之府:the residence of marrow; house of marrow

精明之府:the residence of intelligence; house of intelligence

元神之府:the residence of mind; house of mind

胸中之府:the residence of chest; house of chest

在翻译时,有时候不需要译出表层的文化色彩,直接译出"谜底"即可:

血之府:blood vessels

筋之府:knee joint

肾之府:lumbar region

髓之府:bones

精明之府:head

元神之府:brain

胸中之府:back

2) 医学翻译中的文化传真——异化

1980年3月,杨宪益在澳大利亚的一个"作家周"座谈会上说:"中国应该知道外国的文化遗产,外国也应该了解中国有多么丰富的文化遗产。"中医英译传播的不仅仅是其医学理念,还应传递其特有的文化内涵。例如"木克土"是指肝脏病变进而影响脾胃功能,用归化法翻译为"the liver restricts the spleen",译文符合西医表达习惯,也便于西方读者理解。但这样的翻译是以牺牲中医丰富的文化内涵为代价的,没有把五行与五脏的关系表达出来,造成了文化缺省……,为了保留中医的文化内涵,还是翻译为"wood restricts earth"。(程卫强,丁年青,2012)

魏迺杰(Nigel Wiseman)作为一个以英语为母语的资深译者对中医西传做出了不懈

努力。他一直致力于在中医的英译中保持中医概念的整体性和独立性不被破坏。2000年，他以 Translation of Medical Terms—A Source-Oriented Approach（《中医术语翻译——来源导向方法》）为题完成了他的博士论文，在该博士论文中系统论证了"来源导向"的中医术语翻译原则，认为来源导向的翻译方法应该是专业术语翻译的标准方法，目标导向的翻译方法比较适用于外行读者或其他领域的专家。当前的中医术语翻译的现实却是，目标导向的翻译方法广泛用于以专业读者为对象的中医文献翻译上。由于目标导向翻译无法精确并完整地反映出中医的详细内容，对于中医西传不仅没有帮助，反而有害。（陈晓华，施蕴中，2008）

魏迺杰（Wiseman）的"来源导向"翻译原则和"作者按兵不动，让读者去靠近作者"的异化译法有异曲同工之妙。他在翻译时也一直不遗余力地维护中医的原汁原味，极力反对中医翻译的西医化。比如他最经典的翻译：将"风火眼"译为"wind-fire eye"，而非西医化的"acute conjunctivitis"，将"面色萎黄"译为"withered yellow facial complexion"，保留了 yellow 这个字，将"抽风"译为"tugging wind"，认为这样的翻译能反映出病因，有助于保留中医对此概念的见解。

3）归化与异化的和谐共存

在文化传播的不同阶段，两种译法承担着不同的角色，往往交替使用。在把中医基本理念传播给西方普通受众时，归化译法更可行，然而在一些基本理念已经被接受的基础上，可采用异化译法，让真正有兴趣的读者能深入认识中医药文化，欣赏来自东方文化的"异国情调"，比如"阴阳"和"气"的概念，最初是音译加注，相当于文化诠释；再如"六淫"可译为"six excesses"，并辅以注解："A collective term for the six excessive or untimely climatic influences as external pathogenic factors: wind, cold, summer-heat, dampness, dryness and fire, also the same as six climatic pathogenic factors."。（WHO，2007），在这些术语被西方读者逐渐接受后再直接采用异化翻译。

语言是整个文化体系的一部分，是文化的重要载体，两者相互作用，形成一个不可分割的整体。中医学文献多为古汉语，既包含了医学信息，也往往是经典的文学作品，同时包含了文化信息，带有很强的综合性。在翻译时，一方面要让目的语读者准确理解其中的医学信息，需要采用归化的方式拉近读者与作者的时空距离；另一方面，中医语篇的文学性和文化性又决定了译者不能不再现和重构术语、文本的艺术美，努力保持其原质性，这时需要采用异化的手法。归化与异化的统一和平衡需要译者的智慧，需要在翻译实践中不断探索才能实现。

真正的译者应该能够融合异化与归化，做到和谐共赢。两者并非水火不容，而是并行不悖和相辅相成的，在目的语文化中起着不同的作用，各有其优越性和存在价值。在翻译中，我们始终要辩证地运用两种翻译方法，从而达到译文和源语的和谐共赢。下面将从《医学源流论》摘选一段加以分析：

原文：故病之为患也，小则耗精，大则伤命，隐然一敌国也。以草木之偏性，攻脏腑之偏胜，必能知彼知己。多方以制之，而后无丧身殒命之忧。

译文：Thus the impairment of disease is, if mild, to consume the essence, and if serious, to endanger the patient's life, just like a hidden enemy state. To make use of the cold or warm nature of the drugs to cure visceral sthenia or asthenia requires the full knowledge of both drugs and disease as well as the combined use of various therapies to attack the pathogenic factors. Only by taking such a measure can life be guaranteed.

原文体现了中医典籍中取类比象的语言特点,形象生动,如"隐然一敌国也""知彼知己"。译文中,作者一方面采用异化译法保留了原文中关于"用药如用兵"的文化意象,使比喻语言得到了生动的体现,又巧妙地将"知己知彼"翻译为"the full knowledge of both drugs and disease",可谓独具匠心,是归化和异化有机融合的一个很好的范例。

练 习

Ⅰ. 段落翻译(汉译英)

(1) 中国是世界上人口最多的国家,她幅员辽阔,自然资源十分丰富。高低起伏的山脉,绵延流淌的河流,多变的气候,孕育了成千上万形态各异的动植物。中国人自古以来通过发现、采集、加工、利用这些大自然馈赠的礼物治疗百病,在长期的医疗实践过程中,逐渐总结形成了传统的中国医学理论体系。

(2) 传统中国医学简称中医学。"中医"的名称产生于西汉,原意是"中和之医",以阴阳五行为理论基础,把人体看作形、气、神的整体循环,只有做到中和平衡才是健康。中医治疗的对象是人,目标是把人治好。中医还强调人和自然的统一。一名优秀的中医医师,除了具备专业的传统医学知识和丰富的临床经验外,还需具备深厚的传统文化修养。

(3) 中医主要的治疗手段之一是中药。中药材大部分由植物药构成。药店和药房将药材分类放入中药柜中,柜中分许多格,每格又有多个小格,每小格里存放一种药材。药师依据中医处方,称量抓取药材。患者取药后,可交给药房或药店代煎,也可以回家自己熬制服用。

(4) 中国人的家庭药箱里都会准备些常用、应急的中药:比如治疗小儿疳积的王氏保赤丸,缓解心绞痛的速效救心丸,消炎止血的云南白药,宣肺止咳的川贝枇杷露,舒筋止痛的红花油,清热解毒的板蓝根冲剂,防暑醒脑的人丹和清凉油等。这些中成药有丸、散、膏、丹等多种剂型,在中国代代相传、疗效显著,可在家中自疗自救,也方便外出时携带备用。

(节选自视频材料《中医文化与保健常识》教学片)

Ⅱ. 段落翻译(英译汉)

In the Western Pacific Region, the major system of traditional medicine which originated from ancient China has continued to develop not only in China but also in neighbouring countries and areas, particularly in Japan, the Republic of Korea and Vietnam, with certain variations in accordance with local conditions, i. e. availability of natural resources, indigenous culture and political climate. Different names have been designated for this system of traditional medicine as it developed in various countries, such as Oriental medicine, traditional Chinese medicine, traditional Korean medicine, Kampo medicine and traditional Vietnamese medicine. They are collectively called traditional medicine(TRM) in the Western Pacific Region.

Traditional medicine is a comprehensive system of medicine characterized by its own theoretical basis and practical experience. It includes herbal medicine, acupuncture and other non-medication therapies. Owing to its unique paradigm and remarkable efficacy with fewer adverse effects, this system of medicine has been attracting more and more interest internationally. Considering the recent rapid increase in the worldwide use of TRM, there is a pressing need for a common language, i. e. an international standard terminology.

In 1981, the World Health Organization(WHO) Regional Office for the Western Pacific organized a Working Group for the Standardization of Acupuncture Nomenclature. After 10 years of effort, a consensus on the proposed standard international acupuncture nomenclature was reached by the Regional Office for the Western Pacific's Working Group and then by the WHO Scientific Group in Geneva. In 1991, *A Proposed Standard International Acupuncture Nomenclature* was published by WHO in Geneva and a revised edition of *Standard Acupuncture Nomenclature* (Part 1 and 2) was published by the Regional Office for the Western Pacific in Manila. Practical use has proven these WHO publications to be invaluable contributions to international information exchange on acupuncture. However, the publications are still quite limited, only including nomenclature for the 14 meridians, 361 classical acupuncture points, 8 extra meridians, 48 extra points, 14 scalp acupuncture lines and a few terms related to acupuncture needles. Moreover, to meet the increasing demands of practice, education, research and exchange of information, there is an urgent need to develop standardized terminology and nomenclature for TRM as a whole.

...

Principles for English expression selection

Accurate reflection of the original concept of Chinese terms.

In this context, it should be stressed that each term is a unit of meaning, which is not necessarily equal to the summation of meanings of the constituent original Han characters. According to Chinese philology, a character may have several different meanings and is often more like a syllable in English. Generally a compound word, consisting of two or more characters, provides the specific meaning. However, the meaning of a compound word is different from the separate meanings of its components. Furthermore, the appropriateness of an English equivalent should be judged primarily by its accuracy in reflecting the medical concept of the Chinese original.

No creation of new English words.

All the English terms included in this document are those that have been collected in universally recognized English dictionaries. If there are exceptions, they are derived from available English words with some grammatical modifications.

Avoidance of pinyin(Romanized Chinese) use.

For certain TRM terms, it is extremely difficult to determine English equivalents, and many publications use pinyin. However, it should be stressed that Romanized Chinese is still Chinese and pinyin is not a real translation. In addition, Han characters are similar in Chinese, Japanese and Korean, but the pronunciation differs greatly. The titles and author names of classical texts are described in the original pronunciation.

Consistency with WHO's Standard Acupuncture Nomenclature.

Especially for the terms of acupuncture and moxibustion, IST followed the English translation in *Standard Acupuncture Nomenclature*, Part 1 and 2 revised edition which was published by the WHO Regional Office for the Western Pacific in 1991.

Use of Western medical terms

Since both traditional and modern medicines aim at maintaining health and treating diseases, there must be some overlap between the two systems of medicine in concept and hence in terminology. On such occasions, the only difference exists in wording. When a traditional term in Han character has a corresponding Western medical term expressing the same concept, use of that Western medical term is not only reasonable but also necessary. Otherwise, creation of a new English term from the original term in Han character would cause confusion. On the other hand, improper use of Western medical terms is misleading and therefore is excluded from this document.

Standard terminology versus literal translation

In this document, most terms in English correspond well to the primary translation of the Chinese original, but there are exceptions.

Because of historical backgrounds, many terms have alternative names. Even in the State Standard promulgated by the Chinese Government some alternative names are still retained, for there are many classical works using different terminology in Chinese, which are still of practical significance. When translating these terms, particularly from a literal approach, each alternative name should have its rendering, and as a result, one single concept may have several expressions in English. In fact, this diversity in English equivalents is of no technical significance.

Because of the Chinese custom of word formation, some characters are added or deleted simply for linguistic or rhetoric purpose. Since the addition or deletion is of no technical significance, it is unnecessary to reflect the change of wording in the international standard terminology.

Because of the evolution of TRM, the original concepts of some traditional medical terms have been changed or only one of the multiple concepts has been adopted at present. In this case, the English expression of the contemporary concept should be regarded as the standard.

In short, the international standard terminology is closely related to the appropriate translation, but it is not a simple conversion of the translation.

(节选自 WHO International Standard Terminologies on Traditional Medicine in the Western Pacific Region)

Ⅲ. 下列英译文均来自中国古代典籍作品，将其回译为汉语

(1) Those who know me will say my heart is sad and bleak; Those who don't know me may ask me for what I seek. （冯友兰译）

(2) The wise man delights in water; the good man delights in mountains. The wise move; the good stay still. The wise are happy; the good endure. （冯友兰译）

(3) The wise are free from doubts; the virtuous from anxiety; the brave from fear. （冯友兰译）

(4) The superior man is always happy; the small man sad. （冯友兰译）

(5) I built my hut in a zone of human habitation,
Yet near me there sounds no noise of horse or coach,
Would you know how that is possible?
A heart that is distant creates a wilderness round it.
I pluck chrysanthemums under the eastern hedge,
Then gaze long at the distant summer hills.
The mountain air is fresh at the dusk of day;
The flying birds two by two return.
In these things there lies a deep meaning;
Yet when we would express it, words suddenly fail us.

(translated by Arthur Waley)

(6) Man on earth,
Good at birth.
The same nature,
Varies on nurture.
With no education,
There'd be aberration.
To teach well,
You deeply dwell.
Then Mencius' mother,
Chose her neighbor.
At Mencius' sloth,
She cut th' cloth.

（赵彦春译）

(7) Nature says few words. Hence a squall lasts not a whole morning and a rainstorm continues not a whole day.

(8) He who stands on tiptoe does not stand firm. He who strains his strides does not walk well. He who reveals himself is not luminous. He who justifies himself is not far famed. He who boasts of himself is not given credit. He who prides himself is not chief among men.

(9) The student of knowledge aims at learning day by day; the student of Tao aims at losing day by day. By continual losing, one reaches doing nothing. By doing nothing, everything is done. He who conquers the world often does so by doing nothing. When one is compelled to do something, the world is already beyond his conquering.

(10) Disaster is the avenue of fortune, and fortune is the concealment for disaster.

第三章　西医词汇及其翻译

To Cure Sometimes, To Relieve Often, To Comfort Always.
　　　　　　　　　　　——E. L. Trudeau(特鲁多)
有时会治愈；常常是帮助；总是在安慰。
Nature, time, and patience are the three great physicians.
自然、时间和耐心是三个伟大的医生。
Sound in body, sound in mind.
有健全的身体才有健全的精神。
As rust eats iron, so care eats heart.
锈能蚀铁，忧能伤人。
Work is father of appetite, grandfather of digestion, and great-grandfather of health.
劳动是食欲的父亲，是消化的祖父，是健康的曾祖父。
Sloth, like rust, consumes faster than labor wears.
懒惰犹如铁锈，其腐蚀之快，比劳作更甚。

（编者译）

第一节　西医词汇的特点

英国在发展的历史中曾经多次遭遇外邦入侵，每一个入侵国都在大不列颠诸岛上留下了自己语言和文化的痕迹，因此英语词汇来自多种语源，医学词汇亦如此。

1. 多源性

英语在发展的过程中吸纳了大量外来语的语言要素，是世界上最具多源性的语言。医学英语词汇因此分为本族语(native word)词源和外来语(loanword)词源。本族语词源是由古英语发展而来，其中的医学词汇极少，且多为单音节词，它们诠释了当时人们对自然、社会及自身的认识与理解，其中表示人体部位名称的词汇有 bone, hand, arm, eye, foot, ear, chin, heart 等，也有一些最基本的人体解剖术语，如 blood, eye, neck, lung 等，以及与人体基本生理功能和疾患相关的术语，如 yawn, ache, wound, breath, thirst, deaf, swallow, fever 等。

大部分医学英语词汇是外来语，还有些是在演化过程中融入了外来语的词素成分。

如：

1）希腊语词源

Achilles tendon（跟腱），psychogenia（精神障碍），psychotherapeutics（心理疗法），psychoanalysis（心理分析），hepatitis（肝炎），neurology（神经病学），phlebotomy（静脉切开术），aphrodisiac（春药），amnesia（遗忘症），aneurysm（动脉瘤），colon（结肠），coma（昏迷），ectopia（异位），echometer（听诊器），glaucoma（白内障），Hygeian（提倡卫生者），iris（虹膜），larynx（喉），morphine（吗啡），pharynx（咽），ptosis（下垂），stenosis（狭窄），stasis（停滞），somniloquy（梦语）等。

常见的希腊前缀有：hemi-（半，不完全地），tri-（三），a-/an-（无，没有），homo-（相同；像），aut(o)-（自己的），hydr(o)-（与水有关的），micr(o)-（微小的）等；常见的希腊后缀有：-cyte（细胞），-itis（炎，炎症），-penia（缺乏，不足），-ptosis（下垂）；常见的希腊词根有：acou(o)-（听觉，听力），append(o)-（阑尾），arthr(o)-（关节），gastr(o)-（胃），ur-（尿），rhin(o)-（鼻），opt(o)-（视觉，视力），neur(o)-（神经）等。

2）拉丁语词源

caesarean（剖宫产），medicine（医学），clinic（临床），diagnosis（诊断），apnea（呼吸暂停），dystrophy（营养不良），cerebrum（大脑），cornea（角膜），femur（股骨），pelvis（骨盆），aorta（主动脉），bacteria（细菌），muscle（肌肉）等。

常见的拉丁词缀有：mal-（坏；错误），multi-（多个），semi-（半），sub-（在……以下），super-（极；超），syn-（共，合，相同），trans-（横穿；通过），-cide（杀死），-puncture（刺术），-section（剖），-ulc（小）等；常见的拉丁词根有：audi(o)-（音的；声的），cerebell(o)-（小脑），arteri(o)-（动脉），cerebr(o)-（大脑），fibr(o)-（纤维），laryng(o)-（喉），muscul(o)-（肌肉），or(o)-（口腔），ped(o)-（足），saliv(o)-（唾液），spin(o)-（脊柱），spir(o)-（螺旋），urin(o)-（尿）等。

3）阿拉伯语词源

benzoin（安息香），candy（糖果），musk（麝香），sugar（食糖），syrup（糖水），camphor（樟脑），lilac（丁香），alcohol（酒精），elixir（长生不老药），jasmine（茉莉），ill（疾病），pepsin（胃蛋白酶），khan（汗）等。

4）法语词源

cerveau（大脑），cerveau moyen（中脑），cervelet（小脑），nerf cranien（脑神经），endocrine（内分泌），coeur（心脏），foie（肝脏），maladies bénignes（良性的），massage（按摩），lavage（灌洗），chancre（下疳），grandmal（癫痫大发作），hormone（激素）等。

5）德语词源

zinc（锌），nickel（镍），bismuth（铋），aspirin（阿司匹林），biology（生物学），chemotherapy（化学疗法），chromosome（染色体），gene（基因），leukemia（白血病），neuron（神经元），schizophrenia（精神分裂症）等。

6）意大利语词源

influenza（流行性感冒），malaria（疟疾），quarantine（检疫）等。

7）西班牙语词源

mosquito(蚊子),quinine(奎宁)等。

2. 明显的词义理据特征

理据(motivation)是指语言符号(包括发音与拼写等)与其所表达意义之间的联系。医学英语词汇的构成主要以派生词和合成词为主,构词理据非常明显。

医学英语词汇中绝大多数派生词汇都是由有确切含义的词根与词缀构成的,词语的意义基本上都可以从构成成分的意义之和直接推测出来(表3-1)。

表3-1 派生词汇及其词根和词缀

oto(耳)	rhino(鼻)	laryngo(喉)	-logy(学)	otorhinolaryngology(耳鼻喉学)
dacryo（泪）	cysto（囊）	rhino（鼻）	-tomy（切开）	dacryocystorhinotomy（泪囊鼻腔造孔术）
laryngo（喉）	tracheo（气管）	bronchi（支气管）	-tis（炎）	laryngotracheobronchitis（喉气管支气管炎）

这种显著的形态理据特征在一定意义上有助于理解、记忆和翻译医学英语词汇。另外,部分合成词也具有这种形态理据特征,因为很多合成词都是由自由词根结合在一起形成的。如：

heart failure(心脏衰竭)　　genetic engineering(基因工程)

bottle feeding(人工喂养)　　sperm bank(精子库)

brain death(脑死亡)　　chemotherapy(化疗)

factorial trial(析因试验)　　control group(控制组)

red-flag signs(危险症状)　　practicing physician(执业医师)

randomized clinical trial(随机比对临床试验)

diet-and-exercise discussion(关于节食和运动的讨论)

first-contact primary care(首诊初级保健)

但是有些合成词的词义并非各构成成分意思的简单叠加与组合,需要把形态理据与人们对客观世界的认知结合起来,方能推测出语义。如：test-tube(人工受精的)、midwife(助产士),afterbirth(胞衣),drug-fast(耐药的),frostbite(冻疮),heartburn(胃灼热),ugly-duckling stage(出牙期)。

明显的理据特征也有助于译者根据已知的词汇推测新的词汇,例如根据heart attack(心脏病发作)可以推断出anxiety attack(焦虑发作)。对于一些反义词缀,也可以成为理解、识记和翻译的依据。如：

disinfection(消毒)→infection(感染)

post-partum(产后的)→prepartum(产前的)

hyperglycemia(高血糖)→hypoglycemia(低血糖)

endocrine(内分泌)→exocrine(外分泌)

tachyphasia(急语症)→bradyphasia(发言迟缓)

tachycardia(心跳过速)→bradycardia(心跳过缓)

macrocythemia(大红细胞症)→microcythemia(小红细胞症)

macrocephalia(巨头症)→microcephalia(小头症)

leptomeninges(软脑脊膜)→pachymeninges(硬脑脊膜)

intercellular(细胞间的)→intracellular(细胞内的)

3. 层出不穷的新词汇

西医被称为现代医学,科学技术的迅猛发展推动了医学的进步,医学中的新发现、新理论、新概念、新技术和新发明都需要用新的词汇来表达,据不完全统计,每年约有1500个新的医学英语词汇出现。如:clinical engineer(临床工程师),egg bank(卵子库),artificial fertilization(人工授精),light therapy(光治疗),kidney / renal transplant(肾移植),implantation of heart peacemaker(永久性人工心脏起搏器植入术),heart lung machine(人工心肺机),aorto-coronary arterial bypass(主动脉冠状动脉旁路),extracranial-intracranial arterial bypass(颅内-颅外动脉旁路),Ebola virus(埃博拉病毒),SARS[(Severe Acute Respiratory Syndrome)非典(严重急性呼吸综合征)],COVID-19[(Corona Virus Disease 2019)新型冠状病毒肺炎],MERS[(Middle East Respiratory Syndrome)中东呼吸综合征],asymptomatic carrier(无症状携带者),Fecal-oral transmission(粪口传播),nucleic vaccine(核酸疫苗),inactivated vaccine(灭活疫苗),patient zero[零号病人(the first person infected with the virus in an epidemic)]等。

医学文体中经常会出现一些临时复合词。如:prick skin test(点刺皮肤试验),newborn cord blood(新生儿脐血),goblet cell(杯状细胞),dog days treatment(伏天治疗),the fibrous connective tissue(纤维结缔组织),mood-related effects(情绪性作用),anti-inflammatory effects(抗炎作用),antidepressant(抗抑郁药),in a concentration-dependent manner(受浓度影响的方式),steroid-resistant(激素耐药型),steroid-dependent(激素依赖型),chicken-and-egg argument("鸡和蛋"之争),infection-fighting cell(抗感染细胞),urinary tract infection(尿路感染)等。

这些层出不穷的新词汇给译者带来了很大挑战。不断更新词汇储备、了解最新的医学进展、阅读国际医学期刊,是一个成功的译者的必学功课。

4. 词义的变化

医学术语在发展过程中,会经历词义的演变,如词义扩大、缩小、转移等。"allergic"原意指"患过敏症的,过敏的",在普通词汇中指的是"对……有强烈反感的,极讨厌的",如:"He's allergic to study."(他极讨厌读书);"complex"本意是"复杂的",但也可以用来指不健康的心理状态,如:Oedipus complex(恋母情结);"pill"本意指各种药片,但有时候用来专指"避孕药片";"indication"(指示,暗示)在医学术语中指"指征或适应证";"history"(历史,历史记录)在医学术语中指"既往病史";"complaints"(牢骚,委屈)用来指"疾病,症状"。

再看其他例子:

plastic:可塑的;塑料的→外科整形的

labour:劳动;劳工→分娩

appendix:附录;附加物→阑尾

vessel：容器,器皿→脉管,导管
tractor：拖拉机;牵引车→牵引器
obstinate：固执的,倔强的→难治的
pack：包裹→包裹疗法
capsule(拉丁语)：小盒→胶囊
condom(法语)：类似手套的东西→安全套,避孕套
malaria(意大利)：不好的空气→疟疾,瘴气

5. 大量的缩略语

西医术语中有大量的缩略语,主要有下面几种构词方式：

1）首字母缩略法

首字母缩略法是把词或词组的首字母结合起来构成新的单词来表示其词义的构词方法。有些首字母缩略词也会出现词汇中的其他字母。缩略词是按字母逐个读音的。

CT—computerized tomography 计算机体层摄影

BP—blood pressure 血压

GH—growth hormone 生长激素

TB—tuberculosis 肺结核

Ach—acetylcholine 乙酰胆碱

i. v. /I. V. —intravenous 静脉的;静脉注射

i. m. /I. M. —intramuscular 肌内的;肌内注射

IP—inpatient 住院病人

R. B. C. —red blood(cell) count 红细胞计数

MRI—magnetic resonance imaging 磁共振成像

DNA—deoxyribonucleic acid 脱氧核糖核酸

RNA—ribonucleic acid 核糖核酸

有些首字母缩略词是由拉丁语或希腊语直接缩写而成的。如：

a. c. —ante cibum(before meal) 餐前

p. c. —post cibum(after meal) 餐后

AD—auris dextra(right ear) 右耳

AU—auris uterque(each ear) 每耳

h. s. —hora somni(at bedtime) 就寝时

2）首字母拼音法

首字母拼音法的构词方法与首字母缩略法的构词方法相同,它们的差异是由首字母拼音法构成的词汇可以读为一个完整的单词。

AIDS←Acquired Immune Deficiency Syndrome 获得性免疫缺陷综合征

SARS←Severe Acute Respiratory Syndrome 严重急性呼吸综合征

COVID-19 ←Corona Virus Disease 2019 新型冠状病毒肺炎

3）截短法

截短法是用词汇的一部分来表达整个词汇的意义,而把其他部分截去省略的一种构

词方法。截短法非常灵活,构词时可截去词首、词尾或同时截去词首、词尾。有时短语的构成也可以用截短法。如:

Abd—abdomen 腹部

Doc—doctor 医生

Flu—influenza 流感

Cap—capsule 胶囊

aq.—aqua 水

amb—ambulate,ambulatory 行走

CA/ca—carcinoma,cancer 癌

Polio—poliomyelitis 小儿麻痹症

了解西医词汇的构词法可以在很大程度上帮助译者理解、识记和翻译词汇,提高翻译效率。

第二节 西医词汇的翻译

根据上述医学英语词汇的特点,在翻译西医词汇时要留意以下几点:

1. 词义的选择

由于医学英语术语在演变过程中和普通词汇的互相转化,造成了一些词在不同语境中具有不同语义,翻译时需要选择恰当的表述,使文字通顺、得体、规范,以保持术语的严密性和专业性。如:

(1) Other HPV types are responsible for non-genital warts, which are not sexually transmitted.

译文:其他类型的HPV(人乳头瘤病毒)会造成非生殖器湿疣,这些湿疣不会通过性行为进行传播。

"be responsible for..."在一般语境中译为"对……负责",此处译为"是……形成的原因,造成"。

(2) After cardiac and/or pulmonary arrest, the most critical emergency is severe bleeding, especially from a main artery.

译文:心肺骤停后,最危急的情况是严重出血,尤其是主动脉出血。

"arrest"一词有"拘捕、逮捕"的意思,此处指的是"骤停、功能中止"。

(3) All of the septic shock patients were free from heart or renal failure.

译文:所有的感染性休克患者没有出现心脏或者肾脏衰竭。

"failure"一般意为"失败",此处指"衰竭"。

(4) Thyroid storm is a crisis or life-threatening condition characterized by an exaggeration of the usual physiologic response seen in hyperthyroidism.

storm:风暴,此处指危象;exaggeration:夸张,此处指过度反应。

hyperthyroidism:甲状腺机能亢进

译文：甲状腺危象是一种危及生命的紧急状况，其特征是因甲状腺机能亢进而引起的正常生理反应的过度表现。

（5）Experts estimate that surgical complications result in at least one million deaths a year.

译文：专家估计手术并发症每年至少造成一百万人死亡。

"complication"一词有很多义项：①并发症；②复杂，难懂；③纠纷。此处显然指"并发症"。

（6）Some drugs can compromise the immune system.

译文：有些药物会使免疫系统受损。

"compromise"有"妥协；危害；和解；折中"的意思，此处指"使……受损"：to expose somebody or something to danger.

（7）Embryonic stem cells are the source of every cell, tissue and organ in the body.

译文：身体中的每一个细胞、组织和器官都来源于胚性干细胞。

"tissue"有"纸巾；（人、动植物细胞的）组织；织物"的意思，此处指"组织"。

（8）Certain compounds can enter and spread throughout the interior of the cell only after the surface has been punctured.

译文：只有在细胞表面被戳破以后，某些化合物才能进入并散布整个细胞内部。

"cell"有"细胞；电池；牢房；基层组织"的意思。此处指"细胞"。

（9）pathogenic bacteria culture and drug sensitive test on nosocomial infection in general surgical intensive care unit

译文：普通外科对医院感染的病原菌培养与药敏试验

"culture"有"文化；栽培；教养"的意思。此处指"培养"。

2. 术语的表述

医学术语和普通词汇相比，在表述上显得更加规范、客观、严密。在翻译这类词语时要避免使用随意性强的表达。如：

（1）The most common trigger for a hyperglycemic crisis is an infection, such as strep throat, pneumonia, an intestinal virus, or a urinary tract infection.

译文：高血糖危象最常见的诱发因素是感染，如脓毒性咽喉炎、肺炎、肠道病毒，或尿路感染。

（2）People with stress ulcers have a longer ICU length of stay(up to 8 days) and a higher mortality(up to 4 fold) than patients who do not have stress ulceration and bleeding.

译文：应激性溃疡患者的 ICU 停留时间较长（可至 8 天），死亡率高于未发生应激性溃疡和出血的患者（高达 4 倍）。

此处"stress ulcer"意为"应激性溃疡（而非压力溃疡）"。

（3）Women who consumed additional meat or took iron supplements were able to bounce back.

译文：那些增食肉类食品或服用铁离子补剂的女性，能够<u>恢复</u>到健康状态。

（4）An antibiotic is not precisely definable but is usually thought of as a product of microbial metabolism which inhibits growth of other, pathogenic organisms, without substantially affecting any <u>host</u> of the latter.

译文：对抗生素还不能精确地下定义，但通常认为它是微生物代谢的产物，能抑制其他致病微生物的生长，而对后者的<u>宿主</u>没有明显的影响。

（5）The glycerol-glucose procedure, as designed, is inadequate and, therefore, a revision should be made so that further studies address optimization of <u>yields</u> after freezing of the platelets.

译文：如此设计的甘油—葡萄糖（低温保存）技术是不充分的，因此应该改进，进一步研究的方向应是把血小板冷冻后的<u>回收率</u>提高到最佳水平。

（6）Pain due to these causes is usually paroxysmal and possesses the distribution characteristic of <u>the nerves involved</u>, which are <u>tender</u> on pressure.

译文：由这些原因引起的疼痛通常为发作性的，并具有按<u>受累神经</u>分布的特点，压迫该神经有<u>触痛</u>。

（7）However if such <u>water-excluding</u> masses of triacylglycerol appear in the wrong places, for instance in the liver(fatty liver) or in the small vessels(fat embolism), there can be serious consequences.

译文：然而，如果这种<u>斥水</u>的甘油三酯出现于不适当的位置，如在肝脏（脂肪肝）或在小血管（脂肪栓塞），就可能产生严重后果。

（8）A diagnosis is the determination of disease or disorder based on an examination of a patient, the patient's history and <u>complaints</u>, and any laboratory tests.

译文：诊断就是根据病人的体检、病史和<u>主诉</u>以及化验检查，对疾病或病症做出的判断。

（9）Patients with well established pneumococcal pneumonia <u>appear accurately ill.</u>

译文：确诊肺炎球菌性肺炎的患者<u>呈急性病容</u>。

（10）The <u>fingerprint</u> technique had already been extensively used for the quality evaluation and control.

译文：<u>指纹图谱</u>技术在（中药）质量评价和控制当中<u>应用广泛</u>。

3. 构词语素的积累

医学英语词汇中的词缀非常丰富，且意义相对稳定，为确定词义、翻译词汇提供了线索。para-表示周边，构成的词汇有：paranasal（鼻旁的；鼻侧的），parathyroid（甲状旁腺的），paradentitis（牙周炎）；-ia 表示状态，常用于病名：leukemia（白血病），pneumonia（肺炎），ataxia（共济失调）；lev(o)-意为左，向左，如：levocardia（左位心），levodopa（左旋多巴），levoduction（左旋眼）；-oma 意为瘤，如：cerebroma（脑瘤），epithelioma（上皮瘤；上皮癌），hemangioma（血管瘤）；-genesis 意为产生，生成，如：myelogenesis（骨髓发生），pathogenesis（发病机制），dentinogenesis（牙本质生成）。

1）常见前缀派生构词

由表否定的前缀构成的派生词：

由表示否定的前缀构成的派生词：

a-
anemia 贫血
aseptic 无菌的

an-
analgesia 无痛法
anacholia 胆汁缺乏

in-
insanitary 不卫生的
invertebrate 无脊椎动物

由表示相反或向背的前缀构成的派生词：

allo-
allosome 异染色体
allotopia 异位, 错位

anti-
antibiotics 抗生素
anticoagulant 抗凝血剂

contra-; counter-
contraceptive 避孕剂
counterirritant 抗兴奋药

de-
deoxidation 脱氧
dehydration 脱水作用

dis-
dislocation 脱位, 脱臼
disinfection 消毒

ex-
excision 切除

由表示程度或大小多少的前缀构成的派生词：

bi-; di-
bicephalus 双头畸胎
diglyceride 甘油二酯

hemi-; semi-
hemiparalysis 偏瘫
semisynthetic 半合成的

hyper-; super-; supra-
hyperglycemia 高血糖
superlactation 泌乳过多

macro-; mega-
macroglossia 巨舌
megacardia 心肥大

multi-; pluri-; poly-
multicellular 多细胞的
polyuria 多尿症

homo-; iso-
homosexual 同性恋的
isotope 同位素

由表示时间的前缀构成的派生词：

pre-; pro-
preoperative 手术前的
prognosis 预后

post-
postpartum 产后的
posthemorrhagic 出血后的

由表示方位的前缀构成的派生词：

ad-; ana-; epi-
adrenal 肾上腺的
anagenesis 再生
epigastrium 上腹部

ante-; pre-; pro-
anteflexion (子宫) 前屈
premolar 前磨牙
protrude 向前突出

ecto-; extra-; ex-
ectoderm 外胚层
extracorporeal 体外的
exocrine 外分泌的

endo-; sub-
endocrine 内分泌的
subcutaneous 皮下的

infra-; in-
infracostal 肋下的
intravenous 静脉内的

ingestion 摄入
inframammary 乳腺下的

2) 常见后缀派生构词

由动词性后缀构成的派生词：

-ate
degenerate 恶化
defibrillate 除颤

-ize
sensitize 致敏
neutralize 中和

由形容词性后缀构成的派生词：

-ac; -al; -ar
cardiac 心脏的
bronchial 支气管的

-ic; -eal; -ary
hepatic 肝的
esophageal 食道的

-ous; -oid
mucous 黏液的
cystoid 囊样的

tonsillar 扁桃体的	ciliary 睫状的	
-tive; -sive	-ed; -ish; -less	-genic
congestive 充血性的	lubricated 润滑的	pyrogenic 致热性的
supersensitive 过度敏感的	lifeless 无生命的	angiogenic 血管源性的

由表手术类的后缀构成的派生词：

-rrhaphy	-puncture	-pexy
cardiorrhaphy 心（肌）缝合术	cardiopuncture 心穿刺术	enteropexy 肠固定术
nephrorrhaphy 肾缝术	ventriculopuncture 脑室穿刺术	gastropexy 胃固定术
-tomy	-otomy	-ostomy
appendectomy 阑尾切除术	craniotomy 颅骨切开术	gastrostomy 胃造口术
angiotomy 血管切开	colostomy 结肠造口术	

由表疼痛的后缀构成的派生词：

-algia	-odynia
arthralgia 关节痛	crymodynia 冷痛
cephalgia 头痛	omodynia 肩痛

由表病症的后缀构成的派生词：

-osis	-emia	-phasia; -phemia
arthrosis 关节病	hyperglycemia 高血糖	tachyphasia 急语症
anhypnosis 失眠症	septicemia 败血症	aphemia 运动性失语

由表制剂的后缀构成的派生词：

-ant	-cide	-gogue
coagulant 凝血剂	bactericide 杀菌剂	cholagogue 利胆剂
decongestant 减充血药	germicide 杀菌剂	
refrigerant 制冷剂	parasiticide 驱虫剂	

由表药物成分的后缀构成的派生词：

-amide	-caine	-cillin
pyrazinamide 吡嗪酰胺	lidocaine 利多卡因	penicillin 青霉素
nicotinamide 烟酰胺	procaine 普鲁卡因	ampicillin 氯苄西林
cyclophosphamide 环磷酰胺	dibucaine 地布卡因	furbenicillin 呋苄青霉素

4. 构词语素的翻译顺序

医学英语中大部分的合成词可以按照原词的语序来逐个翻译构词语素。如：

intracardiac direct vision operation 心内直视术

light therapy 光治疗

reproductive cloning 生殖性克隆

secretory piece 分泌片

immunological memory 免疫记忆

membrane attack complex 膜攻击复合体

alternative pathway 旁路途径

lymphocyte lineage 淋巴细胞系

secondary organ 外周器官

clonal anergy 克隆失活

MLR(mixed lymphocyte response)混合淋巴细胞反应

cough-equivalent asthma 咳嗽替代性哮喘

sickle cell disease 镰状细胞疾病

opportunistic inflection 机会性感染

DBPCFC(double-blind placebo-controlled food challenge)双盲安慰剂对照食物激发

但是有的语序需要根据汉语的习惯进行调整。如:"total anomalous pulmonary venous connection"译为"完全性肺静脉异常连接"或者"肺静脉连接完全异常"均可; interventional radiotherapy 译为"放射介入术"; adverse food reaction 译为"食物不良反应";"irritable bowel"译为"肠易激"等。

还有的需要进行"本地化",比如"Category B infectious diseases"译为"乙类传染病",而非"B类传染病"。类似的翻译还有:beta-agonist 乙型受体素;hepatitis A/B/C 甲肝、乙肝、丙肝。

练　习

Ⅰ. 翻译下列养生谚语(英译汉)

(1) Sleeping is the best cure for waking troubles.

(2) Anger punishes itself.

(3) Anger begins with folly, and ends in repentance.

(4) All work and no play, makes Johnny a dull boy.

(5) Care brings grey hair.

(6) Laugh at your ills, and save doctor's bills.

(7) No pillow is softer than a clear conscience.

(8) Feed a cold and starve a fever.

(9) Care kills a cat.

(10) The best physicians are Dr. Diet, Dr. Quiet, and Dr. Merryman.

(11) A clown into town is worth more than a dozen doctors.

(12) An apple a day keeps the doctor away.

(13) Always rise from the table with an appetite and you will never sit down without one.

(14) Go to bed with the lamb and rise with the lark.

(15) A closed mouth catches no flies.

Ⅱ. 翻译下列缩略语

(1) n. p. o

(2) p. o.

(3) baso

(4) gtt

(5) chemo

(6) chol

(7) postop

(8) primip

(9) pulv

(10) cath

Ⅲ. 翻译下列术语

(1) infectious microbe or virus

(2) adaptive immune system

(3) neuron overload

(4) malignant tumor

(5) the muscle bundles

(6) fatty liver

(7) ultra violet rays

(8) the lumens of the sinusoids

(9) a 10-year follow up study

(10) the childproof cap

Ⅳ. 借助词根及词缀翻译下列术语

(1) oligomenorrhea

(2) hypermenorrhea

(3) amenorrhea

(4) dysmenorrhea

(5) erythrocyte

(6) leukocyte

(7) hemocyte

(8) germicide

(9) colostomy

(10) cardiopuncture

Ⅴ. 翻译以下段落，注意词语的选择

(1) It is far more likely to be seriously injured by a vaccine-preventable disease than by a vaccine. For example, in the case of polio, the disease can cause paralysis, measles can cause encephalitis and blindness, and some vaccine-preventable diseases can even result in death. While any serious injury or death caused by vaccines is one too many, the benefits of vaccination greatly outweigh the risks, and many more illness and deaths would occur without vaccines.

(2) Symptoms may occur several times in a day or week in affected individuals. For some people the symptoms become worse during physical activity or at night. Failure to recognize and avoid triggers that lead to a tightened airway can be life threatening and may result in an asthma attack, respiratory distress and even death.

(3) Asthma triggers can include cold air, extreme emotional arousal such as anger or fear, and physical exercise.

(4) Asthma is often under-diagnosed and under-treated, creating a substantial burden to individuals and families and possibly restricting individuals' activities for a lifetime.

(5) The strongest risk factors for developing asthma are exposure to indoor allergens such as house dust mites in bedding, carpets and stuffed furniture; pollution and pet dander; outdoor allergens such as pollens and moulds; tobacco smoke and chemical irritants in the workplace.

资料来源：http://www.who.int/features/qa/84/en/2017 年 4 月 20 日

Ⅵ. 短文翻译

Which Kinds of Foods Make Us Fat?

One fundamental and unanswered question in obesity research is what kind of foods contribute most to the condition. Experts variously blame, for example, fatty or sugary fare or foods that lack protein, which may prompt us, unconsciously, to overeat.

For a diet study published this summer in *Cell Metabolism*, researchers randomly assigned one of 29 different diets to hundreds of adult male mice. (The scientists hope to include female mice in later experiments.) Some diets supplied up to 80 percent of their calories in the form of saturated and unsaturated fats, with few carbohydrates; others included little fat and consisted largely of refined carbohydrates, mostly from grains and corn syrup, although in some variations the carbs came from sugar. Yet other diets were characterized by extremely high or low percentages of protein. The mice stayed on the same diet for three months—estimated to be the equivalent of roughly nine human years—while being allowed to eat and move about their cages at will. The mice were then measured by weight and body composition, and their brain tissue was examined for evidence of altered gene activity.

Only some of the mice became obese—almost every one of which had been on a high-fat diet. These mice showed signs of changes in the activity of certain genes too, in areas of the brain related to processing rewards; fatty kibble made them happy, apparently. None of the other diets, including those rich in sugar, led to significant weight gain or changed gene expression in the same way. Even super-high-fat diets, consisting of more than 60 percent fat, did not lead to significant weight gains, and the mice on those diets consumed less food over all than their counterparts, presumably because they simply could not stomach so much fat.

"It looks like consuming high-fat diets, if they aren't extremely high fat, leads to weight gain, if you are a mouse," says John Speakman, a professor at the Chinese Academy of Sciences in Beijing and at the University of Aberdeen in Scotland, who oversaw the study. Speakman and his co-authors believe that the fatty meals stimulated and altered parts of the brains, causing the mice to want fatty food so much that they ignored other bodily signals indicating that they had already consumed enough energy.

资料来源：https：//cn.nytimes.com《纽约时报》

第四章　中医词汇及其翻译

(1) 无恒德者,不可以作医。　　　　　　　　　　　　　(《古今图书集成医部》)
Without solid morality, one cannot become a doctor.

(2) 人法地,地法天,天法道,道法自然。　　　　　　　　　(《老子集注》上)
People follow the principle of the earth, which follows the principle of the heaven, which follows the principle of the Tao, which follows the principle of the nature.

(编者译)

(3) 四时阴阳者,万物之根本也。　　　　　　　　　　(《素问·四气调神大论》)
The changes of Yin and Yang in the four seasons are the roots of all the things in nature.

(4) 天覆地载,万物悉备,莫贵于人。　　　　　　　　　(《素问·宝命全形论》)
The covering of the heavens in the upper and the support of the earth in the lower have paved the way for the creation of all things in nature, among which the most valuable one is man.

(5) 春生夏长,秋收冬藏。　　　　　　　　　　　(《灵枢·顺气一日分为四时》)
Crops germinate in spring, grow in summer, get harvested in autumn and stored in winter.

(李照国译)

和现代医学的词汇相比,中医药词汇似乎是迥然不同的一个体系,它浓郁的人文色彩、大量的比喻、丰富的修辞很难让人将其理解为专业术语。若要理解中医词汇的独特性,必须了解其生成背景。

第一节　中医词汇的哲学背景

中医药文化是中国传统文化的重要组成部分,在其形成理论体系的过程中传统哲学思想贯穿始终。

1. 儒家对中医药的影响

儒家文化是自汉代以后中国传统文化的主流,中国古代有"儒医"之说,许多儒士精通中医,许多医家熟读孔孟之书。

儒家思想对中医的第一个影响是"仁"。儒家思想主要用于治国理政,如不能,则退而求之医人,即"不为良相,当为良医"(范仲淹语)。阳泉在其《物理论》"论医"一文中说:"夫医者,非仁爱之士不可托也,非聪明理达不可任也,非廉洁淳良不可信也。"

第二个影响是"忠孝"。药王孙思邈有言:"君亲有疾,不能疗之者,非忠孝也"。不少医家是出于尽孝而学医的。《四库全书总目提要》中说:"以为惟儒者能明其理,而事亲者当知医也。"金代医学家张从正即把自己的医学专著叫作《儒门事亲》。

第三个影响是"中庸"与"中和"的关联及二者在中医中的应用。儒家提倡"中庸之道",力求达到"致中和"的境界。董仲舒又全面论述了"执中用和"的观点,提出:"是故能以中和理天下者,其德大盛;能以中和养其身者,其寿极命",由此扩展到饮食、劳逸、动静、情志等人们生活的方方面面。中医学中的"阴阳和合""阴平阳秘"以及《黄帝内经》中"怒伤肝,悲胜怒;喜伤心,恐胜喜"等,都是"致中和"最恰当的例证。用药时"升降互补、寒热并用、燥湿相济"的配伍原则,也体现了运动变化之后复归于"和"的平衡状态。

2. 道家对中医药的影响

医道同源,表明了道家乃至道教与中医学在生命的认知上有着同一出发点和始基。先秦道家文化不但影响了中医学基础理论的形成,而且在接下来的两千多年中,医道相互影响、相互渗透,使两股学术源流始终水乳交融,共同兴衰。

道家学说的"道一气"一元论思想说明了自然的可知性。但与此同时,道家的"道"和中医的理一样往往只可意会不可言传:"道可道,非常道""医之为言意也"(《后汉书·方术列传》)。这也为中医术语的模糊性提供了理论依据。

1)道家的生命科学对中医词汇的影响

道家的"生命科学"是整个道家文化的核心部分。《黄帝内经》是较早的具有道家思想内容的中医学理论的奠基之作。此后,中国传统医学逐渐以道教为中心,形成了"道教医学",先秦道家的哲学术语"阴阳"为医家提供了说理的工具,与后来介入中医学的五行成为中医学基础理论的最核心概念。

"飘风不终朝,骤雨不终日":先秦道家展示给世人的斑驳世界永远是运动、变易、充满矛盾转化的。《黄帝内经》中记载的生命现象也是随着天地四时而不断变化着的。如:"寒极生热,热极生寒""重寒则热,重热则寒""味归形,形归气,气归精,精归化……化生精,气生形。味伤形,气伤精,精化为气,气伤于味"(《素问·阴阳应象大论》)。

2)道家的认知方法对中医词汇的影响

老子提出以"虚""静"为观览万物之本。《黄帝内经》中则有朴实的身心健康观:"上古之人,其知道者,法于阴阳,和于术数,食饮有节,起居有常,不妄作劳,故能形与神俱,而尽终其天年,度百岁乃去"。

老子还提出"玄览"的方法,河上公注解为:"心居玄冥之处,览知万物,故谓之玄览"。这一方法为中医学家提供了方法论依据,并形成了以虚形静观、直觉顿悟为特色的中医学认知方法:"持脉有道,虚静为保"(《素问·脉要精微论》)。

3. 中医药产生的人文背景

中医学在人文文化的土壤中蕴生,人文环境决定了中医的理论取向,由此也决定了中医人文文化的三个层面。

政治层面:中医理论从当时封建王朝的政治制度出发,运用了当时社会统治阶层的职务及相互关系来比喻十二脏腑的功能及其相互联系。如："心者,君主之官也,神明出焉。肺者,相傅之官,治节出焉。"

结构层面:中医理论在结构上讲究"天人相应,形神合一",如《内经》所说:"人以天地之气生,四时之法成""人与天地相参也,与日月相应也"。

观念层面:受传统"重道轻器"人文思想的影响,中医重视"形而上"的研讨,而忽视"形而下"的探求。在古代文学艺术创作中,丰富的中医学知识频频被融入其中。屈原在《离骚》中借香草以谓忠良、借莸草痛斥奸邪。《西游记》里的药诗和《红楼梦》中的药对都说明了中医浓厚的人文特色。

第二节　中医词汇的特点

我国绝大多数自然科学的术语来源于西方,它们是以翻译的形式进入汉语体系的,如:万有引力、马力、牛顿、千瓦、立方体等,唯独中医术语形成于古代。独特的人文哲学背景造就了中医不同于任何其他自然科学的独特术语体系,尤其是中医典籍的语言,可谓"其文简,其意博,其理奥,其趣深"。概括起来,具有以下特点:

1. 抽象性与模糊性

和西医术语的精确性相比,中医术语显得抽象而且模糊,给人以深奥晦涩之感。例如"阴阳""精""气""经络""三焦"等术语,完全是中医理论中所特有的概念,在英文中没有对等的词,即使是和西医体系有相似之处的"脏腑"概念在含义上也有不同。中医注重的是相关脏器的功能而非具体的解剖形态,而西医则纯粹从解剖学的角度来描述心、肝、脾、肺、肾,概念并不对等,这就给翻译和理解带来了相当大的挑战。

2. 文学性与人文性

没有任何一门学科的术语像中医用语一样充满了浓郁的文学色彩。尤其是在中医典籍中,广用修辞,看似不符合科技用语的要求。然而近几年人们越来越意识到现代医学中缺失的人文关怀恰恰在丰富的中医语言这一载体中得到了体现。中医术语有着独特的"辞简""文约""言炼"等语言美学特点,具体如下:

节律美:中医典籍往往在叙述和阐发理论术语,在长短错落的散文句子中,融进节奏和谐的韵文,在遣词造句中有对"音乐美、建筑美和绘画美"的追求,使得文章朗朗上口,结构整齐,色彩斑斓。《诗纪匡谬》云:"素问一书,通篇有韵。"再看《灵枢·终始》:"和气之方,必通阴阳,五藏为阴,六府为阳,传之后世,以血为盟,敬之者昌,慢之者亡,无道行私,必得夭秧。"在张仲景的《伤寒论·序》中,排比句式比比皆是,气势跌宕,节奏铿锵:"勤求古训,博采众方""进不能爱人知人,退不能爱身知己""感往昔之沦丧,伤横夭之莫救"。

简洁美:中医学中大量传世医案、医论都是语言简洁性的典范,"言有尽,而意有余"。如:"汗、吐、下、和、温、清、消、补"是中医治法的八大原则,每一个原则都只用一个字就道出了中医治法的精髓和灵魂,可谓"意则期多,字惟求少"。

通俗美:中医往往采用比喻的手法使其术语通俗易懂,比如脉象中的"洪脉、沉脉、迟脉、数脉、滑脉、丝脉",治法中的"提壶揭盖、釜底抽薪、逆水行舟、激流挽舟"等形象生动。症状描写如《伤寒杂病论》中的"弱如葱叶",《灵枢·邪气藏府病形》的"微急为沉厥奔豚",其特点跃然纸上。

含蓄美:"其言曲而中,其事肆而隐",即把主观上认为不美或不雅的事物套上一个文雅的语言符号。"视其前后,知何部不利,利之则愈"中的"前后"分别指大小便;《素问》中用"隐曲"表示"前后二阴"。

3. 历史性

由于中医药学成形于古代,具有文言文的性质,名词术语多为古代汉语,有很多单字词,如"气"。有时词即短句,如"木克土""肺主气",更有古今词义演变以及古文的现代表述等,如"简其平日所服,寒凉者十六,补肝肾者十三"(《杂病广要》),其中,"十六"即十分之六,"十三"即十分之三,翻译时要将其所指明确地表示出来:"... six out of ten are those cold in nature and three out of ten are those for tonifying liver and kidney"(王洁华,2010)。

第三节 中医词汇的分类

中医英语词汇是用来准确表达特有中医概念的专门词汇,从语义学角度可以将中医英语词汇分为以下几类:

1. 基础理论类

基础理论类主要是关于中医基础理论的基本中医英语词汇,具体如下:

阴阳五行:holism(整体观念),yin-yang balance(阴阳平衡),yin-yang conversion(阴阳转化),five elements/phases(五行),overwhelming(相乘),rebellion(相侮),mother and child affecting each other(母子相及),correspondence between nature and human(天人相应),pattern identification/syndrome differentiation and treatment(辨证论治)等。

气血津液:innate essence(先天之精),acquired essence(后天之精),kidney essence(肾精),innate qi(先天之气),acquired qi(后天之气),vital qi(正气),qi transformation(气化),qi movement(气机),homogeny of clear fluid and blood(津血同源),homogeny of essence and blood(精血同源)等。

五脏六腑:viscera and bowels(脏腑),five zang viscera(五脏),six fu viscera(六腑),extraordinary fu-viscera(奇恒之腑),kidney yin(肾阴),kidney yang(肾阳),intercourse between heart and kidney 等。

十二经络:meridian and collateral(经络),eight extra meridians(奇经八脉),twelve meridian divergences(十二经别)等。

形体官窍:body constituent(形体),skin and hair(皮毛),interstices(腠理),orifice of sense organ(官窍),five sense organs(五官),seven orifices(七窍),defense aspect(卫分),qi aspect(气分),nutrient aspect(营分)等。

病因学说：pathogen（病邪），external pathogen（外邪），exogenous disease（外感），six climatic external pathogens（六淫），wind pathogen（风邪），dampness toxin（湿毒），cold toxin（寒毒），seasonal toxin（时毒），seven emotions（七情），phlegm-fluid retention（痰饮），retained fluid（水饮），three types of disease causes（三因）等。

病机：theory of pathogenesis（病机学说），location of disease（病位），nature of disease（病性），flaring up of deficient fire（虚火上炎），superficies cold with interior heat（表寒里热），upper cold and lower heat（上寒下热），deficiency and excess（虚实），sunken middle qi（中气下陷），disorder of qi and blood（气血失调），deficiency of both heart and spleen（心脾两虚），liver qi invading stomach（肝气犯胃），adverse rising of stomach qi（胃气上逆）等。

2. 诊断学类

关于中医诊断的基本英语词汇，可分为四诊（望诊、闻诊、问诊、切诊）、八纲辨证、病因辨证、气血辨证、津液辨证、脏腑辨证、各科辨证、六经辨证、卫气营血辨证、三焦辨证等，具体如下：

望闻问切：four diagnostic methods（四诊），pale white complexion（面色淡白），tongue inspection（舌诊），tongue shape（舌形），fur（舌苔），loss of voice（失音），paraphasia（错语），wheezing dyspnea（喘鸣），cough with dyspnea（咳逆），aversion to wind（恶风），mild fever（微热），vexing heat in the extremities（手足烦热），pulse taking（脉诊），pulse manifestation（脉象），floating pulse（浮脉），slow pulse（迟脉），rapid pulse（数脉），surging pulse（洪脉），thready pulse（细脉），slippery pulse（滑脉），stringy pulse（弦脉）等。

八纲辨证：yin syndrome（阴证），yang syndrome（阳证），syndrome of deficiency of both yin and yang（阴阳两虚证），syndrome of hyperactivity of fire due to yin deficiency（阴虚火旺证），superficies syndrome（表证），interior syndrome（里证），cold syndrome（寒证），heat syndrome（热证），deficiency syndrome（虚证），excess syndrome（实证）等。

病因辨证：syndrome differentiation of etiology（病因辨证），exogenous wind syndrome（外风证），endogenous wind syndrome（内风证），summerheat syndrome（暑证），dampness syndrome（湿证），syndrome of blood stasis syndrome（血瘀证），syndrome of cold-in-blood（血寒证），wind-toxicity syndrome（风毒证）等。

气血辨证：qi and blood differentiation of syndromes（气血辨证），syndrome of qi deficiency（气虚证），syndrome of qi sinking（气陷证），syndrome of qi stagnation（气滞证），syndrome of blood deficiency（血虚证），blood heat syndrome（血热证），disorder of qi and blood（气血失调）等。

津液辨证：fluid and humor differentiation of syndromes（津液辨证），phlegm syndrome（痰证），fluid retention syndrome（饮证），water retention syndrome（水停证），syndrome of turbid fluid depletion（液脱证），syndrome of fighting of wind with water（风水相搏证）等。

脏腑辨证：syndrome differentiation of zang-fu viscera（脏腑辨证），syndrome differentiation of heart diseases(心病辨证),syndrome of deficiency of heart qi(心气虚证),syndrome of deficiency of heart yin(心阴虚证),syndrome of deficiency of lung qi(肺气虚证),syndrome of spleen failing to transport(脾失健运证),syndrome of deficiency of stomach qi(胃气虚证),kidney deficiency syndrome(肾虚证),syndrome of non-consolidation of kidney qi(肾气不固证),syndrome of disharmony between heart and kidney(心肾不交证)等。

各科辨证:pattern of wind-cold obstructing the collateral(风寒阻络证),syndrome of stasis and stagnation due to traumatic injury(外伤瘀滞证),syndrome of liver fire invading head(肝火犯头证),syndrome of heat-toxicity invading tongue(热毒攻舌证)等。

六经辨证:syndrome differentiation of six channels theory(六经辨证),Taiyang disease(太阳病),Shaoyang disease(少阳病),Taiyin disease(太阴病),heat transformation syndrome of Shaoyin(少阴热化证)等。

卫气营血辨证:syndrome differentiation of weifen(卫气营血辨证),weifen syndrome(卫分病),qifen syndrome(气分证),syndrome of stirring blood due to intense heat(热盛动血证),summerheat-heat syndrome(暑热证),summerheat-damp syndrome(暑湿证)等。

三焦辨证:syndrome differentiation of triple energizer(三焦辨证),syndrome of diffusive dampness-heat in sanjiao/triple energizer(湿热弥漫三焦证),dampness-heat in middle jiao/energizer(中焦湿热)等。

3. 临床各科类

和中医临床各科相关的基本中医英语词汇若再细分,还可以分为内科、外科、妇产科、儿科、眼科、耳鼻喉科、骨伤科等,具体如下:

内科:yin disease(阴病),yang disease(阳病),exogenous cold disease(伤寒),miscellaneous disease(杂病),warm-toxin disease(温毒),warm disease(温病),wheezing and dyspnea(哮喘),dyspnea of deficiency type(虚喘),meridian stroke(中经),chronic diarrhea(久泄),water distention(水胀),yin edema(阴水),blood disease(血病),latent fluid retention(伏饮),prolonged fluid retention(留饮),consumptive disease(虚劳)等。

外科:sore and ulcer(疮疡),ulcer(溃疡),cerebral palsy(脑瘫),erysipelas(丹毒),qi tumor(气瘤),herpes simplex(热疮),tinea manuum(鹅掌风),cattle-skin lichen(牛皮癣),internal hemorrhoid(内痔),huhuo disease(狐惑)等。

妇产科:menopathy(月经病),menstrual disorders(月经不调),metrorrhagia(崩漏),inverted menstruation(倒经),threatened abortion(胎动不安),lochioschesis(恶露不下)等。

儿科:fetal weakness(胎弱),infantile asthma(小儿哮喘),spleen gan disease(脾疳),lung gan disease(肺疳),mumps(痄腮),neonatal jaundice(胎黄)等。

眼耳鼻喉:photophobia(羞明),heat lacrimation(热泪),sudden blindness(暴盲),facial paralysis(口眼歪斜),ear sore(耳疮),nasal malnutrition(鼻疳),stony moth(石

蛾),throat obstruction(喉痹),double tongue(重舌)等。

骨伤科:stiff neck(落枕),tendon injury(筋伤),tendon ruptured(筋断),muscle and tendon crispation(筋缩),muscular rheumatism(筋痹)等。

4. 治疗学类

和中医治疗相关的基本中医英语词汇又可分成两类:治则和治法。

治则:orthodox treatment(正治),retrograde treatment(反治),strengthening vital qi to eliminate the pathogenic factor(扶正祛邪),treating same disease with different methods(同病异治),treating the acute before the chronic(先急后缓),treating the exterior before the interior(先表后里)等。

治法:method of treatment(治法),eight methods(八法),diaphoresis(汗法),dispelling cold(散寒),strengthening body resistance for relieving superficies syndrome(扶正解表),ventilating lung(宣肺),clearing method(清法),purgation method(下法),harmonizing method(和法),eliminating dampness(化湿),dissipating phlegm(化痰),invigorating the spleen and dispersing the stagnated liver-energy(疏肝健脾)等。

5. 针灸类

针灸类词汇可分成三类:针法、灸法和拔罐。

针法:techniques of acupuncture and moxibustion(刺灸法),infant acupuncture therapy(小儿针法),facial acupuncture(面针),ear acupuncture(耳针),acupoint(穴位),channel point(经穴),extra point(奇穴),needle-inserting with single hand(单手进针法),arrival of qi(得气)等。

灸法:direct moxibustion(着肤灸),mild-warm moxibustion(温和灸),natural moxibustion(天灸),medicinal moxibustion(药物灸)等。

拔罐:cupping(拔罐),retained cupping(留罐),moving/slide cupping(走罐),medicated cupping(药罐),suction cupping method(抽气罐法),burning cotton method(贴棉法)等。

6. 药物治疗类

关于中草药及运用中草药治疗的相关基本中医英语词汇可分成两类:药物和方剂。

药物:Chinese materia medica(中药),herb(草药),materia medica(本草),genuine regional drug(道地药材),top grade drug(上品),channel entry(归经),incompatibility(相畏),mutual inhibition(相恶),eighteen antagonisms(十八反),nineteen incompatibilities(十九畏),superficies-relieving medicinal(解表药),heat-clearing medicinal(清热药),purgative medicinal(泻下药),tranquillizing medicinal(安神药),qi-supplementing medicinal(补气药)等。

方剂:prescription(方剂),classical prescriptions(经方),sovereign drug(君药),minister drug(臣药),assistant drug(佐药),envoy drug(使药),preparation(剂型),powder preparation(散剂),paste preparation(膏剂),pellet(丹剂),soluble granules(冲剂),decocting pieces(饮片),strong fire(武火),mild fire(文火),administered before meal(饭前服),superficies-relieving formula(解表剂)等。

第四节 中医术语的翻译

中医翻译争议最激烈的领域是术语的翻译,中西医的差异体现得最淋漓尽致的领域也是专业术语。

1. 中医词汇常见的翻译方法

音译:有些术语反映该民族特有的事物、思想和观念,具有很强的民族性,在别的语言中找不到对应词,如"阴""阳""气"宜音译为"yin""yang""qi"。针灸穴位名称宜音译,如"寸口""至阴"分别音译为"cunkou""zhiyin"。

沿用西医现成的术语:如心、肝、脾、肺、肾等解剖学类术语在西医中可找到合适的对应语。虽然中医的脏腑和西医的解剖器官在意义上出入很大,但是为了简便起见,依然采用西医中的术语。此外,"血"译为"blood","阴血"指的也是血,不必译为"yin blood",否则概念重复,直接译为"blood"即可。

约定俗成:即沿用中医译语数千年来比较确切的部分。如:"针""灸"两术语,分别被译为"acupuncture"和"moxibustion",沿用多年,已得到世界各国的普遍接受,尽管这两个词未能体现该术语的中国属性,但重译它们有违语言发展规律,也没有必要。

科技构词法:即借鉴西医语言的构词语素来翻译表达病理变化与治疗方法等类型的中医术语。如:词根 hepat-意为"肝",stagnation 意为"郁结"。"肝郁"可译为"hepatostagnation"。

仿照西医,求同存异:西医术语常用形容词加名词表示因果,如"菌痢"译为"bacillary dysentery","菌毒败血症"译为"toxemic septicemia";而中医病名中的因果关系却常用后置定语表示,如"肾虚不孕"译为"sterility due to the kidney deficiency","肺虚咳嗽"译为"cough caused by lung deficiency",显得比较冗长。不妨借鉴西医术语的章法,将两个术语分别译为"nephrasthenic sterility"和"pulmopenic cough"。

2. 四字中医药术语的翻译

中医词汇中有很多四字词语,可以在深入理解的基础上根据其语法和语义关系进行翻译,但是翻译后的语法结构未必要和原结构保持一致。

偏正关系类:阴阳学说(yin-yang theory);经络现象(channel phenomenon);先天之气(innate qi);后天之气(acquired qi);水液代谢(water metabolism);血液循行(blood circulation);阴阳转化(mutual convertibility of yin-yang);相互消长(mutual waning and waxing);相互制约(mutual inhibition);相互依存(interdependence);五行学说(five-phase theory/five-element theory);奇恒之腑(fu-viscera);元神之府(fu-viscera of mental activity);精明之府(house of bright essence);贮痰之器(receptacle that holds phlegm);水上之源(upper source of water)。

动宾关系类:补其不足(supplementing the insufficiency);温补脾胃(warmly invigorating spleen and stomach);温养脏腑(nourishing the viscera)。

主谓关系类:脾主四肢(spleen governing limbs);肝主疏泄(liver controlling

conveyance and dispersion);中气下陷(sinking of middle-qi);阳常有余,阴常不足(yang is often over abundant while yin is often deficient);肝气不和(disharmony of the hepatic qi);阴阳互根(mutual rooting of yin-yang);阴阳对立(opposition of yin-yang);听力不佳(lowering of auditory acuity);肾气不固(non-consolidation of kidney qi);心主血脉(heart governing blood and vessels);肾主纳气(kidney governing inspiration);肾主水液(kidney governing water metabolism);脾主运化(spleen governing transportation and transformation);木喜条达(wood characterized by growing freely and peripherally);木曰曲直(wood characterized by bending and straightening);火曰炎上(fire characterized by flaring up);土爱稼穑(earth characterized by sowing and reaping);金曰从革(metal characterized by clearing and changing);水曰润下(water characterized by moistening and descending);心肾相交(intercourse between heart and kidney);肝肾同源(homogeny of liver and kidney)。

重叠式动宾关系(动宾+动宾):养阴清肺(nourishing yin and clearing lung-heat);健脾利湿(invigorating spleen and draining dampness);消食化滞(relieving food stagnation);清肝泻火(clearing liver-fire);温肺散寒(warming lung for dispelling cold);和胃理气(relieving the gastric disorder and regulating vital energy);活血化瘀(activating blood circulation to dissipate blood stasis);养血柔肝(nourishing blood to soften the liver)。

宾语前置式动宾关系:虚者补之(相当于补虚者)(treating deficiency syndrome with tonifying methods);实者泻之(相当于泻实者)(treating excess syndrome with purgative methods);散者收之(gathering dispersion);劳者温之(warming consumption);热者寒之,寒者热之(a heat syndrome is relieved with cold-natured herbs, while a cold syndrome is relieved with hot-natured herbs);下者举之(elevating collapse);高者抑之(suppressing the rising);惊者平之(tranquilizing the unease)。

因果关系类:风热头痛(anemopyric headache);肾虚不孕(nephrasthenic sterility)。

条件关系类:阳盛则热(hyperyang generating heat);燥胜则干(predominant dryness causing withering);阴盛格阳(exuberant yin repelling yang);恐则气下(fear leading to qi sinking)。

并列关系类:升降出入(ascending descending, exiting and entering);升降浮沉(ascending, descending, floating and sinking);真寒假热(true cold with false heat);假寒真热(true heat with false cold);敛汗固表(stopping the excessive perspiration and strengthening the superficies);养心安神(refreshing and tranquilizing);阴平阳秘(relative equilibrium of yin-yang);头重脚轻(heavy head and light feet)。

补充说明关系类:阳损及阴(yang deficiency involving yin);阴虚风动(stirring wind due to yin deficiency);肝阳化风(hyperactive liver yang causing wind);热极生风(extreme heat causing wind);血虚生风(blood deficiency causing wind);血燥生风(blood dryness causing wind)。

3. 中医术语中的数字翻译

很多中医术语中包含数字,有的数字需要译出来。如:五行(five phases/elements),

四气(four nature of drugs),五味(five flavors),四诊(four diagnostic methods),八纲(eight principles),五色(five colors),手三阴经(three yin channels of hand),手三阳经(three yang channels of hand),足三阴经(three yin channels of foot),足三阳经(three yang channels of foot),手少阳三焦经(triple energizer meridian of hand lesser yang),七冲门(seven important portals),十二经脉(twelve regular channels)等。还有许多汤剂名称是带有数字的,多表示其中包含的成分,也需要译出来。如:五皮饮(five-peel decoction),五味消毒饮(five-ingredient toxin-eliminating decoction),四物汤(four-ingredient decoction)等。

许多带数字的中医术语高度概括,翻译时既要揭示其内涵,又不能过于冗长烦琐。如:"五运六气"指的是运用五行学说,结合六种气候(风、火、热、湿、燥、寒)的转变,来推断每年气候变化与人体疾病发生的关系,常见的译法有以下几种:

five movements and six climates

five elements' motion and six kinds of weather

five elements' evolution and six kinds of natural factors

five evolutive phases and six climatic changes

以上译法都从某一个方面揭示了术语的内涵,但是考虑到术语应当具有的简洁性,还是第一种译法比较可取。

"五脏"是"心、肝、脾、肺、肾"的合称,常见的译法有:

five solid organs

five viscera

five zang viscera

five zangs

其中,"five zang viscera"最为流行,"five zangs"是该译法的进一步简写,也广为使用。根据约定俗成的原则,这两种译法比较可取。

"六腑"是"胆、胃、大肠、小肠、膀胱和三焦"的合称。常见的译法有:

six hollow organs

six hollow viscera

six fu viscera

six fus

同上,"six fu viscera"和"six fus"比较可取。

三焦是中医独有的名称,其实质很难界定,历来是争议较大的一个术语,常见译法有:

three warmers

three heaters

triple energizer

sanjiao

世界卫生组织在《针灸经穴名称国际标准化方案》中将"三焦"译作"triple energizer",因此流传较广,有约定俗成的趋势。

病因中的"七情"指的是喜、怒、忧、思、悲、恐、惊七种情志活动,常常译为"seven

emotions"。方药中的"七情"指的是药物配伍中的七种作用情况,可译为"seven conditions of ingredients in prescriptions"或者"seven features(of compatibility)",包括:单行(drug used singly),相须(mutual promotion),相使(mutual enhancement),相畏(incompatibility),相恶(mutual inhibition),相杀(counteract toxicity of another drug),相反(clashing)。

"七冲门"指的是整个消化系统中的七个要冲之门,常见的译法有"seven important openings"和"seven important portals"。两种译法在语义上均有可取之处,但后者更具有回译性。

"四气五味"指的是药物寒、热、温、凉四种性能和辛、甘、酸、苦、咸五种药味,可译为"four properties and five tastes and five flavours"。

"五心烦热"中的"五心"指的是胸口、掌心和脚心,译为"vexing heat in the chest, palms and soles"。

有的中医术语虽不含具体数字,却和数字有关,如"奇方"指"药味为单数的方剂",英语没有对应词,可译成"odd-ingredient prescriptions"。

4. 传统医学典籍的翻译

中医药古籍书名的翻译是困扰译者的一个重要难题,原因有三:一是由于时代变迁,有些书名显得隐晦难解、诘屈聱牙;二是其中的文化负载词颇多,意蕴深邃、厚重典雅;三是书名翻译不仅要求达意,更要惜字如金、高度概括。(孙俊芳,2016)

古籍书名的翻译大多采用"拼音+汉字+英语"的方式,这样既便于保持作品的原貌,又便于感兴趣的读者进一步查阅原著。宇文所安认为:"重要术语的翻译皆附加拼音,这个方法虽然笨拙,但它可以不断提醒英文读者,翻译过来的汉语词与它的英文对译其实并不完全是一个意思"。(宇文所安,2003:11-16)

从目前的实践来看,中医药古籍书名大致采用以下方法进行翻译:

直译:《良方》*Wonderful Prescriptions*;《素问》*Plain Questions*;《灵枢》*Spiritual Pivot*;《药性论》*Theory of Medicinal Property*;《医原》*The Medical Origin*;《医学源论》*Medicine Source Theory*;《伤寒来苏集》*An Annotated Edition of Treatise on Febrile Diseases for Renewal of Patients*;《伤寒起景集》*A Collection of Essays on Febrile Diseases*;《古今医统》*Ancient and Modern Medical System*;《冷庐医话》*Medical Cases Recorded in Lenglu*;《古今医者案》*Medical Cases Past and Present*;《本草纲目》*Compendium of Materia Medica*;《新修本草》*Newly Revised Canon of Materia Medica*;《本草图经》*Illustrated Materia Medica*;《妇人良方》*Compendium of Effective Prescriptions for Women*;《备急千金要方》*Golden Prescriptions for Emergency Use*;《箧中方》*A Private Collection of Prescriptions*;《医方集解》*Collection of Prescriptions with Notes*;《广济方》*Guangji Prescriptions*;《太平惠民和剂局医方》*Prescriptions from the Great Peace Imperial Grace Pharmacy*;《朱氏集验方》*Effective Formulas by Doctor Zhu*;《灵苑方》*Magical Formulas*;《外科正宗》*Orthodox External Medicine*。

音译加直译/意译:《太素脉》*The Taisu Pulse*;《丹溪心法》*Danxi's Experiential*

Therapy；《桐君采药录》Tong Jun's Notes of Herbal Medicine；《马王堆汉墓医书》Mawangdui Han Dynasty Medical Books。

音译和直译/意译的结合也是译语与源语的结合。歌德曾说过:"犹如生命演变中的遗传学,在完美的翻译中,译语与源语融合为一,便产生出新的形式,又不抛弃各自原有的成分。"(谭载喜,2004:106)

意译:《医灯续焰》Annotation of Sphygmology；《金镜内台方义》Golden Mirror of Commentaries on Prescriptions from Treatise on Febrile Diseases(研究《伤寒论》方剂的著作);《虚邪论》On Pathogenic Factors("虚邪",致病邪气的通称);《理瀹骈文》Essays on the External Therapeutics of Chinese Medical Theories；《洗冤录》Instruction to Coroners(又称《洗冤集录》,系宋朝法医宋慈所著的世界上第一部系统的法医学著作);《儒门事亲》Instructions on Fulfilling Filial Piety；《黄帝内经》Inner Canon of Yellow Emperor；《针灸甲乙经》A-B Classic of Acupuncture and Moxibustion；《千金方》Golden Prescriptions；《学古诊则》Pulse Diagnosis Following Theories Stated in Inner Classic。

直译加意译:《褚氏遗书》Medical Legacies of Doctor Chu；《济阴纲目》Outline for Women's Diseases；《金匮要略》Synopsis of Golden Chamber；《日华子》Materia Medica Compiled by Rihua Zi。

理解典籍的内容是翻译书名的密钥,切忌从字面简单臆测。如:《运气略》并非 good luck,而是"五运六气"的简称,故译为 Synopsis of Five Phases' Evolution and Six Climatic Factors；《诚书》是一本儿科专著,故译为 Monograph on Pediatrics；《达生编》是一本产科专著,故译为 A Compilation of Obstetrics；《邯郸遗稿》为妇科专著,故译为 Posthumous Manuscripts in Handan City: Theories and Practice of Gynecology and Obstetrics；《过秦新录》为儿科专著,故译为 New Records on Pediatrics；《幼幼新书》也是一本儿科专著,译为 A New Book on Pediatrics；《折肱漫录》是一本临床经验漫谈,典自《左传》"三折肱知为良医",以喻经历久而成良医,故译为 A Collection of Medical Experiences。

在翻译时,有时还需要对书名做一补充说明,如:《扁鹊仓工传》Biography of Bian Que and Cang Gong, The Two Famous Ancient Physicians；《泗源先生岐黄余议》Mr Si Yuan's Commentaries on the Yellow Emperor's Inner Canon；《红炉点雪》A Little Snow on Stove Fire: Key to Treatment of Smallpox 或 A Little Snow on Stove Fire: Key to Treatment of Pulmonary Tuberculosis。

练　习

Ⅰ. 翻译以下带数字的中医术语

（1）五行学说

（2）三因学说

（3）奇经八脉

（4）十五别络

(5) 十二皮部
(6) 十二经筋
(7) 十五络脉
(8) 六淫
(9) 五邪
(10) 一指禅推法
(11) 五志化火
(12) 五腧穴
(13) 八脉交会穴
(14) 足三阳经
(15) 八会穴

Ⅱ. 翻译下列四字中医术语，并根据其语法关系进行归类
(1) 补中益气
(2) 阴阳转化
(3) 阳盛阴衰
(4) 阴盛阳衰
(5) 阴阳偏盛
(6) 阴阳偏衰
(7) 阳盛格阴
(8) 精血同源
(9) 潜阳熄风
(10) 养阴清热
(11) 祛风散寒
(12) 绝对偏盛
(13) 藏而不泻
(14) 泻而不藏
(15) 上焦如雾
(16) 中焦如沤
(17) 下焦如渎
(18) 健脾燥湿
(19) 健脾和胃
(20) 坚者削之

Ⅲ. 翻译下列书名
(1)《丹溪心法》
(2)《景岳全书》
(3)《马王堆汉墓医》
(4)《难经》
(5)《千金要方》

(6)《千金翼方》

(7)《伤寒论》

(8)《神农本草经》

(9)《药性论》

(10)《医经溯洄集》

Ⅳ. 回译下列中医药术语

(1) nearby point selection

(2) retention of needle

(3) phlegm syncope

(4) cold pathogenic disease

(5) consumptive thirst

(6) bian stone

(7) yang jaundice

(8) wind pathogen

(9) retention of dampness-heat in the interior

(10) abnormal urination and defecation

Ⅴ. 下列译文选自李照国所译《黄帝内经》英文版,试将其回译为汉语,然后对照原文

(1) The sages in ancient times who knew the Dao (the tenets for cultivating health) followed [the rules of] Yin and Yang and adjusted Shushu (the ways to cultivate health). [They were] moderate in eating and drinking, regular in working and resting, avoiding any overstrain. That is why [they could maintain a desirable] harmony between the Shen (mind or spirit) and the body, enjoying good health and a long life.

(2) When the sages in ancient times taught the people, they emphasized [the importance of] avoiding Xuxie (Deficiency-Evil) and Zeifeng (Thief-Wind) in good time and kept the mind free from avarice (贪婪). [In this way] Zhenqi in the body will be in harmony, Jingshen (Essence-Spirit) will remain inside, and diseases will have no way to occur.

(3) [Therefore people in ancient times all lived] in peace and contentment, without any fear. They worked, but never overstrained themselves, marking it smooth for Qi to flow. [They all felt] satisfied with their life and enjoyed their tasty food, natural clothes and naive customs. [They] did not desire for high positions and lived simply and naturally. That is why improper addiction and avarice could not distract their eyes and ears, obscenity (淫秽的语言) and fallacy (谬见) could not tempt their mind.

(4) Physically, they tried not to exhaust their body; mentally, they freed themselves from any anxiety, regarding peace and happiness as the target of their life, and taking self-contentment as the symbol of achievement.

(5) Following [the rules of] Yin and Yang ensures life [while] violating them leads to death. Abidance by them brings about peace while violation of them results in disorders.

第五章 医学翻译中的句式

子曰:"不愤不启,不悱不发,举一隅不以三隅反,则不复也。"选自《论语·述而第七》
The Master said, "Never give him enlightenment unless he has racked his brains and yet fails to understand, or unless he has tried hard to express himself but fails to speak. Never teach him more if he cannot extend to three cases from one instance."

(编者译)

第一节 医学学术文体的句式特征

英语中的医学学术文体,在语言上相对比较正式。比较下列两组句子:

例 5-1:When we think of being well, we think of being disease- or illness-free. (Formal)

When we think of being well, we think that we don't have disease or illness. (Informal)

例 5-2:But, plans for end-of-life care can be arranged ahead of time, so that when the time comes, care can be provided as needed without first consulting a doctor. (Formal)

But you can make plans for end-of-life early, so that when the time comes, you don't have to ask a doctor before they can provide necessary care. (Informal)

例 5-3:Such treatment falls under the principle of beneficence. (Formal)

Such treatment belongs to the principle of beneficence. (Informal)

例 5-4:Indeed, admission to the study of medicine and advancement throughout the various stages of one's career are often based solely on what one knows. (Formal)

Indeed, whether one can go to a medical school and whether one can develop throughout the various stages of one's career are often based only on what one knows. (Informal)

(季佩英,孙庆祥,2012:219)

上述各例中的第一个句子明显比较正式,第二个句子则属于非正式用语。翻译此类文本时需要特别留意其句式特征。概括起来,英语中的医学文体往往具有以下句式特征:

1. 广泛使用被动语态

(1) Marijuana is one of man's oldest and most widely used drugs. It has been consumed in various ways as long as medical history has been recorded and is currently used throughout the world by hundreds of millions of people. A fairly consistent picture of short-term effects on users is presented in many publications.

译文：大麻是使用最广泛，历史最长的一种毒品，自有医学史以来，就有使用大麻的记载，目前全世界有数以万计的人们在使用。许多出版物均相当一致地报道大麻对毒品使用者常出现短期效应。

(2) The thick muscle layer of the heart wall is the myocardium, which is lined on the inside with a thin endocardium and is covered on the outside with a thin epicardium.

译文：心肌是构成心脏的一层厚厚肌肉，内面有一层薄薄的心内膜覆盖，外面有一层薄薄的心外膜覆盖。

(3) The rationale of acupuncture analgesia has not been understood but first-class research on it is being done.

译文：针刺镇痛的基本原理尚未弄清，但一流的研究工作正在进行。

(4) Not only hearts and kidneys, but also other parts, which are even more delicate can be transplanted.

译文：不仅心脏和肾，其他更脆弱的器官也能移植。

(5) Hypothetically, a bioweapon would be designed to be highly targeted in its effects, whereas since its outbreak the coronavirus is already on track to become widespread in China and worldwide.

译文：假如是生物武器，其效果必定具有高度的针对性；而自从疫情爆发以来，冠状病毒已经在中国和世界范围内蔓延。（中国日报双语新闻）

(6) In cities where traffic control is not implemented, residents are asked to isolate themselves for 14 days after arriving at their destination.

译文：未实施交通管控的地市，人员抵达目的地后一律集中隔离14天。

(7) Residents in the province are classified into groups of high, medium and low risk based on their recent history of travel, residence and contact, as well as their current health status. Different control measures will be taken for different groups.

译文：根据居民近期旅行史、居住史、病例接触史以及目前健康状况等判断其传播疾病风险，将其划分为高风险、中风险、低风险人员，对不同人群将采取针对性的管控措施。

(8) The inadequacy of the government's response was laid bare by the unmitigated epidemiological and public relations disaster that was the saga of the Diamond Princess cruise ship. (*The Economist*)

译文："钻石公主号"邮轮上严重的流行病和公共关系灾难方面的传言，已将政府应对措施的不足暴露无遗。

(9) One idea that is being explored is using the blood (plasma) from people who are recovered.

译文：目前正在探索的一个办法是使用已被治愈病例的血液（血浆）。

由上例可见，英译汉时，被动语态常译为主动句式，反之，汉译英时则可根据英语习惯，适当使用被动语态。

（1）充分说明当时人们对于疾病的认识已经相当深刻，并同时积累了较为丰富的医疗经验，从而为医学理论知识的整理、规律的总结和理论框架的建构提供了直接资料并奠定了实践基础。

译文：It is sufficiently shown that the recognition of diseases at that times had been rather profound, and a richer medical experience had been accumulated, so that the direct data were given for sorting out the knowledge of medical theory, summarizing the law of medicine and establishing the frame of the theory, and a practical basis was built up. （柴可夫，2010：3-4，122）

（2）武汉已封城一月之久，以战病毒之役。如秋千受力而摆，疫情让世界失衡。中国正奋发图存。

译文：It has been a month since Wuhan was locked down because of the coronavirus. Like a big push on a swing, the epidemic tips the balance in the world, and China is making efforts to keep standing.

（3）中国许多地区都在执行严格的检疫隔离，中国需要这样的举措来应对传染性极强的疫情。

译文：Draconian quarantines are being enforced in many parts of the country. And that was exactly what was needed to deal with a travelling threat like an epidemic.

（4）我国的灭活疫苗有较好的研究基础，甲肝灭活疫苗、流感灭活（裂解）疫苗、手足口病灭活疫苗、脊髓灰质炎灭活疫苗等均已广泛应用。

译文：China has laid a solid foundation for research in inactivated vaccines, which has been widely used to fight hepatitis A, influenza, hand-feet-mouth disease and poliomyelitis.

（5）这两款疫苗可用于大规模接种，并且有国际通行标准来判断疫苗的安全性和有效性。

译文：The two vaccines can be used for large-scale vaccination, and their safety and effectiveness can be judged by internationally accepted standards.

2. 长句多

（1）Thus, due to the action of ultra-violet rays on the skin, substances are produced in the skin which get into the blood and accelerate the processes of metabolism in the various organs of the body.

译文：因此，由于紫外线对皮肤的作用，皮肤里产生一些物质进入血液，可促进人体各器官的代谢作用。

（2）One of the most widely used over-the-counter pain relievers is acetaminophen, a drug that can also be found in more than 600 products aimed at reducing fever and pain from such things as arthritis, backache, headaches, toothaches, cold and flu, muscle aches and menstrual cramps.

译文：最广泛使用的非处方止痛药之一是乙酰氨基酚，这种药物也可以在600多种产品中找到，这些药物主要用于减轻关节炎、背痛、头痛、牙痛、感冒和流感、肌肉酸痛，以及经期痉挛等引起的发烧和疼痛。（Dartmouth，NS某地方报纸，编者译）

（3）Specific research on the toxicity of acetaminophen clearly shows the drug is linked to such things as liver and kidney damage, certain cancers, risk of motor milestone delay and impaired communication skills in 18-month-old children, lower IQ scores and poorer attention span in five-year-olds, physical abnormalities in sexual organ development in children and even death, to name just some of the numerous side effects.

译文：对乙酰氨基酚毒性的具体研究表明，该药物与以下风险相关：18个月大的儿童的肝肾损害、某些癌症、运动里程碑延迟和沟通技能受损；5岁儿童的IQ得分偏低，注意力集中程度偏低；儿童性器官发育异常甚至死亡。此处列举的仅仅是诸多副作用中的一部分。（Dartmouth，NS某地方报纸，编者译）

（4）There certainly will be some people whose lives are saved, but you have to weigh that against maybe thousands of patients who have had to undergo unnecessary procedures, each with its own attendant risks.

译文：这肯定可以挽救一些人的生命，但是你要考虑到成千上万的人要接受不必要的检查，而每次检查都伴随着风险。

3. 大量使用名词化结构

名词化结构将复合句化为简单句，大大简化了句子，在信息量没有减少的情况下减少了分句的出现，使句子显得更加紧凑。

名词化结构往往意味着冗长的定语和修饰词，这一点不太符合汉语的表达习惯，因此在翻译时，可以将名词化结构翻译为短句。如：

Now, the debate has shifted away from the ethics of baby-making and toward the morality of cloning embryos.

译文：现在，争论已经从制造婴儿是否违背伦理的层面转到克隆胚胎是否违背道德的层面上。

例句中有两个名词性词组：the ethics of baby-making 和 the morality of cloning embryos。在这两个名词性词组中，"ethics"与"baby-making"、"morality"与"cloning embryos"分别构成了修饰关系。若将它们译成"制造婴儿的伦理层面"和"克隆胚胎的道德层面"，意思不够明确且不太符合汉语习惯，因而将它们译成主谓分句"制造婴儿是否违背伦理"和"克隆胚胎是否违背道德"。

再看以下例句：

（1）A thrombus may cause sudden closure of the vessel with complete obstruction of the blood flow.

译文：血栓可能会引起血管突然阻塞，造成血流完全中断。

(2) Although the production of transgenic strains of animals carrying foreign genes is now a relatively routine technique in many laboratories, it is unlikely that such methods will be extended to human embryos, both for moral and technical reasons.

译文：尽管目前在许多实验室里，培养这种携带异体基因的动物转基因株是一种比较常规的技术，但由于伦理及技术方面的原因，这些方法不大可能扩展应用于人体胚胎上。

(3) The transmission of a contagious disease involves the transfer of some of the germs from the infected person to another person.

译文：传染病的传播包括感染者身上的一些细菌传给他人。

(4) The formation of urine by the kidney begins when the blood is filtered through capillaries of the renal artery.

译文：血液经过肾动脉的毛细血管过滤时，就开始在肾脏形成尿。

4. 缩略词使用频繁

(1) Male homosexual AIDS patients also show an increased incidence of certain tumors, most commonly Kaposi's sarcoma.

译文：某些肿瘤在男同性恋艾滋病患者中的发生率上升，最常见的是卡波西肉瘤。

(2) Transcription to MRNA is a process very similar to DNA replication and may use some of the same enzymes.

译文：转录给信使 RNA 的过程与 DNA 的复制过程非常相似，且可以用一些同样的酶。

(3) Fatty liver and CAD have several risk factors in common, which are usually considered to account for their frequent coexistence.

译文：脂肪肝和冠状动脉疾病有几个危险因素是共同的，这通常被认为是两种疾病经常并发的原因。

(4) WHO, the World Organisation for Animal Health (OIE), the Food and Agriculture Organization of the United Nations (FAO) and the Global Alliance for Rabies Control (GARC) have established a global "United Against Rabies" collaboration to provide a common strategy to achieve "Zero human rabies deaths by 2030".

译文：世卫组织、世界动物卫生组织（国际兽疫局）、联合国粮食及农业组织（粮农组织）和全球狂犬病控制联盟建立了"联合抗击狂犬病"全球合作，为实现"到 2030 年人类狂犬病零死亡"提出共同策略。

(5) Coronaviruses are a large family of viruses found in both animals and humans. Some infect people and are known to cause illness ranging from the common cold to more severe diseases such as Middle East Respiratory Syndrome (MERS) and Severe Acute Respiratory Syndrome (SARS).

译文：冠状病毒是在动物和人类身上发现的一个大类病毒。有些会传染给人，引起从普通感冒到更严重疾病的各种疾病，例如中东呼吸综合征（MERS）和严重急性呼吸综合征（SARS）。

常用的缩略词还有：

AA＝aplastic anemia 再生障碍性贫血

PCN＝penicillin 青霉素

BAO＝basal acid output 基础酸排出量

BMT＝bone marrow transplantation 骨髓移植

PH＝past history 既往史

Ab＝abortion 流产

cpd＝compound 化合物

5. It 结构多

科技文体的句子往往有很长的主语，为保持句子平衡（end weight），常把主语置于句末，用形式主语 It 代替。

（1）It is impossible to draw a sharp line between normal and high blood pressure.

译文：在正常血压和高血压之间划出一条清晰的界限是不可能的。

（2）It can be seen that there may be a considerable variation of cardiac damage resulting from rheumatic infection, and also that exacerbation are liable to occur even when the rheumatic heart disease has become chronic and almost inactive.

译文：可以看出，风湿性感染引起的心脏损害可能有相当大的变化，并且即使风湿性心脏病已经转为慢性且不再活跃，也容易加重。

（3）The issue with acetaminophen is compounded by the fact that it is contained in a number of different issues, which makes it very easy for people to accidentally overdose by taking these products simultaneously.

译文：对乙酰氨基酚包含在许多不同的药品中，很容易使人同时过量服用这些产品。这一事实使对乙酰氨基酚的问题变得更为复杂。（Dartmouth，NS 某地方报纸，编者译）

6. 科技词汇多

科技文体中有大量专业术语，这些一般可以通过查找词典得以解决，不是翻译中的难点。然而一些由普通名词转化而成的专业术语（两栖词汇）往往造成理解上的混淆，成为翻译的难点。

在词汇的应用上，不同文体呈现不同的特点。如：pertussis 和 whooping cough 都表示百日咳，前者多用于正式文体。再如：

Diphtheria is making a comeback in the former Soviet Union. (informal)

Diphtheria is re-emerging in the former Soviet Union. (formal)

译文：白喉正在前苏联重新出现。

观察以下两栖词汇的应用及翻译：

（1）We try to avoid extrapolating a flu epidemic from mere anecdotal evidence.

译文：我们试着避免从偶发的情况去推断流感传染病情。

比较：No one seems to compile statistics on the standing-desk trend. But anecdotal reports suggest Silicon Valley is embracing the movement.

译文：似乎没有人汇编过有关立式办公桌趋势的统计数据，但<u>零星报告</u>表明，硅谷正在欣然接受这一潮流。

<u>Anecdotal</u> evidence suggests that, in some quarters at least, exporters are starting to balk and seeking to raise their own prices.

译文：<u>坊间证据</u>显示，至少在某些领域，出口商已经开始犹豫不前，希望提高自己产品的价格。

(2) Cancer of the uterus <u>involves</u> the body of the organ in about 1 in 7 cases.

译文：每7例子宫癌中，大约有1例<u>累及</u>宫体。

(3) Myasthenia gravis(MG) is an autoimmune disease which choline <u>receptor</u> antibody mediates, cell immunity depends on and addiment participates.

译文：重症肌无力是乙酰胆碱<u>受体</u>抗体介导、细胞免疫依赖、补体参与的自身免疫性疾病。

(4) Rabies is a vaccine-preventable viral disease which <u>occurs</u> in more than 150 countries and territories.

译文：狂犬病是一种疫苗可预防的病毒性疾病。全球150多个国家和地区<u>存在</u>此疾病。

(5) Rabies is an infectious viral disease that is almost always fatal following the onset of clinical symptoms. In up to 99% of cases, domestic dogs <u>are responsible for</u> rabies virus transmission to humans. Yet, rabies can affect both domestic and wild animals. It is spread to people through bites or scratches, usually via saliva.

译文：狂犬病是一种在出现临床症状后绝大多数情况下会致命的病毒性传染病。在高达99%的人类感染病例中，狂犬病毒都<u>由</u>家养狗<u>传播</u>。狂犬病既可感染家畜，又可感染野生动物，然后通过咬伤或抓伤（通常是经由唾液）传播至人。

7. 广泛使用名词性从句

名词性从句包括主语从句、同位语从句、表语从句等。如：

(1) False-negative test results —<u>tests that indicate you are not infected, when you are</u>—seem to be uncomfortably common.（同位语从句）

译文：假阴性的检测结果——即你已经被感染，但检测表明你没有——似乎是十分常见的现象，而这一现象令人不安。

(2) <u>What the test can't do</u> is telling you whether you're currently sick with coronavirus, whether you're contagious, whether you're fully immune—and whether you're safe to go back out in public.（主语从句）

译文：测试不能告诉你你现在是否感染了冠状病毒，你是否有传染性，你是否完全免疫，以及你在公共场合是否安全。

(3) The good news is <u>that the tests appear to be highly specific</u>: If your test comes back positive, it is almost certain you have the infection.（表语从句）

译文：好消息是，这种检测似乎是高度明确的：如果你的检测结果呈阳性，几乎可以肯定你感染了病毒。

科技文章中经常在人名后面跟着长长的同位语,以表明说话人的身份、专业等。如:

(4) We don't know for certain that the chronic kidney disease of unknown cause in Sri Lanka is the same as in India, Nicaragua, or El Salvador, comments Madeline Scammell, who is part of a team of researchers at Boston University School of Public Health, Boston, MA, USA, studying the Mesoamerican nephropathy.

译文:马德琳·斯卡梅尔表示,我们不能肯定斯里兰卡不明原因的慢性肾病与印度、尼加拉瓜或萨尔瓦多相同。马德琳·斯卡梅尔是美国马萨诸塞州波士顿大学公共卫生学院研究员团队中的一员,她在研究中美洲肾病。(《中医英语水平考试大纲》,编者译)

第二节　医学句式翻译的技巧

英语是形合性语言,常借助连接词等辅助手段,句子结构往往长而不乱,仿佛一棵枝繁叶茂的大树,主干上有很多树枝,每一个树枝又有很多更小的树枝,每个小枝子又有很多花叶点缀其间。而汉语是意合性语言,句式往往相对较短。翻译时根据两者的特点,可采用以下技巧:

1. 化整为零

英语科技文体大量使用长句和定语从句,而汉语由于结构所限,不宜使用过长的定语,翻译时往往需要化整为零,具体可分为:

1) 将长句化为若干小句

(1) Thus, due to the action of ultra-violet rays on the skin, substances are produced in the skin which get into the blood and accelerate the processes of metabolism in the various organs of the body.

译文:因此,由于紫外线对皮肤的作用,皮肤里产生一些物质进入血液,可促进人体各器官的代谢作用。

(2) Scientists who study cells have determined that a single cell may be as large as a tennis ball or so small that thousands would fit on the point of a needle.

译文:研究细胞的科学家已经确定了一个事实——一个单个细胞可能有一个网球那么大,也可能成千上万个细胞合起来才有针尖那么大。

(3) In some cases, through the process of opsonization, antibodies "butter" the surface of some antigens and make them "tastier" to phagocytes, which engulf the antigens.

译文:在某些情况下,通过调理作用的过程,抗体在抗原表面涂上一些"黄油",让吞噬细胞更喜欢吞噬它们。

(4) The relation of the muscle bundles to the tendons is that the muscle bundles are surrounded and held together by the fibrous connective tissue that is continuous with the fibrous connective tissue of the tendonous part of the muscle.

译文:肌束和肌腱之间的关系是——肌束被纤维缔结组织包绕并连接在一起,纤维缔结组织又与肌腱部分的纤维缔结组织相延续。

（5） The white pulp of the spleen produces lymphocytes that migrate to the red pulp and reach the lumens of the sinusoids, where they are incorporated into the blood that is present there.

译文：脾的白髓产生淋巴细胞，淋巴细胞向红髓迁移到达脾窦腔，加入窦内的血液中。

（6） Acute refers to a disease or illness that has a short duration but whose symptoms appear quickly and are severe. Chronic refers to a disease or illness that has a long duration with milder symptoms.

译文：急性指疾病持续时间短，症状出现迅速而严重。慢性指疾病延续时间长，症状和缓。

（7） Behavioral scientists long attributed such differences to personal eccentricities or early conditioning. This thinking was challenged in the late 1950s by a theory labeled chronobiology by physician-biologist Franz Halberg.

译文：长期以来，行为科学家们把这种差异归结为个人怪癖或早期训练。这一见解到了20世纪50年代后期遭遇一个新理论的挑战。生物学家兼内科医生弗朗兹·哈尔伯格称这个理论为"时间生物学"。

（8） The reason that one tissue or organ, such as stomach, can digest food, and another tissue or organ, such as a muscle, can move a limb, is that the cells of each tissue or organ are different.

译文：某一组织或器官（如胃）能消化食物，另一组织或器官（如肌肉）能使肢体运动，其原因是构成每一组织或器官的细胞是不同的。

2）同位语或定语单独成句

（1） To see what is to come, look to Lombardy, the affluent Italian region at the heart of the COVID-19 outbreak in Europe. (*The Economics*)

译文：要想知道接下来会发生什么，那就去伦巴第看看吧。伦巴第是意大利的富裕地区，是欧洲COVID-19疫情的中心。

（2）Viral particles, the transmission vehicle of the coronavirus, must travel within mucus or saliva, and they must enter through eyes, nose or mouth. (*The New York Times*)

译文：病毒颗粒是冠状病毒的传播媒介，它必须通过黏液或唾液传播，并且只能通过眼睛、鼻子或嘴巴进入人体。

（3） The news that the world's wealthiest countries were convening to orchestrate a response to the deadly coronavirus outbreak had resonated across economies like the sound of whirring helicopters bringing relief to a disaster zone. (*The New York Times*)

译文：世界上最富裕的国家召集会议，对致命的冠状病毒爆发做出反应，这个消息在各经济体中回荡着，就像直升机为灾区运送救援物资时发出的嗡嗡声。

（4） A stew of biological factors may be responsible, including the female sex hormone estrogen, which appears to play a role in immunity, and the fact that women carry two X chromosomes, which contain immune-related genes. (*The New York Times*)

译文：造成这个结果的可能是一系列生物因素,其中包括女性的雌性激素,它似乎在免疫系统中起着一定的作用;此外,女性携带两条包含与免疫相关基因的 X 染色体。

3) With 结构单独成句

(1) The pandemic, as the World Health Organization(WHO) officially declared it this week, is spreading fast, with almost 45,000 cases and nearly 1,500 deaths in 112 countries outside China. (*The Economist*)

译文：本周,世界卫生组织正式宣布,COVID-19 正在迅速蔓延,在中国以外的 112 个国家,已有近 4.5 万例确诊病例,近 1 500 人死亡。

(2) With no test, there can be no rise in confirmed cases either. (*The Guardian*)

译文：不做检测,确诊的病例就不会增加。

(3) With a smaller investment, we can also try to get ahead of pandemics by working with communities in hot spots of emerging diseases. (比尔·盖茨讲话)

译文：用较少的投资,我们还可以通过与新发疾病热点地区的社区合作,争取在大规模流行之前采取行动。

(4) Four were positive, with one exhibiting symptoms. (*The New York Times*)

译文：有 4 人为阳性,其中 1 人有症状。

即使是汉译英,有时候也可以把一个长句化为包含若干主谓结构的短句,如:

(5) 面对突如其来的新冠肺炎疫情,中国政府、中国人民不畏艰险,//始终把人民生命安全和身体健康摆在第一位,//按照坚定信心、同舟共济、科学防治、精准施策的总要求,//坚持全民动员、联防联控、公开透明,//打响了一场抗击疫情的人民战争。(习近平主席 2020 年 3 月 26 日 G20 领导人特别峰会重要讲话《携手抗疫 共克时艰》)(1 句中文)

译文：Facing the COVID-19 outbreak that caught us all by surprise, the Chinese government and Chinese people have been undaunted as we took on this formidable task. From day one of our fight against the outbreak, we have put people's life and health first. We have acted according to the overall principle of shoring up confidence, strengthening unity, ensuring science-based control and treatment and imposing targeted measures. We have mobilized the whole nation, set up collective control and treatment mechanisms and acted with openness and transparency. What we fought was a people's war against the outbreak. (5 句英文)

2. 纲举目张

汉语是意合性语言,行文不太讲究句子结构。而英语的句式结构相对严谨,对语法要求较高,所以在汉英翻译时往往需要找到句子的主谓结构,才能立定框架,统领全句,如:

(1) 中医药在历史发展进程中,兼容并蓄、创新开放,形成了独特的生命观、健康观、疾病观、防治观,实现了自然科学与人文科学的融合和统一,蕴含了中华民族深邃的哲学思想。(《中国的中医药白皮书》)

译文：TCM has created unique views on life, on fitness, on diseases and on the prevention and treatment of diseases during its long history of absorption and innovation. It represents a combination of natural sciences and humanities, embracing profound philosophical ideas of the Chinese nation.

这个句子比较长,确定主语是"中医药",谓语动词有五个:兼容并蓄、创新开放、形成、实现、蕴含。可以确立英语句式:"TCM has created A. It represents B, embracing C."。将"兼容并蓄"和"创新开放"当作修饰语,有效融合了几个谓语动词。

(2) 在数千年的发展过程中,中医药不断吸收和融合各个时期先进的科学技术和人文思想,不断创新发展,理论体系日趋完善,技术方法更加丰富,形成了鲜明的特点。(《中国的中医药白皮书》)

译文：During its course of development spanning a couple of millennia, TCM has kept drawing and assimilating advanced elements of natural science and humanities. Through many innovations, its theoretical base covered more ground and its remedies against various diseases expanded, displaying unique characteristics.

(3) 当前,国际社会最需要的是坚定信心、齐心协力、团结应对,//全面加强国际合作,凝聚起战胜疫情强大合力,携手赢得这场人类同重大传染性疾病的斗争。(习近平主席2020年3月26日G20领导人特别峰会重要讲话《携手抗疫 共克时艰》)

译文：At such a moment, <u>it is imperative</u> for the international community <u>to strengthen</u> confidence, <u>act</u> with unity <u>and work together</u> in a collective response. We must comprehensively step up international cooperation and foster greater synergy <u>so that</u> humanity as one could win the battle against such a major infectious disease.

此句用一个 it 结构句把 to strengthen,act 和 work together 连接了起来;又用 so that 结构把汉语句子中隐含的前后逻辑关系凸现出来,使句子前后的关联性更强更明显。

(4) 中方秉持人类命运共同体理念,愿同各国分享防控有益做法,开展药物和疫苗联合研发,并向出现疫情扩散的国家提供力所能及的援助。(2020年3月26日习近平主席G20领导人特别峰会重要讲话《携手抗疫 共克时艰》)

译文：<u>Guided by</u> the vision of building a community with a shared future for mankind, <u>China will</u> be more than ready <u>to share</u> our good practices, <u>conduct</u> joint research and development of drugs and vaccines, and <u>provide</u> assistance where we can to countries hit by the growing outbreak.

原文一个主语后面可以提炼出四个动词,经过逻辑关系梳理,可以把第一个动词"秉持……理念"改为分词短语作状语,其余三个动词并列作谓语,句子的结构关系便一目了然。

3. 确立主语

因为汉语是主题突出(topic-prominent)的语言,遣词造句都围绕主题进行,即使省略主语,也不影响句意的表达,一般不会引起歧义。如:透关射甲,温经散寒,滋补肝肾等,这符合汉语以意合为主的语言特点。

而英语是主语突出(subject-prominent)的语言,不能省略主语,否则句子结构不完整,尤其是当句子中出现多个主语的情况下,如果省略主语,会导致句子表述不清。因此,汉译英的时候首先要确立主语,使句子在结构上衔接,句意上连贯。

1) 根据语义和逻辑关系确立主语

(1) 竭则燋槁

译文:The exhaustion of vitality brings about haggardness (憔悴) and spiritlessness.

(2) 从舌苔能看出五脏的情况。

译文:The condition of the tongue coating thus tells us the condition of the five zang organs.

(3) 要使零散的、自我意识的、局部的、流传于民间的医学实践知识,上升为具有指导性意义的医学理论知识,成为系统的医学知识体系,需要一定的基础和条件。

译文:It needs a certain basis and conditions for Chinese medicine to become a systematical medical system of knowledge, developing from knowledge of sporadic, subjective, local and folk medical practice to a medical theoretical knowledge with guiding significance.

(4) 秦汉时期的中医典籍《黄帝内经》,系统论述了人的生理、病理、疾病以及"治未病"和疾病治疗的原则及方法,确立了中医学的思维模式,标志着从单纯的临床经验积累发展到了系统理论总结阶段,形成了中医药理论体系框架。(《中国的中医药白皮书》)

译文:*The Huangdi Neijing* (*Yellow Emperor's Inner Canon*) compiled during the Qin and Han times offered systematic discourses on human physiology, on pathology, on the symptoms of illness, on preventative treatment, and on the principles and methods of treatment. This book defined the framework of TCM, thus serving as a landmark in TCM's development and symbolizing the transformation from the accumulation of clinical experience to the systematic summation of theories. A theoretical framework for TCM had been in place.(《中国的中医药白皮书》)

(5) 古代哲学观点为医学理论研究提供了思维的框架。尤其是气一元论、阴阳五行等学说,为中医理论体系的形成提供了哲学依据,确立了生命是物质的,是一个阴阳对立统一、运动不息的发展变化过程,疾病可防可治的主导思想;为中医学确立采用整体综合的研究方法、构建独特的中医学体系提供了方法;为阐明人与自然的关系、生命的本质、健康与疾病等重大理论问题奠定了基础,从而为散在的、零碎的医疗性经验的整理、归纳、总结和研究制定了基本的标准和纲领,使中医学逐步系统化、规范化,理论逐步得到升华,促进了中医学理论体系的形成。毋庸置疑,古代哲学思想是中医学理论体系形成的思想基础。(柴可夫,张庆荣,2010:3)

译文:Ancient philosophical views gave a thinking frame for research of medical theory. Especially the doctrines of qi monism, yin-yang and the five phases provided a philosophical evidence for development of theoretical system of Chinese medicine. They established a guiding thinking that the life is of material, a unity of opposites of yin-yang and in an endlessly developmental and changeable process, and also the illness can be both prevented and treated. They provided methods for Chinese medicine to adapt an integral and compound study and establish a unique theoretical system of Chinese medicine. They also built up a basis for Chinese medicine to expound the major theoretical problems such as the relationship between man and nature, the essence of life, and health and disease. Thus they made an essential standardization and guideline in sorting out, summing up and studying the sporadic and odd medical experiences, leading to a gradual systematization and standardization of Chinese medicine, and promoting the initiation of theoretical system of Chinese medicine. Therefore there is no doubt that the ancient philosophical thinking is the thinking basis for establishment of theoretical system of Chinese medicine. (柴可夫,张庆荣,2010:122)

（6）同时期的《神农本草经》，概括论述了君臣佐使、七情合和、四气五味等药物配伍和药性理论，对于合理处方、安全用药、提高疗效具有十分重要的指导作用，为中药学理论体系的形成与发展奠定了基础。（《中国的中医药白皮书》）

译文：The Shennong Bencao Jing (Shennong's Classic of Materia Medica)—another masterpiece of medical literature appeared during this period—outlines the theory of the compatibility of medicinal ingredients. For example, it holds that a prescription should include at the same time the jun(or sovereign), chen(or minister), zuo(or assistant) and shi(or messenger) ingredient drugs, and should give expression to the harmony of the seven emotions as well as the properties of drugs known as "four natures" and "five flavors." All this provide guidance to the production of TCM prescriptions, safe application of TCM drugs and enhancement of the therapeutic effects, thus laying the foundation for the formation and development of TCM pharmaceutical theory.

有时候要根据需要转换主语，如：

（7）High blood pressure is a contradiction for this drug.

译文：高血压患者忌服此药。

（8）这是治疗湿邪困脾的方法，使用芳香化湿药。

译文：This therapy removes splenic retention of pathogenic dampness by the application of fragrant herbs effective in eliminating dampness.

2) There be 句型主语的确立

英语中 There be 句型的主语是 be 动词后面的成分，翻译时可根据需要重新确立，如：

（1）There were more than 500 reports of deaths from coronavirus on Monday, the most death reports in a single day in the United States. (CNN, March 25, 2020)

译文：在周一，媒体报道了超过500例的冠状病毒感染者死亡案例，这是美国有史以来所报道的单日死亡人数最多的一次。

（2）There are simultaneous effort to procure ventilators for the most severe patients. (CNN, March 25, 2020)

译文：与此同时，为救治情况危急的感染者，呼吸机的生产也在加快进行。

(3) At this time, there are no specific vaccines or treatments for COVID-19. However, there are many ongoing clinical trials evaluating potential treatments. (WHO, March 23, 2020)

译文：关于新型冠状病毒肺炎，目前还没有特定的疫苗或治疗方案。但是，许多测试潜在治疗方法的临床试验正在进行当中。

(4) There is a very different air this week than there was last week. (CNN, March 25, 2020)

译文：与上周相比，本周的疫情局势发生了很大的变化。

(5) There were more cases and deaths in this outbreak than all others combined. (WHO, March 23, 2020)

译文：此次疫情的致病率和致死率，比以往其他疫情的致死率之和。

3) 英语形式主语的处理

英译汉时可以去掉形式主语，将句子变为无主句，常规处理方法有以下几种：

It must be noted that... 必须指出

It should be noted that... 应当指出

It is reported that... 据报道

It has been proved that... 业已证明

It will be seen from this that... 由此可见

It is believed(thought, considered, reputed, regarded) that... 据认为

It is generally considered... 一般认为

It is stated(claimed, declared, announced, alleged) that... 据说

It may be said(expected, hoped, anticipated) that... 可以说（预期）

It is concluded that... 结论是

It is estimated(predicted) that... 据估计，预计

It is supposed(assumed, hypothesized, postulated) that... 据推测，假设

It must be admitted(remembered, pointed out) that... 必须承认（记住，指出）

It cannot be denied that... 无可否认

It has been mentioned that... 上文已经提到

It has been illustrated that... 据图所示，据说明

It should be repeated that... 应该重复指出

It is generally accepted(agreed) that... 普遍认为

此外，英语中形式主语搭配的状况千差万别，可根据具体情况灵活翻译，如：

(1) It is not yet clear how the coronavirus is transmitted. (*The Economist*)

目前人们尚不清楚冠状病毒是如何传播的。

(2) It's upsetting for me to have to ration out COVID-19 testing to my patients, then have to wait 5-7 days for the results, when celebrities are getting tested with ease

and quick turnaround times. (*The New York Times*)

译文：我①不得不按定量配给病人进行COVID-19测试；②而且必须等5～7天才能得到结果，而名人却可以轻松（指无需配额和等待）地进行测试，迅速拿到结果，这令我深感懊恼。

(3) It's not bad to wipe down the area around you, but it's worth remembering that the coronavirus is not going to jump off the seat and get into your mouth. (*The New York Times*)

译文：擦干净你周围的区域没有坏处，但值得记住的是，冠状病毒不会从座位上跳起来再进到你的嘴里。

4) 英语无灵主语句的处理

英语中还有一些无灵主语句，译为汉语时往往需要重新确立主语。如：

(1) Hospitals across the country are seeing a surge of patients. (CNN, March 25, 2020)

译文：在全国范围内，医院的病人数量都在迅速增长。

(2) But the US may already be seeing the beginnings of this in some areas, marking a new stage of the nation's outbreak. (CNN, March 25, 2020)

译文：但是，美国的一些地区已正出现疫情蔓延的情况，这标志着该国疫情爆发到达了新的阶段。

(3) Italy has seen its second highest daily number of coronavirus deaths after two days of improving figures, but the rate of infections is slowing down. (BBC, March 28, 2020)

译文：在死亡人数下降的两天后，意大利冠状病毒单日死亡数量达到历史第二新高，但所幸其感染率正处于降低状态。

4. 不破不立

现代汉语的双音节词语比较多，常用二四六八结构。两个字的如：行走、站立、应答、失败、狭窄等；四个字的如：温文尔雅、毕恭毕敬、小心翼翼、光辉灿烂、丰富多彩等；六个字的如：不自由，毋宁死；一不做，二不休等；八个字的如：江山易改，本性难移等。翻译时，不必拘泥于原句的结构，可根据英语的语言习惯，打破原来句子中的固定结构，重新组织，如：

(1) 凡为医者。性存温雅。志必谦恭。动须礼节。举止和柔。（《小儿卫生总微论方》）

译文：A doctor should have gentle and graceful temperament, modest attitude, good manners, elegant and gentle behaviors.

这一段是由五个四字结构组成的，翻译成英语后打破了原来的结构，变成一个主谓宾结构：A doctor（主语）should have（谓语）A, B, C, and D（宾语）。

(2) 中医药在历史发展进程中，兼容并蓄、创新开放，形成了独特的生命观、健康观、疾病观、防治观。（《中国的中医药》白皮书）

译文：TCM has created unique views on life, on fitness, on diseases and on the prevention and treatment of diseases during its long history of absorption and innovation.

此处的"兼容并蓄、创新开放"译为"absorption and innovation"。

(3) 壮者之气血盛,其肌肉滑,气道通,营卫之行,不失其常,故昼精而夜瞑。

译文:Strong people are usually vigorous in the day time and fall into a sound sleep during the night, because their qi and blood are vigorous, muscles smooth, meridians functioning normally, and nutritive qi and defensive qi in normal circulation.

(4) 病有浮沉,刺有深浅。

译文:Whether to needle deeply or shallowly depends on the state of diseases.

(5) 因邪热郁肺,蒸液成痰,邪阻肺络,血滞为瘀,而致热毒壅肺,痰瘀互结,血败肉腐化脓,肺络损伤,脓疡溃破外泄而成肺痈。

译文:Accumulation of pathogenic heat in the lung may scorch the fluids and produce phlegm that may obstruct the lung collaterals and cause blood stasis. As a result, there is excessive toxic heat in the lung and phlegm and stasis are mixed, impairing the lung collaterals and causing putrid blood and pus. Once the sore is burst, lung abscess occurs.

(6) 他五岁时得了伤寒,失聪了。

译文:He became deaf at five after an attack of typhoid fever.(把原句的句式结构破句重组,以符合目的语的表达习惯。)

与此相反,英译汉时则尽量考虑汉语的四六八结构,采用地道的汉语表达,如:

(1) Susceptibility to colds varies.

译文:感冒的易感性因人而异。

(2) Depending on the severity of the condition, blood stasis patterns may be treated by one or a combination of three methods.

译文:采用一种还是三种合并疗法治疗血瘀证,还得视病情的轻重缓急而定。

(3) Don't cough more than you can help.

译文:能不咳,就不咳。

(4) The resulting patchwork of laws, people on all sides of the issue say, complicates a nationwide picture already clouded by scientific and ethnical questions over whether and how to restrict cloning or to ban it altogether.

译文:在克隆问题上,各方人士认为,有关是否限制克隆、如何限制克隆或索性禁止克隆的科学及伦理问题已经使全国性立法变得扑朔迷离。而由此产生的那些东拼西凑的法律又只会使全国性立法更加步履维艰。

在翻译时,即使不用四六八结构,也可以大胆打破原文句式的限制,译出符合汉语表达习惯的句子,如:

(1) If it is not digested and accumulates in the stomach and intestines, it not only fails to benefit the body but even becomes a disease evil.

译文:如果食物没被消化,反而积在肠胃,它不仅无益于身体健康,反倒成为病邪。

原文本身是并列关系,翻译成汉语后改成了转折关系。(将原文的并列关系词改为

转折关系词）

（2）In the Sui and Tang Dynasties, TCM physicians made significant breakthroughs in disease causation and pattern differentiation thanks to their research into diseases and patterns.

译文：隋唐时期，医家们不懈探索，对临床疾病、证候逐渐深入研究，在病因学和证候学方面均有重大突破。（打破原文语序）

（3）Physicians' understanding of the properties and indications of some medicinals based on their clinical experience were different from their predecessors.

译文：随着临床经验的累积和丰富，医家们发现有些药性、主治与前人认识有所不同。（重组义群）

5. 形态转化

英语是静态的语言，名词、介词使用频繁。英语科技文体中常大量使用名词性结构。而汉语则呈现动态的特点，动词使用比较多。此外，英语被动句多，汉语主动句多。翻译时可以根据各自的语言特点进行词性、正反、主动与被动之间的转换。如：

Man was, is and always will be trying to improve his living conditions.

译文：人类过去、现在和将来始终都在改善生活条件。

在翻译时常见的转换方式有：

1）形容词转换为动词

（1）Rheumatic and certain infectious diseases are commonly responsible for diseases of the heart valves.

译文：风湿性疾病和某些传染病常引起心脏瓣膜疾病。

（2）Most anesthetics will dissolve in fat readily and some are soluble in water.

译文：多数麻醉药易溶于脂，少数溶于水。

2）名词转化为形容词

（1）People come in all sizes and shapes.

译文：人有高矮胖瘦。

（2）This experiment was a success.

译文：这次实验很成功。

（3）The treatment depends on the severity of the condition.

译文：治疗视病情轻重缓急而定。

3）形容词转化为名词

若三者兼备，则反映机体脏腑功能强健，气血充盈。

译文：Simultaneous appearance of the three reflects strong functions of the zang-fu organs and sufficiency of qi and blood.

4）介词转换为动词

英语中大量的介词及介词短语可以翻译为动词及动词短语，其中比较著名的例子是林肯总统演讲中的"government of the people, by the people, for the people"，译为"民有、民治、民享政府"，医学英语中同样如此。如：

Blood flows through the dilated microvasculature is initially rapid, but soon slows because a concomitant increase in vascular permeability and loss of plasma water raises the viscosity of the blood.

译文：流经扩张的微血管的血流速度最初很快，但由于血管通透性的相应增加，以及血浆水分的丧失提高了血液的浓度，所以血流速度很快减慢。

5) 名词转换为动词

(1) Second, the existence of further therapeutic options for the underlying illness must be addressed.

译文：其次，必须申明，对主要疾病作进一步治疗的选择依然存在。

(2) Insertion of the DNA from the cells of one species into another, such that the recipient replicates the inserted DNA and therefore expresses its genetic information, is the principle of genetic engineering.

译文：遗传工程的原理是，将某一种族的细胞 DNA 植入另一种族，使接受者复制出植入的 DNA 并表达该 DNA 的遗传信息。

(3) Kumar said that the Indian government's unprecedented decision to restrict the movement and daily life of its 1.3 billion citizens for three weeks was the best chance the country had to identify potential virus hotspots and it offered precious time to order and manufacture sorely needed protective gear and ventilators. (CNN)

译文：库马尔说，印度政府史无前例地决定在三周内限制13亿公民的行动和日常生活，这是该国确定潜在病毒热点的最佳机会，为订购和制造急需的防护装备和通风机提供了宝贵的时间。

6) 分词短语转换为句子或短句

英语中的分词短语译为汉语时往往转化为一个小句。如：

(1) More people died of COVID-19 in Iran, bringing the country's overall toll to more than 1,500. (VOA, March 22, 2020)

译文：在伊朗，越来越多的人因新型冠状病毒肺炎而死亡，该国总死亡人数已超过1 500人。

(2) Italy's government says it will extend the nationwide lock-down, warning that life would not immediately return to normal even after the worst was over. (BBC, March 22, 2020)

译文：意大利政府表示，其将延长全国封锁的时间，警示称即便最糟糕的情况过去了，社会生活也将不会立马恢复正常。

(3) The United Nations is launching a two billion dollar funding drive to help vulnerable countries fight COVID-19, saying all of humanity is now at risk. (ABC, March 27, 2020)

译文：联合国正启动20亿美元资金的项目，来帮助那些发展比较落后的国家抗击新型冠状病毒肺炎，并称全人类现在都处于危险状况之中。

(4) Deaths due to dementias more than doubled between 2000 and 2016, making it

the 5th leading cause of global deaths in 2016 compared to 14th in 2000. (WHO, May 23, 2018)

译文：由于其在2000—2016年的翻倍致死率，在全球致命疾病排行中，痴呆症从2000年的第14位跃至2016年的第5位。

（5）The outbreak initially shut down great reaches of manufacturing in China, <u>threatening the global supply chain for a vast array of goods, from auto parts to electronics.</u> Then it went global, assailing industry from South Korea and Japan to Italy and Germany.（*The New York Times*）

译文：疫情最初导致中国制造业大规模停产，威胁到从汽车零部件到电子产品等一系列商品的全球供应链。然后，它走向全球，从韩国、日本到意大利和德国，对工业造成冲击。

（6）When economies struggle and workers are threatened with joblessness, central banks nudge interest rates lower, <u>making credit cheaper, encouraging businesses and households to borrow, spend and invest.</u>（*The New York Times*）

译文：当经济陷入困境，工人面临失业威胁时，央行就会调低利率，降低信贷成本，鼓励企业和家庭借贷、消费和投资。

（7）As a result, some analysts said, visitors might be wary of coming to Japan, <u>wondering whether there are thousands of undetected cases.</u>（*The Economist*）

译文：一些分析人士说，游客可能会因此担心去日本，不知道是否还有成千上万的病例未被发现。

（8）For weeks, the World Health Organization resisted declaring the coronavirus outbreak a pandemic, <u>fearing that doing so would incite panic across the globe.</u>（*The Economist*）

译文：几周以来，世卫组织一直拒绝宣布冠状病毒疫情为大流行，担心这样做会在全球引起恐慌。

7）正反转换

除了词性转换外，还有的采用正反转换的译法，即肯定表达和否定表达之间的转换。

气不摄血：qi failing to control blood

眼无光彩：dull eyes

胎死不下：retention of dead fetus

水不涵木：water failing to nourish wood

口角不闭：graping corners of the mouth

胎动不安：threatened abortion

肺气不宣：failure of lung qi in dispersion

胃气不降：failure of stomach qi to descend

脾不统血：spleen failing to manage blood

8）主动与被动转换

比较普遍的现象是将英语中的被动语态译为主动语态，又分为以下几种情况：

1) 使用原有主语

(1) For now, most of this tech has been deployed in China, though it's worth keeping an eye out for it elsewhere. Like the virus, the deployment of this next-generation tech is bound to spread. (Fox News)

译文：目前，这些技术中的大部分已经在中国使用了，然而其他地区也需要关注。随着病毒的扩散，新一代技术的推广也必须跟上。

(2) This year though hanami events have been cancelled across the country as authorities attempt to slow the spread of the coronavirus. (BBC)

译文：今年，由于政府试图减缓冠状病毒的传播，"花见"活动已在全国范围内取消。

(3) As of early Tuesday morning, the coronavirus has been blamed for 74,000 deaths globally. (NBC News)

译文：截至周二清晨，冠状病毒已导致全球7.4万人死亡。

(4) Fauci said Sunday that people must be prepared for a resurgence next year, which is why officials fighting the pandemic are pushing for a vaccine and clinical trials for therapeutic interventions, so "we will have interventions that we did not have" when this started. (Fox News)

译文：福西星期天说，人们必须为明年的病毒复发做好准备，这就是为什么抗疫官员正在推动疫苗和治疗干预的临床试验，因此在复发时"我们将拥有我们之前没有的干预措施"。

2) 转换成汉语无主句

(1) Examinations should be carried out to exclude tuberculosis, bronchial carcinoma and intrabronchial foreign body.

译文：应进行各种检查以排除结核病、支气管癌和支气管内异物。

(2) Much has been learnt about their clinical features, course and prognosis.

译文：关于其临床特征、病程及预后，已知详尽。

(3) No smallpox strains have been seen in people since the 1980's.

译文：自20世纪80年代以来，没有在人体内发现天花病毒毒株。

3) 处置式（把/将/使句式）

(1) Prevention of such disease as diphtheria, smallpox, poliomyelitis and measles has been accomplished by active immunization.

译文：主动免疫使白喉、天花、骨髓灰质炎和麻疹这样的病得以预防。

(2) The blood flow may be increased by more rapid and vigorous heart action.

译文：心脏活动加快和增强可使血流增加。

4) 惯用被动式译法

(1) It is estimated that more than 90 antigenically different strains of known types of respiratory viruses cause the common cold syndrome. (WHO)

译文：据估计，在已知的呼吸道病毒中有90种以上抗原不同的菌株能引起感冒综合征。

（2）It has been recommended that people with asthma should avoid unnecessary interactions. (WHO)

译文：建议哮喘患者避免不必要的交流。

（3）It is recommended to replace the surgical masks every 2 to 4 hours. (WHO)

译文：建议每2～4小时更换一次手术口罩。

（4）It is well known that the disease might be communicated from one individual to another. (WHO)

译文：众所周知,这种疾病可能人传人。

6. 举一反三

中医术语有一定的规律性,将类似的句式归纳起来,就可以分门别类,举一反三,同类同译。中医很多术语是句子的形式,但考虑到术语的特点,译为英语时常常变为一个短语。

1)"A 主 B"类

心主血脉：heart governing blood and vessels

肝主筋：liver governing tendons

肝主疏泄：liver controlling conveyance and dispersion

肾主骨：kidney governing bones

肾主生殖：kidney governing reproduction

肾主水液：kidney governing water metabolism

肾主纳气：kidney governing inspiration

胃主腐熟：stomach governing/controlling decomposition

脾主四肢：spleen governing limbs

脾主升清：spleen governing ascending clear

脾主运化：spleen governing transportation and transformation

大肠主津：the large intestine dominating liquid

小肠主液：the small intestine dominating fluid

胆主决断：gallbladder dominating decision

2)"A 与 B 相表里"类

胆与肝相表里：interior-exterior relationship between gallbladder and liver/the gallbladder is interiorly and exteriorly related to the liver

肺与大肠相表里：interior-exterior relationship between lung and large intestine

心与小肠相表里：interior-exterior relationship between heart and small intestine

脾与胃相表里：interior-exterior relationship between spleen and stomach

肾与膀胱相表里：interior-exterior relationship between kidney and bladder

肺合大肠：lung and large intestine in pair

3)"A 曰……"类

木曰曲直：wood characterized by bending and straightening

火曰炎上：fire characterized by flaring up

金曰从革：metal characterized by clearing and changing

水曰润下：water characterized by moistening and descending

土爱稼穑：earth characterized by sowing and reaping

4)"A 为 B 所胜"类

金为火之所胜：metal being restricted by fire

金为木之所不胜：metal being un-restricted by wood

木为金之所胜：wood being restricted by metal

木为土之所不胜：wood being un-restricted by earth

火为水之所胜：fire being restricted by water

火为金之所不胜：fire being un-restricted by metal

土为木之所胜：earth being restricted by wood

土为水之所不胜：earth being un-restricted by water

水为土之所胜：water being restricted by earth

水为火之所不胜：water being un-restricted by fire

5)"A 在……为……，其华在……"类

心在体合脉，其华在面：The heart is linked to vessels in body and gloss in face.

心在窍为舌：The heart is linked to tongue in orifice.

心在液为汗：The heart is linked to sweat in secretion.

心在志为喜：The heart is linked to joy in emotion.

心与夏气相通应：The heart and the summer-qi are interlinked.

脾在体合肌肉，主四肢：The spleen is linked to muscles in body dominating four limbs.

在官窍为口，其华在唇：The spleen is linked to mouth in orifice reflecting its brilliance on lips.

脾在液为涎：The spleen is linked to saliva in secretion.

脾在志为思：The spleen is linked to thinking in emotion.

脾主长夏，脾气旺于四时：Spleen is linked to long summer-qi and the spleen-qi is vibrant in long summer.

肝在体合筋，其华在爪：The liver is linked to tendons in body manifesting its splendor in nails.

肝在液为泪：The liver is linked to tears in fluid.

肝在志为怒：The liver is linked to anger in emotion.

肝与春气相通应：The liver and spring-qi are interlinked.

"开窍"的"窍"含有一定的比喻色彩，比如"舌"并非"窍"，而是反映之意，故可以译为：

心开窍于舌：the heart reflected on the tongue

肝开窍于目：The liver reflected on the eyes

脾开窍于口：The spleen reflected on the mouth

肺开窍于鼻：The lung reflected on the nose

肾开窍于耳：The kidney reflected on the ears

同时中医又有"A 为 B 之窍"的说法，此处的"窍"指的是"苗窍"，可译为"signal orifice"。如：

目为肝之窍：the eyes are(as) the signal orifices of the liver

口为脾之窍：the mouth is(as) the signal orifice of the spleen

鼻为肺之窍：the nose is(as) the signal orifice of the lung

耳为肾之窍：the ears are(as) the signal orifices of the kidney

"其华在"可以用"flourish"来翻译，给人赏心悦目之感。如：

心，其华在面：the heart flourishing on the face

肝，其华在爪：the liver flourishing on the nails

脾，其华在唇：the spleen flourishing on the lips

肺，其华在毛：the lung flourishing on the hair

肾，其华在发：the kidney flourishing on the hair

6)"……者……之"类

句式"……者……之"常用来表示"某治法治疗某病"，是宾语前置的一种表达，可以采用分词短语的方式翻译。如：

实者泻之：treating excess syndrome with purgative methods

虚者补之：treating deficiency syndrome with tonifying methods

热者寒之：treating heat syndrome with cold methods

寒者热之：treating cold syndrome with heat methods

客者除之：eliminating exopathogens

逸者行之：regulating disorder

留者攻之：expelling stagnation

燥者濡之：moistening dryness

急者缓之：alleviating spasm

散者收之：gathering dispersion

劳者温之：warming consumption

坚者削之：removing hardness

下者举之：elevating collapse

高者抑之：suppressing the rising

惊者平之：tranquilizing the unease

同样，段落翻译也可以举一反三，将相似的句式归类翻译。

原文：肾在体合骨，生髓，通脑，其华在发，在窍为耳及二阴，在志为恐，在液为唾，与自然界冬气相通应。肾与膀胱相表里。

译文：Being linked to bones in body, the kidney generates marrow and reflects its brilliance in hair; it is linked to orifices in ears and two yins; it is linked to fear in emotion; it is linked to spittle in secretion; the kidney and winter-qi are interlinked. The kidney and the bladder form an external-internal relationship.

原文：肺在体合皮，其华在毛，在窍为鼻，在志为悲（忧），在液为涕，与秋气相通应。肺与大肠相表里。

译文：The lung is linked to skin, reflecting its gloss in hair, to nose in offices, to sorrow and worry in emotion, to fluid in nose secretion, and corresponds to autumn-qi. The lung and the large intestine form an internal-external relationship.

7) There be 句式

英译汉也有很多固定句式，可以举一反三。如：英语中常常有"There is no evidence/indication that..."的表述。

（1）There is no evidence that regularly rinsing the nose with saline has protected people from infection with the novel coronavirus.

译文：没有证据表明定期用盐水冲洗鼻子能保护人们免受新型冠状病毒的感染。

（2）There is no evidence from the current outbreak that eating garlic has protected people from the novel coronavirus.

译文：目前的疫情没有证据表明食用大蒜可以保护人们免受新型冠状病毒的侵袭。

（3）There is some limited evidence that regularly rinsing the nose with saline can help people recover more quickly from the common cold.

译文：有一些有限的证据表明，定期用生理盐水冲洗鼻子可以帮助人更快地从普通感冒中恢复过来。

（4）At present, there is no evidence that companion animals/pets such as dogs, cats can be infected with the virus.

译文：目前没有证据表明狗、猫等陪伴类动物/宠物会被感染该病毒。

（5）Based on the virus genome and properties there is no indication whatsoever that it was an engineered virus.（《中国日报》双语新闻）

译文：根据病毒基因组和特性，没有任何迹象表明它是一种工程病毒。

此外，还有其他形式的 There be 结构。如：

（6）There is immense scope for mixed messages and inconsistent instructions about testing and when to stay isolated at home.（*The Economist*）

译文：有关检测以及何时在家隔离的混合消息和前后矛盾的指令在很大的范围都存在。

（7）As of Wednesday, there were 847 confirmed cases of COVID-19 (and six deaths) in or just offshore of Japan.（*The New York Times*）

译文：截至周三，在日本本土或近海地区已累计确诊了847例新冠病毒肺炎病例（包括6例死亡）。

（8）There's been increased attention on this in recent weeks, with the unsettling spread of the coronavirus around the world.（*The New York Times*）

译文：最近几周，随着冠状病毒令人不安地在世界各地传播，（飞机清洁问题）受到越来越多的关注。

8) ... appears to do 句式

（1）The Fed appears to have taken action not out of some misplaced dream that lower interest rates are an antidote to the economic contagion, but in the hope of altering the psychology around it. (*The New York Times*)

译文：美联储的降息行动似乎并不是出于某种幻想,即降息是应对传染病蔓延下的经济的良药,而是希望改变人们对此的心理反应。

(2) They underscored an uncomfortable truth animating fears about the virus: Policymakers tasked with limiting its economic damage <u>appear to</u> be laboring under the assumption that their tool kit is nearly empty. (*The Economist*)

译文：他们凸显了一个令人不快的事实,导致人们对病毒的恐惧愈发加深:负责限制病毒经济损害的政策制定者们,似乎认为他们手上根本就没有什么可用的工具。

(3) But generally, celebrities of all kinds <u>appear to</u> have had a far easier time getting diagnoses. (*The Economist*)

译文：但总的来说,各类名人似乎都更容易得到诊断机会。

9)... requires... 句型

(1) It could also <u>require</u> a shift in attitudes towards workers who turn up while sick and potentially infectious, from plaudits for their diligence to scorn for their lack of consideration. (*The Economist*)

译文：同时我们还要对那些已经生病或具有潜在传染性仍去上班的员工转变态度,以前会赞扬他们的勤奋,而今却鄙视他们缺乏考虑。

(2) Countering pandemics <u>requires</u> all sorts of public action, from forging new social norms to devising vaccines that authorities have the duty to supply. (*The Economist*)

译文：抗击流行病需要采取各种各样的公共行动,从制定新的社会规范到研发当局有义务提供的疫苗。

(3) That <u>requires</u> governments to guarantee a decent level of sick pay, and rules on sick leave that do not punish responsible citizens. (*The Economist*)

译文：这就要求政府确保合理的病假薪酬水平,并且制定出对具有责任心的公民不施加惩罚的病假规定。

10)... implies/proves that... 句型

(1) Official data <u>imply</u> that few people are back behind desks and conveyor belts. The number of trips taken on February 9th, the last day of the holiday(for most) and usually a peak time for travel, was 85% lower than the equivalent day last year. (*The Economist*)

译文：据官方数据显示,很少有人回到了办公桌前和传送带后。2月9日对于大多数人来说是假期的最后一天,通常也是通行的高峰期,但今年这一天的交通通行量比去年同期减少了85%。

(2) Access has <u>proved</u> uneven across the country, even as guidelines for who qualifies have broadened and the laboratories conducting tests have expanded, from the federal Centers for Disease Control and Prevention to state health departments and then

to hospitals and private labs. (*The Economist*)

译文：事实证明，全国各地获取测试的机会不平衡，即使指南中适用于测试的人群范围扩大，并且可进行测试的实验室也有所增加——从联邦疾病控制和预防中心到州卫生部门，再到医院和私人实验室。

(3) That could prove a threat to economic activity. (*The Guardian*)

译文：这被证明是对经济活动的一种威胁。

(4) But the relief proved underwhelming. (*The New York Times*)

译文：但事实证明，这些行动没多少抚慰的作用。

11) The problem hits/ is... 句型

(1) But when the problem hits the supply side—that is, when businesses have difficulty making their goods because they cannot secure raw materials, cannot get their products to market or encounter some other impediment—cutting interest rates tends to be futile. (*The Economist*)

译文：但是当供应端出了问题——也就是说，当企业因无法获得原材料，无法将产品运送上市或遭受其他方面的困难而难以制造产品时——降息往往是徒劳的。

(2) Part of the problem is that Zhengzhou, the capital of Henan Province, requires those entering the city to undergo a 14-day quarantine. (*The Economist*)

译文：出现这一问题的原因之一在于，河南省会郑州市要求进入该市的人必须接受为期 14 天的隔离。

(3) The problem is that relatively few countries are paying much attention to it. (*The New York Times*)

译文：问题是没有多少国家对此给予重视。

7. 语序调整

1) 陈述与判断语序调整

汉语往往是先进行铺垫和陈述，再做价值判断；而英语则是先进行价值判断，然后做出陈述。翻译时要根据目的语的表达习惯予以调整。如：

(1) It is important to remember that stopping treatment specifically aimed at curing an illness does not mean discontinuing all treatment.

译文：停止某种疾病的专门治疗并不意味着停止所有治疗，记住这一点很重要。

(2) Some have suggested that possessing a body of knowledge and a set of skills that can be applied in the practice of medicine defines what it means to be a physician. (季佩英，孙庆祥，2012：213)

译文：有人提出，成为一名医生意味着拥有一套知识体系和可以在医学实践中运用的技能。（编者译）

(3) He also discovered that the same patterns could be detected in heart and metabolic rates and body temperature.

译文：他还发现，心率、新陈代谢的速度以及体温变化都可以检测到同样的规律。

(4) Behind the scenes there are anchors of China's disease control work: putting

the city under lockdown, shutting down public transportation, canceling flights and trains, and closing schools and factories. (WHO)

译文：封锁城市、停止公共交通、取消航班火车、关停学校工厂，这些措施背后的核心是中国的防疫工作。

(5) The change in policy came despite Patrick Vallance, the UK's chief scientific adviser, saying that as few as 5,000 people in Britain—0.00008 per cent of the population—might be infected at that point. (NBC News)

译文：英国首席科学顾问帕特里克·瓦兰斯（Patrick Vallance）表示，当时英国可能只有 5 000 人（占英国人口的 0.00008%）被感染，但当局还是改变了政策。

(6) President Trump and leading business figures are increasingly questioning the wisdom of a prolonged shutdown of the American economy—already putting millions out of work—to curb the spread of the coronavirus pandemic. (*The New York Times*)

译文：为遏制冠状病毒蔓延而使美国经济长期停摆，致使数百万人失业，特朗普总统和商界领袖们越来越多地质疑这种做法是否明智。

(7) 他还强调要紧抓窗口期。全国范围内和北京市基本阻断疫情传播，虽有境外输入和零散病例发生，但疫情防控总体可防可控、可预期，因此现在是在确保疫情防控前提下，加快复工复产复业，全力以赴恢复正常生产生活的最佳窗口期，要紧紧抓住，不可错失良机，我们拖不起也拖不得。

译文：He also highlighted the importance of seizing the critical window to resume work and production, and bring people's lives back to normal as transmission of the epidemic has been basically interrupted in Beijing and nationwide, although there were still imported and sporadic cases.

2) 倒装句、被动句等语序调整

(1) Forgotten are the 1.8 million people worldwide who die from tuberculosis each year.

译文：全世界每年有 180 万人死于结核病，这一点已经被人遗忘。

(2) Instead of performing at a steady, unchanging rate, our systems function on an approximately 25-hour cycle.

译文：我们的身体系统运行的周期大约是 25 小时，速度并非稳定不变。

汉译英的位置互换往往方向相反。如：

(1) 主症未解，变症已生，病情复杂。

译文：It is a complicated case because complications set in before the prime symptoms are relieved.

(2) 色脉合参可以判断疾病的病机，病情的轻重顺逆等。

译文：Judgment of the pathogenesis, seriousness, recovery from or deterioration of a disease is based on the comprehensive consideration of both complexion and pulse manifestation.

(3) 在中方最困难的时候，<u>国际社会（主语）</u>许多成员给予<u>中方（宾语）</u>真诚帮助和支持，我们(主语)会始终铭记并珍视这份友谊(宾语)。

译文：At the most difficult moment in our fight against the outbreak, China (主语) received assistance and help from a lot of members of the global community (宾语). / Such expressions of friendship (主语) will always be remembered and cherished by the Chinese people (宾语).

3) 论点与出处语序调整

英语往往先讲论点，然后再注明出处；而汉语则先说出处，后说具体论据。如：

(1) Death from stroke was more than halved, according to results published in the *Journal of the American College of Cardiology*.

译文：根据发表在《美国心脏病学会杂志》的研究结果，吃辣的人死于中风的风险也减少了一半以上。

(2) "An interesting fact is that protection from mortality risk was independent of the type of diet people followed," said study lead author Marialaura Bonaccio, an epidemiologist at the Mediterranean Neurological Institute. (Neuromed)

译文：研究的首席作者、地中海神经病学研究所的流行病学家玛利亚劳拉·伯纳西欧说："一个有趣的事实是，这种防护死亡风险的作用与人们遵循的饮食类型无关。"

偶有反例，如：

(3) Chinese passengers who are going to fly from 26 countries, including the United States, Italy and Spain, to China are required to submit their health information prior to boarding the plane, the country's civil aviation regulator said on Tuesday.

译文：民航局周二表示，从美国、意大利、西班牙等26国回国的中国籍旅客需在乘坐航班前填报个人健康信息。（央视新闻 新华网）

(4) The capital, a center for international exchanges, still bears the brunt of the risks as the worldwide spread of the COVID-19 pandemic is accelerating, said Xu, noting that there is no chance to call off the city's prevention and control work in a short time.

译文：徐和建表示，在全球新冠肺炎疫情不断加速蔓延的态势下，作为国际交往中心的首都北京，仍然首当其冲地承担着风险，疫情防控在短期内完全结束是不可能的。

(5) Ian Johnson, a nutrition researcher at Quadram Institute Bioscience in Norwich, England, praised the "high-quality observational study" for its "robust methods".（《中国日报》双语新闻）

译文：英国诺威奇 Quadram 生物科学研究所的营养学研究员伊恩·约翰逊称赞了这项"高质量的观察性研究"及其"稳健的方法"。

8. 词量增删

英语重形合，汉语重意合。中医语言讲究言有尽而意无穷，在用语上有文学化色彩，句式工整、修辞丰富。在翻译实践中，可以通过对中医汉语隐形词的增补，使译文忠实传递原文信息，又符合目标语的语言习惯。但词量的增减需要防止两个倾向：一个添枝加叶，任意发挥；二是避难就易，肆意删节。

1）增词法

（1）风火相煽,高热,惊厥,抽搐。

此句隐去了动词。"风火相煽"指"在热病过程中,由于热邪过盛,肝风内动,风盛则火愈烈"。

译文：Incitement between wind and fire leads to high fever, convulsion and tic.

（2）风热犯肺,肺失清肃而咳嗽气粗。

译文：Invasion of the lung by wind-heat impedes the purifying and descending function of the lung, leading to cough and a deep and hoarse voice.

中文隐去了表示因果关系的动词,英译时可以添加上去。如：

（1）里有热,身不恶寒,反恶热,故不欲近衣。

译文：Internal heat results in aversion to heat instead of aversion to cold, and dislikes of wearing more clothes.

（2）湿热内阻,二便不利。

译文：Retention of dampness-heat in the interior may give rise to difficulty of urination and defecation.

（3）中风后遗症,半身不遂,口眼歪。

译文：Sequela of apoplexy is marked by hemiplegia, and deviation of the eye and mouth.

（4）凡病若发汗、若吐、若下、若亡津液,阴阳自和者,必自愈。(《伤寒论·辨太阳病脉证并治中第六》)

译文：In any illness, if sweating is induced, or if vomiting or if purgation has been used, and if depletion of body fluids occurs, when yin and yang spontaneously harmonize, the patient will be self-cured.（增补表条件、时间的逻辑连接词）

英译汉有时候也需要根据上下文适当添加词语,以确保意思的完整表达。如：

（1）Overconsumption of sweet or fatty foods causes impairment of splenic transformation.

译文：过食甜腻食物会影响脾的运化功能。

（2）Frequent urination, bed-wetting, and incontinence may be due to a deficiency of qi.

译文：尿频、遗尿和小便失禁多由气虚引起。

（3）Drugs used in the treatment of heart diseases can produce heart block.

译文：某些用于治疗心脏病的药物能引起心脏阻滞。

2）减词法

汉语常常为了修辞而使用意义重复的词语,在翻译时应该略去不译。另外,不必要的套话和不言而喻的词语也要略去不译。如：

（1）《达生篇》产科专论,以简要而通俗的文字记述了产前事宜、产后要旨和胎产、临产、产后等诸病的治疗方药和调养方法。

译文：*On Obsterics* describes in simple and plain language about care taken before and after childbirth and treatment of related disorders.

（2）万全主张"调理但取其平，补泻无过其极"。

译文：Wan Quan proposed expelling and tonifying were used together.

（3）瘟疫有强烈的传染性，而疫病侵袭人体发病与否，与正气盛衰、病邪毒力强弱有直接关系。

译文：Epidemic disease was strongly infective and its contraction depended on one's vital qi and the power of pathogenic factors.

（4）心合小肠，肺合大肠。

译文：The heart is in pair with the small intestine while the lung with the large intestine.

（5）促使病人进食，则是真补之道，其他补养药物只能是辅助性的。

译文：Promoting food intake was extremely important and tonics were only supplementary.

（6）口噤不语见于中风病。多因肝风内动、气血瘀滞所致。

译文：Lockjaw is seen in stroke caused by stirring of liver-wind and stagnation of qi and blood stasis.

"口噤"指"牙关禁闭，口不能开"，当然不会说话了，所以"不语"略去不译。因为"肝风"总是在体内的，所以"内"字不必翻译。

（7）在临床治疗上，他提倡滋阴降火之法，善用滋阴降火之剂。

译文：In clinical treatment, he always proposed replenishing yin to purge fire with corresponding formulas.

（8）道家倡导的养生思想和方法，已经成为中医预防疾病的理念。

译文：Taoist ideas and methods of health preservation have become part of disease prevention in TCM.

（9）脉有胃气则生，脉无胃气则死。

译文：When a pulse is felt with stomach qi, one will survive, on the contrary, death occurs.

"脉无胃气"没有采取重复的译法，而用"on the contrary"（与此相反）来表示。

练 习

Ⅰ. **翻译句子（英译汉）**

（1）Small harmful substances that make their way into the alveoli are destroyed by the fourth line of defense, the macrophages.

（2）Diagnosis is made at direct laryngoscope, when replacement of the prolapsed ventricle may be effected by the blade of the laryngoscope or by forceps.

（3）The emphasis in this section is on the morphological aspects of the inflammatory process visible to the pathologist rather than on the pharmacological and biochemical events.

(4) There seems little doubt, therefore, that when a peptic ulcer, is in a stage of causing symptoms, direct exposure of it to hydrochloric acid will usually induce typical ulcer pain.

(5) There have been at least 160,698 cases of coronavirus that have been detected and tested in the United States through US public health systems. (CNN, March 31, 2020)

(6) A range of potential treatments including blood products, immune therapies and drug therapies are currently being evaluated. (CNN, March 25, 2020)

(7) Older patients and individuals <u>who have underlying medical conditions or are immunocompromised should contact their physician early in the course of even mild illness</u>. (CNN, March 24, 2020)(留意画线部分的翻译)

(8) A therapeutic could be available well before a vaccine. Ideally this would reduce the number of people who need intensive care including respirators. (*The Economist*)

Ⅱ. 翻译下列含有被动句的句子（英译汉）

(1) More than half of all deaths in low-income countries in 2016 were caused by the so-called "Group I" conditions, which include communicable diseases, maternal causes, conditions arising during pregnancy and childbirth, and nutritional deficiencies. (WHO, May 24, 2018)

(2) Public health experts have warned the US could "become Italy," where doctors in hospitals filled with COVID-19 patients have been forced to ration care and choose who gets a ventilator. (CNN, March 25, 2020)

(3) The virus is transmitted to people from wild animals and then spreads in the human population through direct contact with the blood, secretions, organs or other bodily fluids of infected people. (WHO, May 24, 2018)

Ⅲ. 翻译下列含有动词不定式的句子（英译汉）

(1) To limit the damage as far as possible, trust and information are of the essence. (*The Guardian*)

(2) Follow advice given by your healthcare provider, your national and local public health authority or your employer on how to protect yourself and others from COVID-19. (WHO, 2020)

(3) Official guidance advised people to practice good hygiene and wash their hands. It was also suggested that people could prepare two weeks' worth of food and water, as well as other household goods, if they felt it necessary.

Ⅳ. 翻译下列含有状语从句的句子（英译汉）

(1) Stay at home if you begin to feel unwell, even with mild symptoms such as

headache and slight runny nose, until you recover. (WHO, 2020)

(2) A big thing is to go along with the "shut down" approach in your community so that the infection rate drops dramatically to let us go back to normal as soon as possible. (比尔·盖茨讲话)

(3) Tan Desai also emphasized that, in addition to mobilizing the strength of various government departments, it is also necessary to mobilize the strength of the whole society and the entire population so that countries can make progress in the anti-epidemic action. (*The New York Times*)

Ⅴ. 英汉段落互译

(1) 接种疫苗使得中国消除了脊髓灰质炎,并极大地减少了疫苗可预防疾病(比如风疹、乙型脑炎、脑膜炎和乙肝)在儿童中的发病率。1992—2014年,得益于乙肝疫苗的使用,避免了1.2亿例乙肝病毒感染和2 800万例慢性感染。因为接种疫苗,今天的中国儿童几乎免于乙肝困扰,这意味着他们在未来罹患肝硬化和肝癌等重病的风险都大大降低。(http://www.wpro.who.int/china/mediacentre/releases/2018/20180803-Immunizations-Save-Lives/en)

(2) For many years, chili has been hailed for its therapeutic properties, and now researchers have found that eating chili peppers regularly can cut the risk of death from heart disease and stroke. Carried out in Italy, where chili is a common ingredient, the study compared the risk of death among 23,000 people, some of whom ate chili and some of whom didn't.

第六章　医学文体翻译（一）

林无静树，川无停流。

《世说新语·文学第四》

In the woods no silent trees grow; In the streams no stagnant currents flow.

（编者译）

楂、梨、橘、柚，各有其美。

《世说新语·品藻第九》

Tangerine and pomelo, haw and the pear, different they may appear, beauty and excellence they share.

（编者译）

文体，是指独立成篇的文本体裁，是文本构成的规格和模式，反映了文本从内容到形式的整体特点。医学文本的翻译整体而言属于科技翻译范畴，然而医学是科学中最人文、人文中最科学的一个领域，随着人们对医学人文的日益关注，有些学者开始留意文学作品中的生命文化与生命叙事，如诗人拜伦和雪莱在诗中表达的对疾病（肺结核）的回应等。"癌症叙事""艾滋叙事"等医学主题的文学作品则是从患者的视角叙述对疾病的体验和经历。这些研究唤醒了人们敏锐的意识，使冰冷的医学语言变成对生命和死亡深层次的观照，而中西医也在彼此的对话与论争中进行人文互鉴。

随着新冠肺炎在全球的蔓延，和疫情有关的标语、新闻、评论、公告、微信分享等层出不穷，渗透至人们生活的各个方面。医学和人们的生活密不可分，医学翻译也越来越呈现多元化的色彩。

而科学研究性文章也是一种信号，信号必须被对方接受和理解，否则就毫无用处。因此，科研文章应该尽可能清晰简洁，修辞、转义用法等应减少到最低限度。

在《如何撰写和发表医学论文》（*How to Write and Publish Papers in the Medical Sciences*）一书中，胡特提出了一篇好的科研论文应该具备流畅、清晰、准确、经济、优美的品质，如表6-1所示。（王燕，2016：5-6，编者译）

表 6-1 好的科研论文应该具备的品质

Fluency 流畅性
Forward-moving sequence of thought 思维顺序的展开
Elements of critical argument in the right sequence 论证要素按正确次序
Narrative sequence in the right order 叙事序列按正确次序
Paragraph connected 段与段之间的关联
Forward-moving line of thought in each paragraph 每段中思路的展开
No slowing or interruptions from obvious devices of style; from unclear, sluggish, excessively long sentences; or from graceless terms 没有对某些明显格式的延缓或中断,没有含糊不清、拖沓或过于冗长的句子,没有不雅用词
Clarity 清晰性
Clear structures and movement of content 结构清晰,内容的进展
Clear connections of paragraphs 段与段之间清晰的连接
Intent of each paragraph clear as its outset; each paragraph limited to that intent; no paragraph unclear because it includes more than needed for that intent 每段开头点明主旨;每段要限于此目的;每一段都不包含任何与主旨无关的信息
Clear use of modifiers 修饰语的清晰使用
Unambiguous antecedents for pronouns 代词的先行词不存在歧义
Right choice of verb tenses for the sequences of actions 动作的顺序时态正确
Accuracy 准确性
Correct choice of words and terms 词汇和术语的准确选择
No misspelled words 没有错误拼写
Right verb tenses for discontinuity or continuity of actions 行为的间断或持续时态正确
Economy 经济性
No unneeded words or phrases 没有不必要的词或短语
Verbs rather than abstract nouns 使用动词而非抽象名词
No unneeded clauses 没有不必要的从句
Grace 优美性
The qualities of fluency, clarity, accuracy, and economy 流畅、清晰、准确和经济的品质
Correct sex references 性别指称正确
Humane terms and phrases 人性化的术语和短语
Standard formal usage 标准正规的用法

下面将介绍几种常见的医学文体及其常用的翻译方法。

第一节 记叙文

和医学相关的记叙文主要包括患者对病情的描述、患病的感受和经历,或者医生、家人等以第三人称的方式对病人情况的描述等,往往比较主观,带有浓厚的个人色彩。

例文 1:

One morning, I stepped out of bed and put my feet on the floor. Suddenly, a mean little man jumped out from under the bed and stabbed an ice pick through my left foot.

Figuratively speaking, yes.

I took another step and he stabbed it again. This went on all day. Step, stab, scream. Over the next few days, I started limping. My whole body hurt. Even my hair. I kept thinking that the little man would get tired of stabbing me and go pick on somebody else. We often take things for granted until we lose them or they start to hurt.

My brother deals with pain every day. He's also blind and suffers from cerebral palsy, needs a walker to walk, doesn't take much for granted. I had to wonder: What would he think about my foot?

Finally, after a week of pain, I went to see a very nice foot doctor. The doctor studied my foot, took X-rays, shook his head, and said the little man's name: Arthur Itis, or Arthritis.

I knew it well. I'd often heard it hissed angrily by my grandparents and parents, all attacked by Arthur's ice pick when they got older.

"Wait," I said. "Doesn't Arthur usually just pick on old people?"

The doctor smiled, looking at my chart. "How old are you?"

I gave him a look. "Never mind," I said. "Can you fix it?"

"Well," he said, "We can try."

He listed several options and I chose the injection. It didn't hurt much. Not half as much as the ice pick.

That was yesterday. This morning, I awoke, took a few careful steps and… Hallelujah! It hurt just a bit, but no ice pick. I looked under the bed. No sigh of Arthur. Maybe he was hiding in the closet, waiting for another day. But for now, he was gone, and I was grateful. My mind began to race with plans to do all the things I'd been putting off for days: unpack, clean the house, wash my hair…

Then it hit me. Another stab. Not in my foot. In my heart. I remembered that I hadn't called my brother in a long time.

It's easy to take some things for granted. But it should never be the people we love.

译文：

一天早晨，我从床上爬起来，双脚触地。突然，从床底下跳出来一个刻薄的小矮人，举起冰锥对准我的左脚刺了下去。

虽是比喻的说法，的确感觉如此。

我又迈了一步，他又刺了一下。这样持续一整天。抬脚、刺痛、尖叫……没几天，我走路就一瘸一拐了。我全身都开始疼痛，甚至直达发梢。我不停地期待这个矮子刺我刺得厌倦了，转而去欺负其他人。我们总是将一切视为理所当然，直到失去它们或者它们开始受伤。

我弟弟很少将一切视为理所当然。他每天都要面对疼痛，同时还双目失明，忍受脑瘫带来的痛苦，需要借助助行器才能行走。我不禁想：他会如何看待我的脚呢？

疼痛持续一周后，我最终去看了一个非常好的脚疾医生。他仔细看了看我的脚，拍了X光片，摇了摇头，对我说出了那个小矮人的名字：关杰衍，关节炎。

我对它很熟悉了。我经常听到祖父母和父母气愤地说出这个名字，他们老年时都受到了"关杰衍"冰锥的攻击。

"等等，"我说。"'关杰衍'通常只欺负老年人，对吗？"

医生笑了，看着我的病历，问道："你多大了？"

我看了看他，说："算了，你能治好吗？"

他说："我们可以试试。"

他提供了几种疗法，我选择了注射。不那么疼。不及冰锥刺痛的一半儿。

那是昨天的事了。今天早上起来，我试着小心走了几步……哈利路亚，感谢上帝！只是轻微疼痛，没有冰锥的刺痛了。我检查床底，没有发现"关杰衍"的踪影。也许他躲在壁橱里，等着某天再出现。但是现在，他已经走了，我非常感恩，脑子里开始飞快筹划耽延了几天的计划：叠衣服、扫房间、洗头发……

突然又疼了一下，我再次被刺中，这次不是在脚上，而是在心上。我想起很长时间没有给弟弟打电话了。

我们很容易把某些事物视为理所当然，但不应该是我们所爱的人。

例文2：

2020年3月31日，中国日报社与清华大学以"云直播"形式共同举办了一期主题为"抗击新冠肺炎疫情，全球命运与共"的线上"新时代大讲堂"。下面的这篇例文来自新冠肺炎疫情下一位坚守武汉的美籍老师在"新时代大讲堂"讲述的故事（中文为译文）：

My name is Megan Monroe. And I have been in China for 98 days. We've been quarantined for 56 of those days, and I've been free for 42 of those days.

我叫梅根·梦露。我来到中国已经98天了，其中56天在隔离，其余42天我都可以自由行动。

I am part of a company called Pro-Stage. And I am over here so that I can be a good role model for kids and eventually become a theater, dance and public speech teacher. We got to work with the kids one on one and in person before. And now we've been working with students online.

我的公司叫 Pro-Stage。我在这里是想给孩子们做好榜样,将来打算成为戏剧、舞蹈和公共演讲方面的教师。我们之前是与孩子一对一教学的,现在都是在线教学了。

In the beginning of the quarantine, I got in contact with the U. S. embassy that's located in Beijing. And they called me back after a few days, saying that they could help me with departure assistance, so that I could get out of here.

刚开始隔离的时候,我和北京的美国大使馆联系,他们过了几天打电话给我,说可以帮我回国,暂时离开这里。

But the United States is charging its citizens($1,100) 7,700 *yuan*, to fly out of here and then get quarantine for two weeks.

但是,我要向美国缴纳 1,100 美元,就是 7,700 元,才能坐飞机离开,再去那边隔离 14 天。

I didn't really want to waste my money on that. And my mom thought that I would be safer here in my apartment than on a plane with a lot of people.

我不想这样浪费钱,我妈妈也觉得待在这边的公寓里,比跟许多人一起坐飞机要安全。

So I'm just here and I'm trying to be positive about everything. And I wish I had gone home, but I'm glad that I didn't go home because I've been able to communicate with so many people and be a very real open news source for everybody.

我就留在了这里,我也在尽量保持乐观的心态。我后悔过没回家,但现在我很庆幸,因为我有机会跟许多人沟通,为大家提供真实、开放的信息。

We started making TikToks on the first day of the quarantine, because we wanted to exhibit what was actually happening. After that it's become our way of being positive news.

隔离第一天,我们就开始在抖音上发视频,因为我们想展示真实的情况,然后这就成了我们传播正能量的渠道。

When I posted one of my videos, someone said, obviously, you're not going to get the virus because you're white. But that's not how the virus works. It's spread all over the world now. It doesn't care what your race is.

我发视频的时候,有人说,你是白人,肯定不会感染病毒。但病毒不是这样的,现在已经扩散到了全世界,并且与种族完全无关。

People that are saying that are just racist against Chinese people. So I think that everyone just needs to take a step back and meet each other in the middle, so that we can mitigate all of the negative effects that have been coming from this.

那样说的人是针对中国人的种族主义者。我觉得大家应该各退一步,相互妥协一下,这样才能消除疫情带来的种种负面影响。

My daily life has definitely changed.

我的日常生活也发生了很大变化。

Before the quarantine, I would wake up and come into the office and do various tasks. And I'd spend the weekends going grocery shopping and exploring the city of Wuhan.

隔离之前,我起床后就去公司完成工作,周末会出去采购,同时逛逛武汉。

One time I jumped onto the metro link and I just took it very far in one direction. And I ended up at East Lake, which is actually a really pretty lake that's famous in Wuhan. Since then I haven't really been able to go outside much.

有次我在地铁上,一直坐到了终点站,最后到了东湖,那是武汉的著名景点,很美。那之后我就没什么机会出去了。

On the first day when we went to the supermarket, all of the vegetables had been taken off the shelves, and bought, and everybody was running around trying to get instant noodles and rice and other things for their home.

隔离开始第一天,我们去超市,蔬菜都被买光了,大家都赶着抢方便面、大米,还有其他日用品。

After a couple of days, it settled down, and you could go to the grocery store pretty regularly.

过几天情况就好多了,可以去日常采购了。

But then after the quarantine got more strict, they started delivering groceries to communities. In our community, they have grocery deliveries and you can order a big bag of vegetables or eggs and fish and garlic and stuff.

但是隔离进一步严格之后,食品杂货都是专人送到社区了。我们的社区有专门的送货员,你可以在线下单,买蔬菜、鸡蛋、鱼、大蒜什么的。

Someone from the community will bring in a couple orders of bread and will stand out on the basketball court and knock off their name on the piece of paper, so that we can make sure that everybody's getting what they ordered.

社区还有专人运送大家订的面包,就在篮球场上,用纸标好各个订单的名字,方便大家拿取自己的订单。

Chinese people have been very resilient during this time. And it makes a lot of sense, especially in Wuhan.

这段时间,中国人民真的百折不挠。效果也是显著的,尤其是在武汉。

For when this virus continues to spread, I think that everyone needs to look at other countries and especially look towards China to see what China has done for this virus.

因为病毒还在继续扩散,我觉得大家都该借鉴他国,尤其是借鉴中国,看中国怎么应对疫情。

Because we can only overcome this together.

因为只有齐心协力才能战胜疫情。

(摘自《中国日报》双语版官方公众号 2020 年 4 月 12 号文)

第二节 应用文体

1. 新闻报道

新闻报道有其固有的格式和行文风格,和医学相关的新闻一般涉及国家医疗政策、医保、流行病或瘟疫等方面。下例摘选自《中国日报》2020年3月9日的双语新闻:

Makeshift hospitals built to treat novel coronavirus infected patients with mild symptoms in Wuhan, Hubei Province, the epicenter of the outbreak, are expected to wrap up operation around March 10, China Central Television reported on Sunday.

据央视3月8日报道,新冠肺炎疫情爆发地湖北省武汉市临时改建的方舱医院有望在3月10日全部休舱。方舱医院主要用来治疗新冠肺炎轻症患者。

Since Feb 5, 14 makeshift hospitals in the city have been operating, with the longest running for 33 days, and treating more than 12,000 cases, it said.

报道称,自2月5日以来,武汉市共有14家方舱医院接诊患者,其中运行时间最长的为33天,共收治新冠肺炎轻症患者12 000多人。

As of Monday morning, 12 of the 14 hospitals have suspended operation, with their patients either discharged or transferred to designated hospitals, it said.

截至3月9日上午,14家方舱医院中已有12家休舱,患者均已出院或转移到了定点医院。

随着各种自媒体的盛行,公众号也成了新闻发布的重要渠道。下例摘自公众号WhereZhengzhou第464期的推文:

疫情下的郑州七"度"
Zhengzhou's Attitude Facing the Epidemic

着眼大局(高度)——Think in big picture

不失时机(速度)——Lose no time

不漏细节(深度)——Ignore no detail

不留角落(广度)——Leave no corner

不遗余力(力度)——Spare no effort

从"暂停"到"重启",快速切换(跨度)——Enable quick switch from "Pause" to "Restart"

全力投入,奉献爱心(温度)——Devote the whole love

一座有担当的城市,在困境中至少要具备七个维度:高度、速度、深度、广度、力度、跨度和温度。

That's what Zhengzhou, as a responsible and loving city, has responded to the recent adversity.

面对突然爆发的新型冠状病毒肺炎疫情,郑州迅速给予回应,将人们的健康和安全放在首位,进行了详细而全面的抗病毒部署,实施了极其严格的内部控制,同时为重灾区提供了帮助,并使企业开始有秩序地复工复产。凭借高度的责任感和实际行动,面临猖獗的病毒疫情,郑州仍立于不败之地。郑州,这座拥有 3 600 年历史的新一线城市兼国家交通枢纽,经受住了严峻的考验,用大爱与无畏温暖着这里的居民和工作者。

Facing the sudden outbreak of the novel coronavirus pneumonia, Zhengzhou has responded in no time, put people's health and safety at top priority, made the detailed and comprehensive anti-virus deployment, implemented the strictest internal control while lending a helping hand to the hardest hit area, and set out on orderly resumption of business and work. The great sense of responsibilities and real actions make Zhengzhou undefeatable in front of the rampant virus. Zhengzhou, a city with 3,600 years of history, a new first-tier city and a national transportation hub, stands the tough test successfully and wins the hearts of all people living and working here with her love and heroic deeds.

疫情防控在升级,经济发展更要升级。

We should strengthen epidemic prevention and control on one hand and ensure the stability and continuous growth of the economy on the other hand.

1月24日,郑州"新冠肺炎疫情防控工作专题会"召开。会上强调,压实责任、细化举措,内防扩散、外防输入,要把做好疫情防控作为头等大事,全力保障好人民群众生命安全和身体健康。郑州的战"疫"正式打响。

On January 24, a special meeting on the prevention and control of novel coronavirus pneumonia was convened. The meeting underlined that we should clarify responsibilities and make detailed measures to prevent import of the infected from external areas and prevent spread in internal areas. The epidemic prevention and control should be given top priority, and every effort should be made to safeguard people's lives and health. Zhengzhou declared war against the epidemic.

2月11日晚,郑州市委、市政府印发《郑州市关于应对新型冠状病毒肺炎疫情促进经济平稳健康发展的若干举措》的通知,围绕加大疫情防控力度,支持企业有序复工复产出台了30条措施促进全市经济平稳健康发展。

On the evening of February 11, the CPC Zhengzhou Municipal Committee and Zhengzhou Municipal Government issued a notice on Measures of Zhengzhou City to Cope with the Outbreak of Novel Coronavirus Pneumonia and Promote the Stable and Healthy Economic Development. With focus on strengthening support for epidemic prevention and control and promoting enterprises to resume production in an orderly manner, 30 measures were introduced to boost the steady and healthy development of the city's economy.

今天的郑州,是 GDP 过万亿、人口超千万的特大城市,是经济高质量发展的国家中心城市,是功能性口岸数量最多、种类最全的内陆城市,是抢先打造国际交通枢纽门户、对外开放体系高地和参与国际合作高地的要塞城市。因此,郑州维持经济长期向好发展的基本条件不仅没有改变，而且会不断升级。

Today's Zhengzhou is a megalopolis with a GDP of over one trillion yuan and a population of over ten million. It is a national central city with high-quality economic development. It is an inland city with the largest number and greatest diversity of functional ports. It is an important city taking the lead in building a gateway of the international transportation hub and a pacesetter of opening up and in participating in international cooperation. Therefore, Zhengzhou's sound economic fundamentals will remain unchanged and be constantly improved.

面对突发事件，所谓高度，就在于是否能够以强烈的责任感扛起使命、把准方向，高屋建瓴，在迅速应对的同时体现前瞻性。

In the face of emergencies, thinking in big picture can keep us aware of our responsibilities to shoulder mission, help us see clearly and see far to make quick response and forward-looking decisions.

岐伯山医院 10 天拔地而起
The Qiboshan Hospital rose from the ground in just 10 days

"我将用我所学、尽我全力、科学救治、精准施策、不惧生死、不畏挑战、不辱使命、不负重托、勠力同心、共抗疫情！" 2 月 13 日上午，郑州市第一人民医院传染病医院出征仪式上，来自郑州市 8 家医院的 226 名 "逆行天使"，右手握拳、庄严宣誓，他们正式进驻河南版 "小汤山" ——郑州岐伯山医院。

"I will use what I have learned and try my best for scientific and precise treatment. I will not fear death and be up for the challenge. I will fulfill my mission and live up to my promise to fight against the epidemic!" On the morning of February 13, 226 brave medical staff from eight hospitals in Zhengzhou made a solemn oath with their right hands clenched at the opening ceremony of the Hospital for Infectious Diseases of Zhengzhou First People's Hospital. Later, they officially entered the "Zhengzhou Qiboshan Hospital", Henan's version of "Xiaotangshan Hospital".

"岐伯山医院"项目正式完成验收移交，总体工期为 10 天。

Zhengzhou Qiboshan Hospital was officially accepted and handed over after intense construction of only 10 days.

此时的"郑州速度"，不仅体现了经济高速发展，更体现了市民对社会保障的充分信任。15 天下发 16 条防控通告，从网格排查到闭环管控，从暂停诊所到实名买药，从启用社区扫码登记到明确企业复工要求……信息一目了然，方法可学可用，第一时间抵达掌心、抵达人心。

"Zhengzhou speed" once reflected how people described its high-speed economic development; now it conveys people's highest praise to its efficient and trustworthy social security practices at this critical moment. Within 15 days, 16 prevention and control notices were issued. Messages inform residents of the updated measures and requirements ranging from grid-based screening to closed-loop control, from clinics' suspension of business to real-name drug purchase, from online registration in each community to definite requirements for enterprises to resume production. The latest information and easy-to-use measures reach people the first time, making people feel assured.

网上之所以铺天盖地出现"硬核郑州"的字眼儿,正是因为"郑州速度"把一颗颗焦虑、茫然的心凝聚在了一起,释放出无限的力量。

People follow Zhengzhou's every firm move on the Internet. Seeing Zhengzhou is making greatest efforts at quickest speed, we know we are together; we will fear nothing and we can overcome any difficulty with the infinite power of all joining together.

……

我们隔离病毒但不隔离爱。

We isolate the virus but not the love.

2月1日,中国铁路郑州局集团有限公司筹措支援的2万只口罩等防疫物资从郑州东站通过G545次列车发往武汉。

On February 1, 20,000 masks and other anti-epidemic supplies raised by China Railway Group Limited were sent to Wuhan by train G545 from Zhengzhou East Railway Station.

2月6日,由河南爱心企业捐赠、长通物流免费运输的6.5吨污水处理药剂,从郑州出发紧急送往武汉火神山医院。

On February 6, 6.5 tons of sewage treatment agents donated by Henan charity enterprise and transported by Changtong Logistics for free were sent from Zhengzhou to Wuhan's Huoshenshan Hospital.

经过近50分钟的飞行,2月9日,河南第五批医疗队从郑州抵达武汉,这其中也包括郑州人民医院的15位医护人员。出征之前,郑州人民医院急诊科男护士刘洋和队友们一起剃了光头,他们说这样的发型既方便又不易感染,是为了自己的安全,更是为了大家一起打赢这场没有硝烟的战争。

After a flight of nearly 50 minutes, the fifth medical team arrived in Wuhan from Zhengzhou on February 9, including 15 medical staff from People's Hospital of Zhengzhou. Liu Yang, a male nurse at the Emergency Department of People's Hospital of Zhengzhou, shaved his head with his teammates before they moved on. "Such a hairstyle is convenient and not easily infected. This is not only for our own safety, but also for the purpose of winning this smokeless war," they said.

截至2月23日,河南共派出14批次1 241名队员组成的医疗队驰援湖北。除了奔赴武汉的医护人员,留守的郑州人也在默默地为战疫献爱心。

As of February 23, Henan has sent a total of 14 medical teams of 1,241 members to assist Hubei. In addition to the medical staff going to Wuhan, the Zhengzhou people who stayed behind are also quietly contributing to the fight against the epidemic.

面对疫情,我们隔离病毒,但不隔离爱!城市管理者有足够的智慧与担当,企业和市民有充分的自律与爱心。郑州的胸怀,让生活在这里的每一个人都感到温暖。

In the face of the epidemic, we isolate the virus, but not the love! We are confident that the joint efforts of each individual and enterprise under the wise leadership of responsible leader teams can create a warm and peaceful place for everyone living and working in this city.

这篇双语推文虽然个别地方的翻译有待进一步推敲,但是两种语言都很符合自媒体报道的行文风格,对"七度"翻译的处理也很巧妙。

2. 学术会议邀请函

学术会议邀请函在书写格式上和普通函件相似,只是其中包含了很多医学相关术语。会议函件和学术会议的专业主题密切相关。邀请函既要表达对受邀者的诚挚敬意,形式上又要不失庄重得体。

1) 面向全体与会者的邀请函

此类邀请函要把会议举办的主题、时间、地点、主题发言人、会议主要特色等陈述清楚,以便潜在与会者做出选择。如下例中英文对照邀请函:

世中联翻译专业委员会换届大会暨
第七届学术年会第一轮会议通知

为进一步推进中医翻译领域的国际合作与学术交流,探讨中医药与中国文化走向世界的战略和策略,定于 2016 年 10 月在中国湖南省长沙市召开"世界中医药学会联合会翻译专业委员会"换届大会暨第七届学术年会,会议由"世界中医药学会联合会翻译专业委员会"主办,湖南中医药大学承办,具体事宜如下:

一、会议主题
中医药文化国际传播与中医外语教育
二、会议时间与地点
会议时间:2016 年 10 月 21—23 日
会议地点:中国湖南省长沙市湖南中医药大学
三、会议日程
10 月 21 日参会人员注册报到,22 日大会学术交流,23 日离会。
四、征文内容
1. 中医药翻译的理论、方法和标准研究
2. 中国文化走出去战略背景下的中医药文化对外交流研究
3. 中医典籍翻译历史、现状与趋势研究
4. 中医外语教育学科建设、人才培养和发展趋势研究
5. 中医药名词术语翻译及其国际标准化研究
6. 中医国际教育与合作的现状与发展研究
7. 中医外语语料库建设与中医国际文献研究
8. 中医双语教学与留学生教育研究
9. 中医翻译专业研究生培养发展与问题研究

10. 中医翻译家的学术思想研究

11. 其他相关论题

此次会议将收集参会者的相关未公开发表的学术、教研论文,将评选出其中的优秀论文,颁发优秀论文证书,并推荐到国内相关的学术期刊发表。

五、投稿须知

1. 论文采用 Microsoft Word 文档格式,正文(含参考文献)字数 8 000 字以内。摘要 200 字以内,需列出 3 至 5 个关键词。

2. 投稿截止日期为 2016 年 9 月 20 日,论文电子稿请发送至邮箱:sct_wfcms@vip.sina.com。

六、报名截止日期

请于 2016 年 10 月 10 日前将参会回执(见附件)以电子邮件的形式发送至 sct_wfcms@vip.sina.com。

七、联系方式(略)

世界中医药学会联合会翻译专业委员会
2016 年 3 月 3 日

General Assembly & Seventh Annual Academic Conference of WFCMS Specialty Committee of Translation First Announcement & Call for Presentation

To further promote the international dissemination, exchange and development of Chinese medicine and Chinese culture, the General Assembly and the Seventh Annual Academic Conference of WFCMS Specialty Committee of Translation, hosted by Hunan University of Chinese Medicine, will be held in Changsha, Hunan Province, China from Oct. 21 to 23, 2016. More details are as follows.

1. Conference Theme

The international dissemination of Chinese medicine and foreign language teaching in Chinese medicine

2. Conference Date and Venue

Date:Oct. 21 to 23, 2016

Venue:Hunan University of Chinese Medicine (Changsha, Hunan Province, China)

3. Conference Schedule

Oct. 21:check-in

Oct. 22:academic exchange

Oct. 23:check-out

4. Conference Topics

(1) Research on the theories, methods and standards of TCM translation

(2) Research on the foreign exchange of TCM culture in the context of Chinese culture going-out strategy

(3) Research on the history, status quo and trend of the translation of TCM Classics

(4) Research on discipline construction, talent cultivation and development trend of foreign language education of TCM

(5) Research on the translation of TCM terminology and its international standardization

(6) Research on the status quo and development of international education and cooperation of TCM

(7) Construction of TCM foreign language corpus and research on TCM international literature

(8) Research on bilingual teaching of Chinese medicine and education for foreign students

(9) Research on development and issues of postgraduate education for students majoring in Chinese medicine translation

(10) Research on the academic thoughts of TCM translators

(11) Related topics

The conference will collect unpublished academic papers of the attendees and the exceptional ones will be issued a certificate and recommended for publishing in related domestic journals.

5. Submission Details

(1) Papers submitted should be in the form of Microsoft Word document. The body of each paper(including references) should be in less than 8,000 words, with an approximately 200-word abstract and 3 to 5 key words.

(2) The deadline for the submission of papers is Sept. 20, 2016. Please send your paper to the following e-mail address: sct_wfcms@vip.sina.com.

6. Registration deadline

Please fill in and send the registration form(in Attachment) to sct_wfcms@vip.sina.com before Oct. 10, 2016.

7. Contacts

Omitted

WFCMS Specialty Committee of Translation
Mar. 3, 2016

2) 面向个人的邀请函

对特别的受邀者除了要对会议做出说明外,还要对受邀人在该领域的成就表达敬意,并呈现出人文关怀和亲密问候,带有一定个人化的色彩。如:

March 16, 2017

Junfang Sun

School of Foreign Languages

Henan University of Chinese Medicine

Zhengzhou, Henan Province

156 Jinshui East Road, Zhengzhou, Henan, China

Dear Professor Sun,

Because of your insightful translation services to my team for their talks at Henan University of Chinese Medicine in last November, it is my privilege to invite you to provide bilingual support for mixed Chinese and American audience and speakers at the third conference for East-West Integrative Medical Practice and Scientific Technology for Allergies & Wellness, to be held May 12, 2017 through May 15th, 2017 at the Icahn School of Medicine at Mount Sinai in New York City. Our previous conference in October of 2016 brought together experts from the Massachusetts Institute of Technology, the University of Virginia, New York University, Albert Einstein School of Medicine, the U.S. National Institutes of Health, and other institutions as well as Mount Sinai. Among our topics were asthma, food allergies, mast cell diseases, and atopic dermatitis, and the openness of the U.S. medical environment to "alternative treatment" which includes traditional Chinese medicine. These scientists and practitioners and more will be joining us in May, including representatives of the U.S. Food and Drug Administration and National Institutes of Health, and the Science and Technology Counselor of consulate General of P.R. China.

You showed such professionalism and wonderful rapport with our team when we visited Henan University of Chinese Medicine that I am convinced you will enhance communication of the cutting-edge science that will be presented at our conference. It is our hope that the exchange of ideas and technology will lead to better outcomes for patients around the world.

We understand that you will be funded by the Chinese Government, your University, or other entities for this conference.

Best wishes,

Min Li, MD

Conference Committee Chair

尊敬的孙教授:

2016年11月,当我和我的团队访问河南中医药大学的时候,您精彩的翻译给我们留下了深刻的印象。我非常荣幸地邀请您参加将于2017年5月12日在纽约市西奈山伊坎医学院举办的,为期三天的(2017年5月13日至15日)第三届"过敏和健康东西方结合医学实践与科学会议"。在2016年10月举办的上一届会议中,我们邀请了来自麻省理工学院、弗吉尼亚大学、纽约大学、阿尔伯特·爱因斯坦医学院、美国国家卫生研究院,以及包括西奈山医学院等其他机构的专家学者。会议的讨论主题包括哮喘、食物过敏、肥大细胞疾病,特应性皮炎等疾病,以及当前美国医疗界对包括传统中医学在内的"替代疗法"越来越开放的态度。这些专家、学者、医生,以及美国食品药品监督管理局和美国国家卫生研究院的代表、中国驻纽约总领事馆科技参赞都将会在 5 月的会议中出席。

在我们访问河南中医药大学的时候,您展现了专业水准的学术翻译工作和与我们团队融洽的合作关系。我深信,您的参与将极大地推动本次交流会议在前沿科技方面的发展。我们希望通过在创新和技术方面的交流能给世界各地患者带来更好的福音。

最后,我们理解您会使用由中国政府,或河南中医药大学,或其他单位提供的资助来参加本次会议。

此致
敬礼

李敏 博士
会议委员会主席

3. 学术会议发言人简介

医学专业人士的个人简介根据用途和使用场合的不同而详略不等,主要涵盖职位、学历、研究方向、主要学术经历、学术成就等,会涉及荣誉称号、奖项、学术组织、专著、头衔、论文题目等内容。学术会议发言人简介大多为本人撰写,涵盖个人的职位头衔、学术成就、学术经历等,篇幅相对不大。如:

Paul M. Ehrlich, MD, was educated at Columbia University, trained in pediatrics at Bellevue Hospital at NYU, and did his allergy and immunology fellowship at Walter Reed Army Medical Center. He practices at Allergy and Asthma Associates of Murray Hill, where he was a founding partner, and is clinical assistant professor of pediatrics at New York University School of Medicine. He is a fellow of the American Academy of Pediatrics, the American Academy of Allergy, Asthma & Immunology, and the American College of Allergy, Asthma & Immunology. He has been featured as one of the New York's top pediatric allergists in *New York Magazine for* the last ten years. He is past President of the New York Allergy and Asthma Society. He is also co-author of *Asthma Allergies Children: A Parent's Guide* and blogs at asthmaallergieschildren. com.

保罗·埃利希,医学博士,毕业于哥伦比亚大学,在纽约大学贝尔维尤医院接受儿科培训,在沃尔特·里德陆军医疗中心完成过敏和免疫学培训。他在默里山过敏和哮喘协会任职,同时也是该部门的创始人之一。他是纽约大学医学院儿科临床助理教授。他是美国儿科学会,美国过敏、哮喘和免疫学学会,美国过敏、哮喘和免疫学学院的成员。过去十年来《纽约杂志》一直评价他为纽约顶级儿科过敏专家之一。他曾经担任纽约过敏和哮喘协会会长,著有《哮喘、过敏症儿童:家长指南》,博客为 asthmaallergies children. com 。

需要特别注意的是,机构、学术团体等名称中的实词首字母要大写。如:

国家中医药管理局:National Administration of Traditional Chinese Medicine

世界中医药学会联合会:World Federation of Chinese Medicine Societies(WFCMS)

中国民族医药学会:China Medical Association of Minorities(CMAM)

名老中医学术思想及临床经验研究:Research on Academic Thoughts and Clinical Experience of Prestigious TCM Physicians

国家中医药管理局"十二五"重点学科:Key Discipline in the 12th Five-Year Plan of National Administration of TCM

科学技术进步奖:Science and Technology Progress Award

重点学科建设单位:Key Discipline Construction Institutions

仲景传承创新中心:Zhongjing Inheritance and Innovation Center

涉及的著作名称用斜体,文章题目要用双引号。

4. 学术会议PPT

PPT是提纲式的文本,除了结论或小结部分会有完整的句子外,大多数内容是以短语形式出现的。很多信息是片段性的,是主讲人思路的提示。对于译者而言,往往需要先理清主讲人的思路,对所讲内容有完备的了解,才能进行有效的翻译。必要时要和主讲人进行个人沟通。因PPT容量所限,翻译时尽量避免冗长的表述。

Online Rating Sites 网上评估站点

- ＞50 rating sites for healthcare professionals
- (不到50个医护专职人员的评价网站)
- Most use commercially available databases to compile lists
- (大部分采用商购的数据库编辑列表)
- Most are free to customers(大部分对顾客免费)
- All allow healthcare providers to claim and manage their profile
- (均许可医疗服务提供者修改和掌握他们的资料)
- All offer search function and rating service(均提供搜索及评价功能)
- Most use basic categories(常见分类)

—Ease of getting an appointment(预约是否容易)

—Amount of time provider spent with patients(与病人在一起的时间)

—Wait times(候诊时间)

—Staff courtesy(员工礼貌)

—Bedside manner(病床前的态度)

5. 广告

广告的首要特点是要吸引人,然后才是传递关于产品的信息。下面这则口罩广告采用了拟人化的手法,在翻译时也要通过恰当的语言表述把产品"可爱""诚实"的特点展示出来。

Hi! My name is Masky. Before you use me...

大家好！我的名字是小口罩！请你详细了解我之后再跟我亲密接触哦～

WASH AND STERILIZE ME THOROUGHLY!

请先对我进行彻底的清洗和消毒！

I was born with no certification. Facilities didn't support germ identification so I may have been contaminated on the way to your door.

我没有政府颁发的出生证，也没有经过严格的体检，所以我在去您家的路上可能已经接触过一些别的污染源了。

I have...

但是我可以……

①4 layers of fabric that keep droplets from you or others away from each other.

提供 4 层防护来阻止您或其他人的飞沫接触到彼此。

②A pouch for extra filtering that's handy for washing. (I love baths, please wash me regularly after use!)

容纳额外的过滤层，也能更方便你的清洗。（我非常喜欢洗澡，使用后请定期帮我做清洁吧！）

③Adjustable ties. GENTLY pull my strings until my loops are out of the fabric. Retie to the desired length, GENTLY pull the loop back in the fabric, and you're done! (If the elastic's not long enough, please contact my creator.)

调整自己耳绳的长度好让我更加适合你。调整方法：轻轻拉动我的耳绳直到抽出绳结。调整绳结的位置，轻轻地将绳结再拉回布料藏起来，即可完成！（如果耳绳不够长，请与我的妈妈联系。）

My comrades and I CANNOT, sadly, fight off COVID-19, but we can help. The smart people say that our strongest comrades, the N95 warriors, are most effective on the frontlines. If one(or more) of them is lazing about on your shelf, please give them a kick and send them where they belong!

虽然我和我的弟兄姐妹们无法抗击 COVID-19，但我们还是希望可以提供力所能及的帮助。据前线战报，我们最强大的战友 N95，是奋战在一线最可靠的战士。如果他们中有在架子上睡着了或是在家里别的地方迷路了，请将他们派到自己应该去的战场上吧！

And the back text：

For more information on masks, check the CDC page：

更多有关口罩的详细信息，请查看美国疾病控制与预防中心网站：

https://www.cdc.gov/coronavirus/2019-ncov/hcp/ppe-strategy/face-masks.html

第三节 科普文体

科普文体介于正式的学术论文和普通文体之间,旨在普及医学常识,是非专业人士能够读懂的医学文章。

Endocrine System

Why is it that some people reach excessive height and some are dwarfs? Most commonly it is due to abnormal secretion during childhood of a hormone called somatotropin(Growth Hormone) by the pituitary gland. Produced in small amount by endocrine glands, hormones affect the function of many vital organs of our body. This passage gives a brief description of the major endocrine glands, the hormones released by them, and the function of each.

The endocrine system consists of a widely distributed group of glands that release specific chemical substances called hormones. Unlike the exocrine glands that secrete chemical substances onto the surface of the body or into specific organs, the endocrine glands, no matter which hormones they produce, secrete their hormones directly into the bloodstream rather than into ducts leading to the exterior of the body.

The endocrine system is a network of glandular structures that function in close coordination with the nervous system. Like the nervous system, the endocrine system controls and integrates many bodily functions. Processes under direct endocrine control include growth, reproduction, cellular metabolism, and the regulation of blood levels of many important nutrients. In contrast with the rapid electrical responses of the nervous system, the endocrine system uses hormones to generate responses that are more cyclical in nature, occurring over hours or days rather than seconds or minutes. Integration of nervous and endocrine influences on the body occurs in the hypothalamus, a structure of the central nervous system...

译文:

内分泌系统

为什么有的人身材高大而有的人身材矮小?最常见的原因系儿童期垂体腺所产生的生长激素分泌异常所致。激素由内分泌腺少量产生,但却影响身体许多重要器官的功能。本文简要描述主要的内分泌腺,它们分泌的激素以及各自的功能。

内分泌系统由一组释放激素即特异化学物质的腺体构成,其分布广泛。与分泌化学物质于体表或特定器官的外分泌腺不同,内分泌腺无论产生何种激素,均直接分泌入血流,而不是进入通向体外的导管。

内分泌系统是一组与神经系统密切合作的腺性结构,它像神经系统一样控制并协调机体的多种功能。直接受内分泌控制的过程包括生长、生殖、细胞新陈代谢以及多种重要营养物的血液水准调节。与神经系统快速的电反应形成对照,内分泌系统利用化学物质产生更具周期性质的反应,发生于数小时或数天中,而非几秒钟或几分钟。神经与内分泌对身体作用的结合发生在中枢神经系统中的下丘脑……

科普性文章和正式的学术性医学文章相比,显得更轻松活泼,经常使用第二人称。如:"If you eat too much, your stomach produces more acid, and the contents of your overly full stomach can be forced back up into the esophagus, which runs in front of the heart, giving you heartburn."。

修辞手法也相对丰富。如:

(1) A healthy artery is like a rubber tube. (simile 明喻) It is smooth and flexible, and blood flows through it freely.... An artery with artherosclerosis is more like a clogged pipe. (simile 明喻) Plaque(斑块) narrows the artery and makes it stiff.

译文:健康的动脉就像一根橡皮管,光滑而灵活,血液流动自由。动脉粥样硬化更像是一根堵塞的管子,斑块使动脉变得狭窄而僵硬。

(2) In this case, gastrin makes the stomach's juice-secreting cells pour out more juices. It is as if the person who went out of the back door ran around the corner and signaled someone in another house to turn on the water faucets. (simile 明喻)

译文:在这种情况下,胃泌素使分泌汁液的细胞分泌更多的汁液。这就好像一个人从后门跑到拐角处,向另一户人家发出信号,让他们打开水龙头。

(3) The flu virus is a trickster(personification 拟人), constantly changing its surface antigens, so that our immune systems need to relearn how to fight it every time it adopts a new costume.(季佩英,孙庆祥,2012:29)

译文:流感病毒诡计多端,不断变化其表面抗原,这样它每换一套新衣都使我们的免疫系统需要重新学习如何与之战斗。

(4) In 1969, Surgeon General William Stewart, testifying before Congress, said that we could "close the book on infectious disease."(metaphor 隐喻) Antibiotics and vaccines had left the medical community flush with a string of impressive victories, from penicillin to polio. That war, they thought, was almost over.(metaphor 隐喻)(季佩英,孙庆祥,2012:26)

译文:1969年,美国卫生局局长威廉·斯图尔特在国会听证时说,我们可以"给传染病画上句号了"。抗生素和疫苗带来了一个接一个了不起的胜利,从青霉素的发现到脊髓灰质炎的防治等凡此种种,让医学界欣喜不已。他们认为这场战争几乎结束了。

(5) And everyone in the infectious-disease field fears the day when a powerful new strain of flu sweeps the world. "The war has been won,"(metaphor 隐喻) one scientist recently quipped. "By the other side."(metaphor 隐喻)(季佩英,孙庆祥,2012:27)

译文:每一位在传染病领域的工作者都害怕,终有一日一种强大的新型流感菌株会席卷全球。"战争胜利了,"最近有位科学家嘲弄道,"是对方(传染病)获胜。"

(6) Today, antibiotics have become a victim of their own success. Antibiotics have been used so extensively that many are becoming powerless against diseases they used to cure. Like other once bright, shiny, new tools, antibiotics have become worn out—

and less effective and incisive over time as a result, simply because we haven't used them right. Bacteria are increasingly resistant to existing antibiotics, and while new drugs have been developed, the pace of discovery has not kept up with the pace of bacterial resistance.

译文：如今，抗生素已成为自身成功的牺牲品。抗生素的使用如此广泛，有一些抗生素已对它们从前可以治愈的疾病束手无策。<u>就像其他一度明光锃亮的新工具一样，抗生素已经破旧不堪</u>，效果会越来越弱，究其原因就是我们没有正确使用。细菌对现有抗生素越来越耐受，当然也有新药出来，但新药研发的速度远跟不上细菌耐药的速度。

丰富的比喻，通俗的语言，流畅的行文，使原本深奥的医学原理变得简单易懂，也增加了可读性。翻译时应尽量以明白晓畅的语言译出来。以雅译雅，以俗译俗。

第四节　政府公文

政府公文指的是政府公开表明医疗政策或对某一医疗体系支持的文件，表达的是官方立场和态度，故其行文相对客观、正式，句子较长。翻译时应留意用词的准确性、客观性和内在的逻辑性。下列片段摘自2016年12月6日国务院新闻办公室发表的《中国的中医药》白皮书：

中国高度重视中医药事业发展。新中国成立初期，把"团结中西医"作为三大卫生工作方针之一，确立了中医药应有的地位和作用。1978年，中共中央转发卫生部《关于认真贯彻党的中医政策，解决中医队伍后继乏人问题的报告》，并在人、财、物等方面给予大力支持，有力地推动了中医药事业发展。中华人民共和国宪法指出，发展现代医药和我国传统医药，保护人民健康。1986年，国务院成立相对独立的中医药管理部门。各省、自治区、直辖市也相继成立中医药管理机构，为中医药发展提供了组织保障。第七届全国人民代表大会第四次会议将"中西医并重"列为新时期中国卫生工作五大方针之一。2003年，国务院颁布实施《中华人民共和国中医药条例》；2009年，国务院颁布实施《关于扶持和促进中医药事业发展的若干意见》，逐步形成了相对完善的中医药政策体系。

China lays great store by the development of TCM. When the People's Republic was founded in 1949, the government placed emphasis on uniting Chinese and Western medicine as one of its three guidelines for health work, and enshrined the important role of TCM. In 1978, the Communist Party of China (CPC) Central Committee transmitted throughout the country the Ministry of Health's "Report on Implementing the Party's Policies Regarding TCM and Cultivating TCM Practitioners," and lent great support in areas of human resources, finance, and supplies, vigorously promoting the development of TCM. It is stipulated in the Constitution of the PRC that the state promotes modern medicine and traditional Chinese medicine to protect the people's health. In 1986, the State Council set up a relatively independent administration of TCM. All provinces, autonomous regions, and municipalities directly under the central government have established their respective TCM administrations, which has laid an organizational basis for TCM development. At the Fourth Meeting of the Seventh National People's Congress, equal emphasis was put on Chinese and Western medicine, which was made one of the five guidelines in China's health work in the new period. In 2003 and 2009, the State Council issued the "Regulations of the People's Republic of China on Traditional Chinese Medicine" and the "Opinions on Supporting and Promoting the Development of Traditional Chinese Medicine," gradually forming a relatively complete policy system on TCM.

中国共产党第十八次全国代表大会以来,党和政府把发展中医药摆上更加重要的位置,作出一系列重大决策部署。在全国卫生与健康大会上,习近平总书记强调,要"着力推动中医药振兴发展"。中国共产党第十八次全国代表大会和十八届五中全会提出"坚持中西医并重""扶持中医药和民族医药事业发展"。2015年,国务院常务会议通过《中医药法(草案)》,并提请全国人大常委会审议,为中医药事业发展提供良好的政策环境和法制保障。2016年,中共中央、国务院印发《"健康中国2030"规划纲要》,作为今后15年推进健康中国建设的行动纲领,提出了一系列振兴中医药发展、服务健康中国建设的任务和举措。国务院印发《中医药发展战略规划纲要(2016—2030年)》,把中医药发展上升为国家战略,对新时期推进中医药事业发展作出系统部署。这些决策部署,描绘了全面振兴中医药、加快医药卫生体制改革、构建中国特色医药卫生体系、推进健康中国建设的宏伟蓝图,中医药事业进入新的历史发展时期。

Since the CPC's 18th National Congress in 2012, the Party and the government have granted greater importance to the development of TCM, and made a series of major policy decisions and adopted a number of plans in this regard. At the National Conference on Hygiene and Health held in August 2016, President Xi Jinping emphasized the importance of revitalizing and developing traditional Chinese medicine. The CPC's 18th National Congress and the Fifth Plenary Session of the 18th CPC Central Committee both reiterated the necessity to pay equal attention to the development of traditional Chinese medicine and Western medicine and lend support to the development of TCM and ethnic minority medicine. In 2015, the executive meeting of the State Council approved the Law on Traditional Chinese Medicine (draft) and submitted it to the Standing Committee of the National People's Congress for deliberation and approval, intending to provide a sounder policy environment and legal basis for TCM development. In 2016 the CPC Central Committee and the State Council issued the Outline of the Healthy China 2030 Plan, a guide to improving the health of the Chinese people in the coming 15 years. It sets out a series of tasks and measures to implement the program and develop TCM. The State Council issued the Outline of the Strategic Plan on the Development of Traditional Chinese Medicine (2016 - 2030), which made TCM development a national strategy, with systemic plans for TCM development in the new era. These decisions and plans have mapped out a grand blueprint that focuses on the full revitalization of TCM, accelerated reform of the medical and healthcare system, the building of a medical and healthcare system with Chinese characteristics, and the advancement of the healthy China plan, thus ushering in a new era of development for TCM.

政府公文语言严谨规范，术语界定清晰，逻辑结构严密，具有权威性。翻译时避免使用含糊不清、主观色彩、情绪渲染的词汇，译文中的选词自然也要符合该文体特点。

第五节　学术性文体

学术性文体指的是医学专业的毕业论文、期刊论文、学术会议报告等。

国际著名的四大医学期刊 *NEJM*，*LANCET*，*JAMA*，*BMJ* 上每年都有大量的中国论文刊登。我国国际科技论文数量连续多年名列前茅，SCI 数据库 2016 年收录中国科技论文 32.42 万篇，占世界份额的 17.1%。（李力，2017）

SCI(Science Citation Index，科学引文索引)和 Medline 是目前国际公认的两大文献数据库，所收录的期刊覆盖世界上重要且有影响力的研究成果。SCI 收录的世界生物医学类期刊约有 2000 种，涉及类别约 50 个。2016 年收录中国科技期刊 185 种，均为英文期刊。

Medline 是在线医学文献分析和检索系统。Medline 收录了 1966 年以来世界 70 多个国家和地区出版的 3400 余种生物医学期刊的文献。目前每年递增 30 万～35 万条记录，其中 75% 是英文文献，70%～80% 文献有英文摘要。Medline 收录的中国科技期刊 195 种，要求论文有英文摘要。

中华医学会系列杂志汇集国内 141 种医学杂志，其中 1 种被 SCI 收录（《中华医学杂志》英文版），23 种被 Medline 收录，这 23 种杂志在各自医学专业领域均名列前茅。其投稿基本要求包括：研究论文要有高质量的英文摘要。投稿国内外主流医学杂志，英文摘要是标配。

这些数据给我们的启示是，中国科技工作者以发表论文的方式快速融入国际学术交流，发展速度惊人，因此学术论文的翻译需求量激增。这一点应引起翻译界的关注：交流互鉴成为趋势、潮流，医学翻译也应该在这种潮流中立于不败之地。

好的论文 ＝ 好的研究 ＋ 好的写作（好的翻译）

虽然 BMJ 的编辑认为影响我国作者发表文章的最主要原因不是英文写作水平，而是论文本身的科学质量；但是，毋庸置疑，对于英语非母语作者在国际刊物上发表论文，英文写作水平常常是重要障碍。

建议一：遵照国际性刊物的论文写作模式和规则，可参照《向生物医学期刊投稿的统一要求》(*Uniform Requirements for Manuscripts Submitted to Biomedical Journals*)，它由国际医学杂志编辑委员会（ICMJE）制定。

建议二：避免中国式英语，经常阅读英语为母语的国外作者撰写的英文论文。词汇和表达方式要符合国外高质量论文和杂志的语言习惯。中国作者写英文论文往往习惯用汉语的思维和表达方式,常常词不达意,甚至造成误解。

建议三:经常阅读国际著名医学杂志,了解国外高质量医学论文的写作方式。世界著名的医学杂志有严格的审稿制度和评价论文的标准,其刊登的论文结构严谨、质量较高、语言地道。经常阅读此类杂志是学习的好途径。

此外,还要了解国际杂志上论文写作的形式、发表的指导、要求和讨论。如:BMJ要求论文后注明伦理学批准情况、临床研究的注册情况、利益竞争的声明及每位作者的具体贡献等。

下面主要就学术论文的标题及摘要进行简单阐述:

(一) 学术论文标题

论文题目力求精练,做到言简意赅。但同时需要提供关于论著要义尽可能多的学术信息,题目中出现的术语可以和关键词互补,对研究进行准确的界定。往往包含:研究对象、研究结论等。具体如下:

1. 论文标题的书写格式

1) 每个实词的首字母大写

所有实词(名词、动词、形容词、副词、数量词等)的首字母大写,3个或4个字母以下的冠词、连词、介词全部小写(有些期刊要求标题中的所有介词,不论字母多少,均一律小写),如:Numerical Alteration of Chromosome 8 in Pleural Effusions(胸腔积液中8号染色体数目变化)

2) 题名第一个词的首字母大写,其余词均小写,如:Insulin resistance is the most important risk factor of deteriorating glucose tolerance in subjects with normal glucose tolerance(胰岛素抵抗是糖耐量正常人群糖耐量恶化的最重要危险因素)

2. 论文标题的词汇特征

1) 简化冠词

英文题名中的冠词有简化的趋势,可用可不用的冠词均可不用。所以,英文题名开头第一个词不得用 The,And,An 和 A。

2) 省略谦辞

受各自文化的影响,英语论文标题注重新信息突出、结构清晰,而中国人则习惯使用"初探""浅谈""粗谈""也论"等表示自谦的字眼,即使是权威性很强的文章也是如此。英汉翻译中宜将这些谦辞略去,以突出主要信息。

3) 介词的使用

英语标题往往以名词开头,而名词与介词又密不可分。在翻译中,要留意名词和介词的搭配,不可随意乱用,常用搭配如下:

……的进展　　advance in...
……的建议　　proposal for...
……的方法　　method for...
……的应用　　application of...
……的研究　　study of/on; research of/on...

4) 避免缩略词的使用

医学论文标题应该尽量避免使用英文缩写词,确实需要用缩略词时,应该在第一次出现时用全称,缩写附在后括号。如:

Effects of proliferation and apoptosis of C6 qlioma cells with triplex forming oligonucleotides(TFO)

有些名词缩写已被本领域读者广泛接受,如 DNA、RNA 等,可以在题目中出现,其他情况尽量使用全称。

5) 标题字数

文章标题宜简不宜繁,能用一行文字表达的,最好不用两行。超过两行会削弱印象。如:

The Effect of Diet on Statistical Risk in Patients with Coronary Artery Disease

可以简化为:Coronary Artery Disease:Diet and Statistical Risk

确有必要的可以在主标题后面增加副标题,进一步界定研究主题,如:

Promotion of rapid testing for HIV in primary care(RHIVA2):a cluster-randomised controlled trial

3. 标题句式特征

医学期刊的学术论文标题一般采用偏正结构的名词性短语,如:

Clinical study of bacteria culture and drug sensitive test after the excision of acute appendicitis

常见的句式有以下几种:

1) "中心词+定语"

(1) The effect of A on B/ effects of A on B,如:The effect of the primary tumor location on the survival of colorectal cancer patients after radical surgery(*International Journal of Medical Sciences*)

Effects of the Geometrical Structure of a Honeycomb TCP on Relationship between Bone / Cartilage Formation and Angiogenesis(*International Journal of Medical Sciences*)

也有稍微复杂一些的,如

Clinicopathological Significance and Antitumor Effect of MPHOSPH1 in Testicular Germ Cell Tumor(*Journal of Cancer*)

(2) The role of/for A in B,如:

The Pivotal Role of Thymus in Atherosclerosis Mediated by Immune and Inflammatory Response(*International Journal of Medical Sciences*)

(3) Outcomes of A for B,如:

Outcomes of Laparoscopic Total Gastrectomy for Elderly Gastric Cancer Patients(*Journal of Cancer*)

(4) ... value of A in B,如:

The Prognostic Value of Cyclin-Dependent Kinase 5 and Protein Phosphatase 2A in

Gastric Cancer(*Journal of Cancer*)

(5) Identification of A as B,如:

Identification of Five Genes as a Potential Biomarker for Predicting Progress and Prognosis in Adrenocortical Carcinoma(*Journal of Cancer*)

(6) Feasibility and Efficacy of A in B,如:

Feasibility and Efficacy of Simultaneous Integrated Boost Intensity-Modulated Radiation Therapy based on MRI-CT fusion in Patients with Brain Metastases of Non-Small Cell Lung Cancer(*Journal of Cancer*)

(7) The Efficacy and Safety of A in B(……运用于……的有效性及安全性),如:

The Efficacy and Safety of Anti-Epidermal Growth Factor Receptor Monoclonal Antibodies in Nasopharyngeal Carcinoma: Literature-Based Meta-Analyses(*Journal of Cancer*)

(8) Current status of...,如:

Current status of endovascular treatment for dural arteriovenous fistula of the transverse-sigmoid sinus: A literature review (*International Journal of Medical Sciences*)

2) 完整句子做标题

完整句子做标题,句末没有句号。这种情况较少见,偶见于某些英美医学杂志。下列文章标题均来自《国际医学科学杂志》(*International Journal of Medical Sciences*):

(1) Elevated mRNA Levels of AURKA, CDC20 and TPX2 Are Associated with Poor Prognosis of Smoking-Related Lung Adenocarcinoma Using Bioinformatics Analysis

(2) RKIP-Mediated NF-κB Signaling Is Involved in ELF-MF-Mediated Improvement in AD Rat

(3) RIPK1 Inhibition Enhances Pirarubicin Cytotoxic Efficacy through AKT-P21-dependent Pathway in Hepatocellular Carcinoma

(4) Decreases in Paraoxonase-1 Activities Promote a Pro-inflammatory Effect of Lipids Peroxidation Products in Non-Smoking and Smoking Patients with Acute Pancreatitis

(二) 学术论文摘要

1. 摘要格式

英文摘要是一篇文章的概括和总结。翻译时首先要符合科研思维方式;其次要按照固定的格式(一般为四段式):

- 目的
- 方法(研究设计、研究地点、研究对象、主要结局、评价指标)
- 结果
- 结论

1) BMJ 英文摘要举例

Antibiotic prescription strategies and adverse outcome for uncomplicated lower respiratory tract infections: prospective cough complication cohort(3C) study

Objective

To assess the impact on adverse outcomes of different antibiotic prescribing strategies for lower respiratory tract infections in people aged 16 years or more.

Design

Prospective cohort study.

Setting

UK general practice.

Participants

28,883 patients with lower respiratory tract infection; symptoms, signs, and antibiotic prescribing strategies were recorded at the index consultation.

Main outcome measures

The main outcomes were reconsultation with symptoms of lower respiratory tract infection in the 30 days after the index consultation, hospital admission, or death. Multivariable analysis controlled for an extensive list of variables related to the propensity to prescribe antibiotics and for clustering by doctor.

Results

Of the 28,883 participants, 104(0.4%) were referred to hospital for radiographic investigation or admission, or both on the day of the index consultation, or were admitted with cancer. Of the remaining 28,779, subsequent hospital admission or death occurred in 26/7332(0.3%) after no antibiotic prescription, 156/17628(0.9%) after prescription for immediate antibiotics, and 14/3819(0.4%) after a prescription for delayed antibiotics. Multivariable analysis documented no reduction in hospital admission and death after immediate antibiotics(multivariable risk ratio 1.06, 95% confidence interval 0.63 to 1.81, $P=0.84$) and a non-significant reduction with delayed antibiotics (0.81, 0.41 to 1.64, $P=0.61$). Reconsultation for new, worsening, or non-resolving symptoms was common[1443/7332(19.7%), 4455/17 628 (25.3%), and 538/3819(14.1%), respectively] and was significantly reduced by delayed antibiotics(multivariable risk ratio 0.64, 0.57 to 0.72, $P<0.001$) but not by immediate antibiotics(0.98, 0.90 to 1.07, $P=0.66$).

Conclusion

Prescribing immediate antibiotics may not reduce subsequent hospital admission or death for young people and adults with uncomplicated lower respiratory tract infection, and such events are uncommon. If clinicians are considering antibiotics, a delayed prescription may be preferable since it is associated with a reduced number of reconsultations for worsening illness.

2) 柳叶刀英文摘要举例

Promotion of rapid testing for HIV in primary care (RHIVA2): a cluster-randomised controlled trial

Background

Many people with HIV are undiagnosed. Early diagnosis saves lives and reduces onward transmission. We assessed whether an education programme promoting rapid HIV testing in general practice would lead to increased and earlier HIV diagnosis.

Methods

In this cluster randomised controlled trial in Hackney(London, UK), general practices were randomly assigned(1:1) to offer either opt-out rapid HIV testing to newly registering adults or continue usual care. All practices were invited to take part. Practices were randomised by an independent clinical trials unit statistician with a minimisation program, maintaining allocation concealment.

Neither patients nor investigators were masked to treatment allocation. The primary outcome was CD4 count at diagnosis. Secondary outcomes were rate of diagnosis, proportion with CD4 count less than 350 cells per μL(微升), and proportion with CD4 count less than 200 cells per μL(微升). This study is registered with ClinicalTrials.gov, number ISRCTN63473710.

Findings

40 of 45(89%) general practices agreed to participate: 20 were assigned to the intervention group(44,971 newly registered adult patients) and 20 to the control group (38,464 newly registered adult patients), between April 19, 2010, and Aug 31, 2012. Intervention practices diagnosed 32 people with HIV versus 14 in control practices.

Mean CD4 count at diagnosis was 356 cells per μL(SD 254) in intervention practices versus 270(SD 257) in control practices(adjusted difference of square root CD4 count 3.1, 95% CI,1.2 to 7.4; $P=0.16$); in a pre-planned sensitivity analysis excluding patients diagnosed via antenatal care, the difference was 6.4(95% CI, 1.2 to 11.6; $P=0.017$).

Rate of HIV diagnosis was 0.30(95% CI,0.11 to 0.85) per 10,000 patients per year in intervention practices versus 0.07(0.02 to 0.20) in control practices(adjusted ratio of geometric means 4.51, 95% CI,1.27 to 16.05; $P=0.021$). 55% of patients in intervention practices versus 73% in control practices had CD4 count less than 350 cells per μL(risk ratio 0.75, 95% CI, 0.53 to 1.07).

28% versus 46% had CD4 count less than 200 cells per μL(0.60, 0.32 to 1.13). All patients diagnosed by rapid testing were successfully transferred into specialist care. No adverse events occurred.

Interpretation

Promotion of opt-out rapid testing in general practice led to increased rate of diagnosis, and might increase early detection of HIV. We therefore recommend implementation of HIV screening in general practices in areas with high HIV prevalence.

2. 摘要中的高频句式

1) 阐述背景

(1) ...requires.../...is(are) required for...

……需要……；……为……所必需

(2) ...is essential for...

……对……至关重要

(3) ...is(are) regarded as...

被认为是……（用以说明某事物的特点、性质）

(4) ...play a...role in...

在……中起……作用

2) 阐述研究目的

(1) To determine...

为了确定……（用于表述研究目的）

(2) To test this hypothesis...

为了验证这个假设……（用于表述研究目的）

3) 阐述方法

(1) We determined/tested/measured/assessed...

我们确定了/检测了/测量了/评估了……

(2) We randomly divided/grouped/separated...into...

我们随机将……分成/分组/分配到……

也可以用被动语态：

(3) was/were determined/tested/measured/assessed...

……被确定/检测/测量/评估

(4) ...were randomly divided/grouped/separated into...

……被随机分成/分组/分配到……

(5) We compare A with B

我们比较了 A 和 B

4) 阐述结果

(1) We found/discovered that...

我们发现……

(2) We identified...

我们鉴定了……

(3) ...was confirmed/validated...

……得到证实

(4) There was/were no significant difference(in...) between A and B

A 和 B 之间在……方面无显著差异

(5) A was/were significantly higher/lower(in...) than normal A

在……方面显著高于/低于正常

5）阐述结论

(1) We conclude that...

我们的结论是……

(2) These results/findings/data indicate that...

这些结果/发现/数据显示……

(3) These experiments demonstrate that...

实验证实……

国内一般医学期刊对英文摘要的要求相对简单，与其他期刊论文的摘要相似，举例如下：

《黄帝内经》"过用"思想的辩证本质、逻辑方法及当代价值

摘要："过用"思想是《内经》病因学说的核心理论。在理论建构过程中，《内经》将认识对象作为一个整体的动态发展过程来考察，运用了分析与综合、归纳与演绎的逻辑思维方法，深刻反映了其辩证思维本质。这种本质对于指导人们准确理解中医哲学与文化的内在意蕴、合理养生和防病治病都有着重要的现实意义与理论价值。

关键词：黄帝内经　过用思想　辩证本质　逻辑方法

The Dialectical Nature, Logical Method and Contemporary Value of "Excess Theory" in *Inner Canon of Yellow Emperor*

Abstract："Excess Theory" is the core theory of *Inner Canon of Yellow Emperor*. In theory construction process, *Inner Canon of Yellow Emperor* recognizes the object as a whole to examine its dynamic development process, by using the logical thinking methods of analysis and synthesis, inductive and deductive, profoundly reflecting its dialectical nature of thinking. This nature is of great practical significance and theoretical value in leading people to accurate understanding of the inner meaning of traditional Chinese medicine philosophy and culture, reasonable health maintenance and disease prevention.

Keywords：*Inner Canon of Yellow Emperor*, Excess Theory, dialectical nature, logical method

练　习

Ⅰ. **翻译下列论文标题（汉译英）**

(1) 不同医学高校学报英文参考文献的比较与分析

(2) 2007—2016 年成都市一院儿科住院死亡病例分析

(3) 儿科住院医师工作现状和流失情况分析与对策

(4) 一个糖尿病肾病(nephropathy)相关新基因的筛选、克隆和序列分析

Ⅱ. 翻译下列发言人简介(英译汉)

Scott N. Smith, MD is the Elliot and Roslyn Jaffe Professor of Pediatrics, Allergy and Immunology and Chief of the Division of Allergy and Immunology in the Department of Pediatrics. He is Medical Director of the Clinical Research Center, a component of Conduits—the Institutes for Translational Sciences at Icahn School of Medicine at Mount Sinai. Dr. Smith is a clinician and clinical researcher in the Jaffe Food Allergy Institute at Mount Sinai. His clinical research interests, funded in part by the National Institutes of Health and Food Allergy Research and Education include: the clinical manifestations of food allergy, allergic diseases caused by specific foods such as peanuts, tree nuts, seafood and milk, the natural history of food allergy, environmental risk factors for food allergy, diagnostic issues in food allergy, epidemiology of food allergy, psychosocial issues associated with food allergies, the genetic epidemiology of food allergy, and the development of educational materials about food allergy aimed toward health care providers and parents.

Ⅲ. 将下列短文译成汉语

Arthritis

Arthritis is a term often used to mean any disorder that affects joints. Symptoms generally include joint pain and stiffness. Other symptoms may include redness, warmth, swelling, and decreased range of motion of the affected joints. In some types other organs are also affected. Onset can be gradual or sudden.

There are over 100 types of arthritis. The most common forms are osteoarthritis (degenerative joint disease) and rheumatoid arthritis. Osteoarthritis usually occurs with age and affects the fingers, knees, and hips. Rheumatoid arthritis is an autoimmune disorder that often affects the hands and feet. Other types include gout, lupus, fibromyalgia, and septic arthritis. They are all types of rheumatic disease.

Treatment may include resting the joint and alternating between applying ice and heat. Weight loss and exercise may also be useful. Pain medications such as ibuprofen and paracetamol(acetaminophen) may be used. In some cases, a joint replacement may be useful.

Osteoarthritis affects more than 3.8% of people while rheumatoid arthritis affects about 0.24% of people. Gout affects about 1 to 2% of the Western population at some point in their lives. In Australia about 15% of people are affected, while in the United States more than 20% have a type of arthritis. Overall the disease becomes more common with age. Arthritis is a common reason that people miss work and can result in a decreased quality of life. The term is from Greek arthro- meaning joint and -itis meaning inflammation.

(来源:https://en.wikipedia.org/wiki/Arthritis 2017-05-26 访问)

Ⅳ. 翻译下列片段(汉译英)

人类在漫长发展进程中创造了丰富多彩的世界文明,中华文明是世界文明多样性、多元化的重要组成部分。中医药作为中华文明的杰出代表,是中国各族人民在几千年生产生活实践和与疾病作斗争中逐步形成并不断丰富发展的医学科学,不仅为中华民族繁衍昌盛作出了卓越贡献,也对世界文明进步产生了积极影响。

中医药在历史发展进程中,兼容并蓄、创新开放,形成了独特的生命观、健康观、疾病观、防治观,实现了自然科学与人文科学的融合和统一,蕴含了中华民族深邃的哲学思想。随着人们健康观念变化和医学模式转变,中医药越来越显示出独特价值。

新中国成立以来,中国高度重视和大力支持中医药发展。中医药与西医药优势互补,相互促进,共同维护和增进民众健康,已经成为中国特色医药卫生与健康事业的重要特征和显著优势。

第七章 医学文体翻译(二)

良弓难张,然可以及高入深;良马难乘,然可以任重致远;良才难令,然可以致君见尊。是故江河不恶小谷之满己也,故能大。圣人者,事无辞也,物无违也,故能为天下器。

《墨子·卷一》

A good bow is hard to draw, but it can reach high and pierce deep; a nice horse is hard to ride, but it can carry heavier loads and make longer journeys; talented people are hard to command, but they can bring honor to the lord. Therefore, rivers never refuse small streams, so they can have mighty currents. Sages never hesitate to undertake challenging tasks and accept other people's opinions, so they can become pillars of the state.

第六章系统阐述了医学文体的类别及翻译,本章单独介绍几种常用的医学文体的翻译体例,主要包括病历、医学评估表、药品说明书、口头医学文体等。

第一节 病历

病历(case history)是记载某个病例的症状、体征、各种检查结果、某些个人因素和社会因素、诊断、治疗的过程。它既是诊治疾病的重要依据,也是医学科研的重要资料;同时,它还具有法律效力,是解决医疗纠纷和保险理赔的重要证据。因此,无论是临床医生书写病历,还是译者翻译病历,都要确保原文和译文简、明、达意。

目前国际上对病历内容无统一格式要求。一般入院的完整病历(complete case history),其主要项目包括:

一般项目 General Data; Biographical Data
主诉 Chief Complaints(C. C.)
现病史 Present Illness(P. I.)
既往病史 Past(Medical) History(P. H.)
家族史 Family History(F. H.)
个人史/社会史 Personal History(Per. H)/Social History
下文分项阐述。

1. 一般项目

包括以下内容：

姓名 Name

性别 Sex

年龄 Age; Exact Age(实足年龄)

种族 Race

宗教信仰 Religious Group

职业 Occupation

住址 Address

婚姻状况 Marital Status

病历可靠性 Reliability

供史者 Supplier/Complainer of History

记录日期 Date of Record

需要注意的是，病历上的时间采用 24 小时的国际记录方式。如：2014 年 2 月 14 日下午 2 时 5 分应写成 14-02-2014,14:05(英式)或 02-14-2014,14:05(美式)。请看下例：

General Data：

Name：XXX

Age：Twenty One

Sex：Male

Race：Han

Nationality：China

Address：XinYang, Henan

Occupation：Excavator driver

Marital status：Unmarried

Date of admission：Nov 11th, 2015

Date of record：8 p.m., Nov 11th, 2015

Complainer of history：patient's father and himself

Reliability：Reliable

2. 主诉

主诉指的是病人诉说的主要症状，常见症状表达有：

柏油样黑大便 black tarry stools

便秘 constipation

腹泻 diarrhea

不规则发热 irregular fever

苍白 pallor

出血 bleeding/hemorrhage

干咳 dry/nonproductive cough

低热 lower fever

恶心 nausea

肥胖 obesity

纳谷不香 poor appetite

食积 dyspepsia

小便不利 dysuria

门诊病历中的主诉部分,常用省略句。住院病历有用完整句的。

(1) 患者入院主诉严重腹痛,并伴有呕吐两天。

译文:The patient was admitted with a chief complaint of a two-day history of severe abdominal pain and vomiting.

(2) 患者首次就诊时主诉寒战、视力模糊和呼吸困难一天。

译文:The patient was seen in the office for the first time with shivering, blurred vision and difficulty in breathing of one day's duration.

(3) 患者嗜烟,主诉呼吸困难几天。

译文:The patient, heavy smoker, complained chiefly of difficulty in breathing, which annoyed him for several days.

(4) 重复恶心和呕吐六个半月。

译文:Reduplicated nausea and vomiting for six and a half months.

(5) 清晨咳嗽伴淡黄色痰约 10 年。

译文:Early morning cough with whitish yellow sputum for about 10 years.

(6) 入院前 4 天出现进行性腹胀。

译文:Progressive abdominal distention 4 days before admission.

(7) 间断腹痛 4 小时。

译文:Intermittent abdominal pain for 4 hours.

(8) 突然发作剧烈的上腹痛 2 小时。

译文:Sudden onset of sharp epigastric pain for 2 hours.

(9) 头痛伴恶心和呕吐,病程两个月。

译文:Headache with nausea and vomiting two months in duration.

(10) 从昨日起咳嗽发烧。

译文:Coughing and fever since yesterday.

3. 现病史

现病史是从医生的角度进一步描述主诉内容,全面说明现有疾病的起病时间与情况、主要症状的特点、病情发展过程、症状间的关系、诊疗经过、目前病人的身体状况、与现有疾病有直接关系的过去情况等。现病史是病历的重要部分,记述必须全面完整。

1) 起病的性质与特征

暴发性的 explosive/fulminating

缓慢性的 gradual

急症 emergency

偶然察觉 accidentally perceived

偶然发现 occasionally noticed

突然发作 abrupt attack/sudden onset/(attack)began all of a sudden

迅速出现 (a symptom)occurred rapidly

2) 症状的性质与特征

病灶的 focal

不发烧的 afebrile

不可忍受的 unbearable

持续的 continuous

发作性的,阵发的 paroxysmal

急性的 acute

患精神神经症的 psychoneurotic

痉挛的 spastic

3) 出现的频率

反复不定的 recurrent/variable

复发的 relapsing

间歇的 intermittent

偶有发生 occurred sporadically

频繁的 frequent

4) 病情的变化

持续 persist

恶化 be more severe/worsen

复发 have a relapse/recur

改善 improve

好转 be better/improving

缓解 be relieved

加剧 aggravate/be exacerbated

减轻 subside

减少 decline

痊愈 (fully)recover

消失 disappear

愈合 heal

请看以下例句:

(1) 突然他右上腹部出现剧痛。

译文: He suddenly developed a sharp pain in his right upper quadrant of the abdomen.

(2) 他有半年没有出现过这些症状。

译文：He continued free of these symptoms for half a year.

（3）昨晚她的病情恶化了。

译文：She took a turn for the worse last night.

（4）病人在六个半月前突然感到恶心，吃下的食物都吐了，原因不明。他当时没有在意，以为自己吃错了东西。大约两周后，他又出现了恶心和呕吐的症状，同时还感到反胃和胃灼热，于是他去了苏州大学第一附属医院。

内镜检查显示他患有十二指肠溃疡和反流性食管炎。溃疡病理报告为慢性炎症伴淋巴细胞增生。给他开了雷贝拉唑，显示有一定疗效。

但治疗两个月后，上述症状再次出现，且病情加重，他再次到苏州大学第一附属医院做进一步治疗。

腹部 CT、MRI、MRCP 均显示胆管（肝内、肝外胆管）、胰管扩张。此外，腹部 CT 显示胰脏增大，有胰脏分裂的可能。诊断为胰腺炎，对症治疗，但效果不佳。

于是他去了郑州大学第一附属医院。腹部 CT 显示腹腔内淋巴结增大，十二指肠壁增厚。十二指肠壁病理报告诊断为 T 淋巴瘤。

为了确诊，他的家人把病理切片送到了北京的三家中国顶级医院。我们医院的病理科和友谊医院都不能排除 T 淋巴瘤的诊断，但是北京大学医院部的病理科已经诊断出他不是 T 淋巴细胞瘤患者。

一个月前，他到我们医院的急诊科接受治疗。十二指肠壁病理检查显示，急性炎症严重，嗜酸性粒细胞浸润。使用肠饲管，但被堵塞。

8 天前，病人因反复恶心呕吐六个半月而入院，自发病以来，病人体重减轻了 18 公斤。

译文：The patient felt sudden nausea and vomited the food he took in with no recognizable cause about six and a half months ago. He didn't pay attention to it and thought he had eaten something wrong. About two weeks later, the nauseous and vomitory symptoms appeared again and he felt sour regurgitation and heartburn at the same time. So he went to the First Affiliated Hospital of Soochow University.

The endoscopic examination showed he had duodenal ulcers and reflux esophagitis. And the pathological report of the ulcers was chronic inflammation with proliferation of lymphocytes. Then the Rabeprazole which had shown a curative effect was given to him.

But two months later after the treatment, the above-mentioned symptoms appeared again and became more serious, so he went to the First Affiliated Hospital of Soochow University again for further treatment.

The abdominal CT，MRI and MRCP all showed the dilatation of the bile ducts (both the intrahepatic and extrahepatic bile ducts) and the pancreatic ducts. Besides, the abdominal CT showed the enlargement of pancreas with the probability of pancreatic divisum. Then he was diagnosed as pancreatitis and the symptomatic treatment was applied with no obvious effect.

So he went to the First Affiliated Hospital of Zhengzhou University. The abdominal CT showed there were some enlarged lymph nodes in the abdominal cavity and the duodenal wall had became thickened. The pathological examination report of the duodenal wall showed he was diagnosed T lymphoma.

For accurate diagnosis, his family sent the pathological slide to three top hospitals of China in Beijing. Neither the pathology department of our hospital nor the Youyi Hospital could exclude the diagnosis of the T lymphoma, but the pathology department of Peking University Health Science Center had diagnosed that he was not a patient with T lymphoma.

One month ago he went to the Emergency Department of our hospital for treatment. The pathological examination of the duodenal wall showed there was severe acute inflammation with the infiltration of many eosinophils. The intestinal feeding tube was applied but filled.

Eight days ago, the patient was accepted because of "reduplicated nausea and vomit for six and a half months". Since the disease occurred, the patient had lost 18 kg.

注意, 检验结果不要用 positive 或 negative。如:"The biopsy(活检) was negative. The exercise test was positive. The ECG was negative"。建议用 normal 和 abnormal, 如:

Laboratory tests(studies) gave normal results.

Laboratory tests showed normal values.

Laboratory data were normal(or within normal limits).

The result of the biopsy was unremarkable.

The exercise test was abnormal.

The ECG revealed no abnormality.

4. 既往病史

既往病史指的是患者以往的患病或医疗经历。本项目特别需要注意的是时态的使用, 常用一般过去时、过去完成时和过去进行时, 如:

明显的有关病史是 20 年前曾患过十二指肠溃疡, 有 15 年多的严重高血压史。无手术史, 无结核病史, 无其他有关的既往史。

译文: Significant/ notable history was duodenal ulcer 20 years ago. He had suffered from severe hypertension for more than 15 years. No surgical procedures, no history of tuberculosis, and no other pertinent past history.

其他例子如:

(1) The patient was healthy before.

(2) Before he came to our clinic today, the patient had visited clinics at two other hospitals. /Before he came to our clinic today, the patient had been to clinics at two other hospitals.

(3) Last Saturday, his headache suddenly got worse.

(4) The patient was informed to have cancer.

也可以避开时态,用不完整句式表达,如:

No history of infective diseases.

No allergy history of food or drugs.

或者:

Operative history: Never undergoing any operation.

Infectious history: No history of severe infectious disease.

Allergic history: He was not allergic to penicillin or sulfamide.

Respiratory system: No history of respiratory disease.

Circulatory system: No history of precordial pain.

Alimentary system: No history of regurgitation.

Genitourinary system: No history of genitourinary disease.

Endocrine system: No acromegaly. No excessive sweats.

Kinetic system: No history of confinement of limbs.

Neural system: No history of headache or dizziness.

5. 家族史

本项目常用短语有:

familial tendency, presence of hereditary disorders, cause of death of parents, relationship of patient's childhood and adult life, siblings or relatives, contact with diseased individuals, ... be in good health, be healthy, be living and well

常用句式有:

The family history did not reveal...

There was no family history of...

There was no case of... in the family.

Family history was irrelevant to...

Family history showed / revealed...

There was a familial tendency to / toward...

... died of...

常用疾病名称同其余项目有:

cancer, tuberculosis, mental disorder and nervous affection, rheumatism, diabetes, hypertension, cerebral vascular accident, hemophilia, syphilis, tumor, epilepsy, allergy

6. 个人史/社会史

个人史记录与病人健康、现有疾患有关的个人生活情况,有的病历将这部分命名为社会史。个人史主要内容涉及生活嗜好、外出旅游、婚姻及生育、职业和工作环境、月经等与健康相关的因素,下面就重点项目进行分述。

1) 患者的生活及嗜好

包括是否有吸烟、喝酒或吸毒的习惯；是否偏食；业余爱好和性格特点等与疾病有关的问题。

本项目常用词汇有：

不嗜烟酒 do not have the habit of smoking or drinking/do not smoke or drink

毒品 narcotic drugs/narcotics

戒酒 stop drinking

戒烟 give up smoking

烈酒 strong drink/hard liquor/spirits

麻醉剂成瘾 narcoticism

慢性酒精中毒 chronic alcoholism

浓茶 strong tea

浓咖啡 heavy coffee

偏食 partiality for a particular kind of food

挑食 be particular about food

喜欢吃辣（冷、热、甜、咸）的食物 like/prefer hot/pungent（cold, hot, sweet, salty）food

喜欢饮酒 like/enjoy/have a taste of drinking

喜欢运动 be fond of sports

酗酒 be drunk often excessive drinking

有烟瘾的人 a heavy smoker

纵酒 be indulged in drinking

2) 职业和工作环境

有不少疾病与患者的职业或工作环境有关，如：硅肺（silicosis）是矿工长期吸入硅粉尘所致，血吸虫病（schistosomiasis）常出现在接触疫水的人群中。因此，工业毒物、粉尘、放射性物质、有毒化学物质之类的词汇会出现在本项目。

常见词汇有：

对健康有害的物质、职业 substances & occupations harmful to the health

滴滴涕 DDT（dichloro-diphenyl-trichloroethane）

敌百虫 dipterex

敌敌畏 DDVP（dichlorvos）

放射性物质 radioactive substances

粉尘 dust

高疟区 highly endemic malarious areas

焊工 welder/solderer

化肥 chemical fertilizer

矿工 miner

3) 外出旅游

在有些情况下,医生要了解病人是否到过某些地方病(local diseases)或传染病(infectious diseases)的疫区或流行区。

4) 婚姻及生育

常见词汇有：

不能生育 be unable to have children/ infertile/sterile

产褥(期)puerperium,初产妇 primipara,分娩 delivery/labour

初婚(one's)first marriage,分居 separate

个人史多用陈述句,其谓语多用一般现在时、现在完成时、一般过去时和过去完成时,有时也用省略句。看以下案例：

(1) 个人史：患者无工作,与男友同居 2 年,避孕,未怀过孕。她 14 岁来初潮,月经很有规律,周期 28 天,每次持续 4 天,经血量中等。她每天喝一杯啤酒。病人否认抽烟及经静脉注射毒品史。她不偏食,但爱吃零食。

SOCIAL HISTORY：The patient doesn't work. She has lived at home with her boyfriend for two years. The patient has practiced birth control successively. Her menses began at the age of 14. She has regular periods every 28 days that lasted 4 days with moderate menses. She consumes a cup of beer daily. The patient denied smoking and IVDA. Having a habit of eating between meals, the patient is not particular about food.

(2) 个人史：患儿是剖宫产取出来的。母奶不足,基本上靠牛奶喂养。尽管他已八个月了,仍没长出乳牙。

SOCIAL HISTORY：The ill baby was born by caesarean section. On the whole, he has been fed by bottle because his mother has little milk to feed him. No teeth have grown out though he is eight months.

由上述例子可以看出,病历翻译的总体原则是：

(1) 客观性

用词应尽可能客观中性,避免使用 unfortunately,sadly,miserably,unluckily 之类的字眼。如：

<u>Unfortunately</u>, nausea, vomiting and abdominal pain developed since last night, and the patient was brought to ER <u>for help</u>.

改为：The patient was well until last night when nausea, vomiting and abdominal pain developed, and he was brought to the ER.

(2) 简洁性

用词尽可能简洁,避免冗余表达。如：

CT scan of the head <u>was arranged(performed)</u>, which showed subdural hematoma over the left parietal area.

改为：A CT scan of the head showed subdural hematoma over the left parietal area.

另外,还要避免使用太长的句子。如：

The patient went to the hospital and was diagnosed of osteoarthritis, so medications were given and the pain decreased in severity, but she had to take the medicines regularly.

改为：The patient went to the hospital, where a diagnosis of osteoarthritis was made. She took analgesics regularly with some relief of her pain.

(3) 准确性

词汇选择、搭配上要准确，如：

The sputum culture showed Streptococcus pneumonia infection.

改为：The sputum culture yielded(grew) Streptococcus pneumonia.

或者：Bacterial culture was positive for Streptococcus pneumonia.

第二节　医学评估表

医学评估表是家属、监护人或者医生根据患者的日常表现得出的医学观察结果，以作为临床治疗或康复训练的依据，看以下对于特殊儿童进行评估筛选的例子：

CHILD SCREENING FORM 儿童筛选表

FOR PHYSICAL, OCCUPATIONAL AND SPEECH THERAPY 用于物理，职业和言语治疗

Complete form before scheduled intervention or at the beginning of the intervention.
请在治疗开始之前填写表格。

NAME 姓名：

DATE OF BIRTH 出生日期：

Living Arrangements 居住情况：

Please describe your child's living arrangements (Mark all that apply):
请选择儿童的居住情况（请在所有适用的选项上打勾）：

_____ My child lives with parents. 孩子与父母同住

_____ The child's grandparents are the primary caregivers. 孩子主要由祖父母照顾

_____ The child lives in a group home. 孩子住在集体宿舍

_____ The child lives in an orphanage. 孩子住在孤儿院

_____ Other. 其他

ANY KNOWN DIAGNOSIS 任何已知的诊断：

ARE THEY TAKING ANY MEDICATIONS? (Please list) 儿童在服用任何药物吗？（请列出）

WHAT BRINGS YOU HERE? WHAT ARE YOUR PRIMARY CONCERNS? 您因何来访？您主要担心什么？

Has your child ever received therapy before? Select the statement that is the most accurate.

您的孩子以前接受过治疗吗？请按您的实际情况选择：

_____My child has never received therapy. 我的孩子从未接受过治疗。

_____My child currently receives therapy. 我的孩子目前正在接受治疗。

How often do they receive therapy? 多久接受一次治疗？

Describe the therapy 请描述治疗方法：

Child's Formal education (Select one and respond to follow-up questions): 儿童的正规教育（选择一项并回答后续问题）：

_____My child no longer attends school. 我的孩子不再上学了。

When did they stop attending school? 什么时候停止上学的？

Why did they stop attending school? 为什么停止上学？

_____ My child has never attended public or private school. 我的孩子从未上过公立或私立学校。

_____My child is schooled at home. 我的孩子在家接受教育。

Please describe what they are learning. 请描述每天的学习及活动内容。

MOTOR 运动

BODY STRENGTH 身体强壮程度

  TRUNK or CORE：躯干 WEAK / STRONG 弱 / 强

  ARMS：双臂 WEAK / STRONG 弱 / 强

  LEGS：双腿 WEAK / STRONG 弱 / 强

BALANCE 平衡

STANDING ON ONE LEG 单腿站立 YES / NO 能/不能

WALKING A STRAIGHT LINE 走直线 YES / NO 能/不能

FINE MOTOR (USE OF FINGERS) 手指运动 NORMAL / ABNORMAL 正常/异常

GROSS MOTOR 四肢运动 NORMAL / ABNORMAL 正常/异常

MOBILITY 活动性

ROLLING UNASSISTED 自主翻身 YES / NO 能/不能

SITTING UNASSISTED 自主坐 YES / NO 能/不能

CRAWLING 爬 YES /NO 能/不能

STANDING UNASSISTED 自主站立　YES / NO 能/不能
WALKING 走　YES / NO 能 / 不能

JUMPING	跳	YES / NO	能/不能
RUNNING	跑	YES / NO	能/不能
USE OF STAIRS	上下台阶	YES / NO	能/不能

SENSORY PROCESSING 对感觉的反应
SENSORY AVOIDING/SENSITIVITY 对感觉的躲避或敏感程度.
My Child AVOIDS SENSORY CONTACT (EFFORT TO STAY AWAY).
我的孩子拒绝感觉接触（设法躲避）。

COVERS EARS 捂耳朵 YES / NO　　　　　　　　　　　是/ 不是
COVERS EYES 捂眼睛 YES / NO　　　　　　　　　　　是 / 不是

AVOIDS FOOD THAT HAS DIFFERENT TEXTURES.
拒绝口感古怪的食物。　　　　　　　　YES / NO　　是 / 不是

　　My Child DOES NOT ACTIVELY AVOID BUT IS BOTHERED BY SENSATIONS AND TOLERATES THE SENSATION. YES / NO
　　我的孩子不会主动拒绝特殊感觉。虽然不喜欢特殊感觉但可以忍受。　是/ 不是

SENSORY SEEKING 寻求感觉
My child SEEKS SENSORY INPUT.我的孩子寻求感觉接触

PUTS THINGS IN MOUTH	YES / NO	把东西放在嘴里	是 / 不是
JUMPS AROUND	YES / NO	跳跃	是 / 不是
GRINDS TEETH	YES / NO	磨牙	是 / 不是
HUGS	YES / NO	拥抱	是 / 不是
LISTENS TO MUSIC VIDEOS	YES / NO	听音乐视频	是 / 不是
VIBRATIONS	YES / NO	摇摆	是 / 不是
SWINGS	YES / NO	旋转	是 / 不是

　　LOW REGISTRATION 反应弱
　　My child DOES NOT RECOGNIZE SENSORY SIGNS IN THEIR ENVIRONMENT.
　　我的孩子无法识别周围环境中的感觉迹象。

DOESN'T RESPOND TO NAME WHEN CALLED OR TO LOUD NOISES. YES / NO
对呼唤其姓名或很大的声音无反应。是/ 不是
DOESN'T RESPOND TO SMELLS/STRONG ODORS. YES / NO
对强烈气味无反应。是/ 不是
DOESN'T RECOGNIZE SOMEONE TOUCHING THEIR BACK. YES / NO
对触摸他的背部无感觉。是 / 不是
DO ANY OF THESE IMPEDE YOUR CHILD'S ABILITY TO FUNCTION? At home, in the community, or at school? Yes / No
以上这些现象对你孩子的生活有影响吗？如果有，在家，在社区还是在学校？有/ 没有
IF YES, EXPLAIN. 如果有，请解释。比如，偶尔把她打疼却不哭闹。

Does your child demonstrate any of the following BEHAVIORS？您的孩子是否表现出以下任何行为？
OUTBURSTS/TANTRUMS YES / NO 发脾气/易怒 是/ 否

BITING	YES	/ NO	咬人	是 / 否
HITTING	YES	/ NO	打人	是 / 否
SELF-HARM	YES	/ NO	自残	是 / 否
SCRATCHING	YES	/ NO	抓挠	是 / 否
EXCESSIVE RUNNING/JUMPING	YES	/ NO	过度地奔跑/跳跃	是 / 否

OTHER? _____ YES / NO 其他？ 是 / 否

What have you found that helps to stop the behaviors? Or make them better?
你发现哪些措施可以减轻或停止孩子的上述行为？

SPEECH AND LANGUAGE DEVELOPMENT 语言能力
My Child is able to understand others：COMPREHENSION 我的孩子理解他人的能力（理解）

WORDS	NONE	FEW	SOME	MOST
单词	不能	很少	部分	大部分
PHRASES	NONE	FEW	SOME	MOST
短语	不能	很少	部分	大部分
SENTENCES	NONE	FEW	SOME	MOST
句子	不能	很少	部分	大部分

PARAGRAPHS/CONVERSATION	NONE	FEW	SOME	MOST
多个句子或对话	不能	很少	部分	大部分

My child is able to express their needs to others: EXPRESSION 我的孩子的表达能力（表达）

	NONE	FEW	SOME	MOST
WORDS 单词	不能	很少	部分	大部分
PHRASES 短语	不能	很少	部分	大部分
SENTENCES 句子	不能	很少	部分	大部分
PARAGRAPHS/CONVERSATION 多个句子或对话	不能	很少	部分	大部分

Are most people able to understand my child? SPEECH INTELLIGIBILITY
大多数人都能理解我的孩子吗？口齿清晰度

	NONE	FEW	SOME	MOST
WORDS 单词	不能	很少	部分	大部分
PHRASES 短语	不能	很少	部分	大部分
SENTENCES 句子	不能	很少	部分	大部分
PARAGRAPHS/CONVERSATION 多个句子或对话	不能	很少	部分	大部分

ARE THERE CERTAIN SOUNDS THAT ARE DIFFICULT FOR YOUR CHILD TO SAY?
是否有某些声音您的孩子说起来有困难？

My child READS/UNDERSTANDS COMMON WORDS? 我的孩子与常用字？
RECOGNIZES OWN NAME. YES/ NO 认识自己的名字。能/不能 COMMON WORDS IN ENVIRONMENT (RESTROOM, EXIT, STOP, SMILE, ETC.).YES / NO
认识周围环境中的常用字（例如：厕所、出口、停止、微笑 等等）。能/不能

My child DROOLS. YES/ NO 我的孩子流口水。是 / 否

My child has the following SWALLOWING CONCERNS：我的孩子有以下吞咽问题：
FREQUENT COUGHING/CHOKING EPISODES DURING MEALS. YES / NO
进餐期间频繁的咳嗽/噎住或窒息。是/ 否
DIFFICULTY WITH DRINKS SPILLING OUT OF MOUTH. YES / NO
喝水时水从口中流出。是 / 否
FREQUENT ILLNESSES LIKE PNEUMONIA. YES / NO
易患像肺炎之类的常见病。是 / 否
DIFFICULTY CHEWING FOODS. YES / NO
咀嚼食物有困难。是 / 否

DIFFICULTY GETTING FOODS CLEARED FROM MOUTH AFTER SWALLOWING. YES / NO
吞咽食物有困难(不能把食物全部咽下)。是 / 否

My child makes EYE CONTACT DURING CONVERSATION. YES / NO
我的孩子和别人说话时看着对方的眼睛。是 / 否

SELF CARE 自理能力

My Child is able to DRESS independently (no physical or verbal help)
我的孩子能自己穿衣裳(不用大人动手或口头指导)

TAKE OFF SOCKS 脱袜子	ALWAYS 总是可以	SOMETIMES 有时可以	NEVER 不会
PUT ON SOCKS 穿袜子	ALWAYS 总是可以	SOMETIMES 有时可以	NEVER 不会
TAKE OFF SHIRT 脱衬衣	ALWAYS 总是可以	SOMETIMES 有时可以	NEVER 不会
PUT ON SHIRT 穿衬衣	ALWAYS 总是可以	SOMETIMES 有时可以	NEVER 不会
TAKE OFF PANTS 脱裤子	ALWAYS 总是可以	SOMETIMES 有时可以	NEVER 不会
PUT ON PANTS 穿裤子	ALWAYS 总是可以	SOMETIMES 有时可以	NEVER 不会
TAKE OFF SHOES 脱鞋	ALWAYS 总是可以	SOMETIMES 有时可以	NEVER 不会
PUT ON SHOES 穿鞋	ALWAYS 总是可以	SOMETIMES 有时可以	NEVER 不会
TIE SHOES 系鞋带	ALWAYS 总是可以	SOMETIMES 有时可以	NEVER 不会

BUTTONS 纽扣

LARGE, MEDIUM, SMALL 大、中、小	ALWAYS 总是可以	SOMETIMES 有时可以	NEVER 不会
ZIPPERS 拉链	ALWAYS 总是可以	SOMETIMES 有时可以	NEVER 不会
TAKE OFF JACKET/COAT 脱外衣	ALWAYS 总是可以	SOMETIMES 有时可以	NEVER 不会

PUT ON JACKET/COAT 穿外衣	ALWAYS 总是可以	SOMETIMES 有时可以	NEVER 不会

My Child is able to Feed themselves independently (no physical or verbal help).
我的孩子能自己吃东西（不用大人动手或口头指导）。

FINGER FOODS 零食	ALWAYS 总是可以	SOMETIMES 有时可以	NEVER 不会
USING A SPOON 使用勺子	ALWAYS 总是可以	SOMETIMES 有时可以	NEVER 不会
USING A FORK 使用叉子	ALWAYS 总是可以	SOMETIMES 有时可以	NEVER 不会
USING CHOPSTICKS 使用筷子	ALWAYS 总是可以	SOMETIMES 有时可以	NEVER 不会
DRINKING FROM A STRAW 用吸管喝饮料	ALWAYS 总是可以	SOMETIMES 有时可以	NEVER 不会
DRINKING FROM A CUP 用杯子喝饮料	ALWAYS 总是可以	SOMETIMES 有时可以	NEVER 不会

My Child is able to complete their self-care (grooming / hygiene) independently (no physical or verbal help).
我的孩子能够独立完成自我护理（梳理/卫生）（不用大人动手或口头指导）。

BRUSHING TEETH 刷牙	ALWAYS 总是可以	SOMETIMES 有时可以	NEVER 不会
BRUSHING/COMBING HAIR 梳头	ALWAYS 总是可以	SOMETIMES 有时可以	NEVER 不会
BATHING (WASHING BODY) 洗澡	ALWAYS 总是可以	SOMETIMES 有时可以	NEVER 不会
WASHING HAIR 洗头	ALWAYS 总是可以	SOMETIMES 有时可以	NEVER 不会
WIPING AFTER TOILET USE 擦屁股	ALWAYS 总是可以	SOMETIMES 有时可以	NEVER 不会

What else would you like us to know about your child?
您还希望我们了解您的孩子什么？

How did you learn about this project?
您是如何知道我们这个项目的？
What do you hope to gain by participating in this project?
您希望通过参与此项目获得什么？

第三节　药品说明书

药品说明书是指导医生与患者合理用药的重要依据,具有一定的法律效力。在英文中可以译为:Instructions,Directions,Description,Package Insert(或简称 Insert),Leaflet,Data Sheets 等。经过注册的进口药品一般是国家承认的有效药物,其说明书包含:

(1) Drug Names 药品名称

(2) Description 性状

(3) Pharmacological Actions 药理作用

(4) Indications 适应证

(5) Contraindications 禁忌证

(6) Dosage and Administration 用量与用法

(7) Adverse Reactions 不良反应

(8) Precautions 注意事项

(9) Package 包装

(10) Storage 贮存

下面逐一进行介绍。

(一) 药品名称

药品名称的翻译常采用以下几种方式:

音译:按药品英文读音翻译,如:阿司匹林(Aspirin),利多卡因(Lidocaine)等。

意译:根据药品名称所表达的含义翻译。如:叶酸(Folic Acid),胆酸(Cholic Acid),或按其药理作用翻译,如:灭糖尿(Minidiab)(治疗糖尿病药物)等。

音意合译:即部分音译,部分意译,如:戊巴比妥钠(Nembutal Sodium),香豆定(Coumadin)(coumarin 香豆素)等。

谐音意译:音译时,尽可能选用恰切的表意汉字,如:多睡丹(Doriden),好尔睡(Halcion),安嗽灵(Asverin),脉心敏(Motazomin),安痛定(Antodin)等。

药品名称一旦确定,具有一定的约定俗成性和规范性,不可随意杜撰。

(二) 性状

这一项多为常用词,个别化学专业词汇通过查专业词典即可解决。

性状表达高频词汇有:

常用名词:colo(u)r(颜色),taste(味道),molecular formular(分子式),molecular weight(分子量),structure(结构),solubility(溶解度),injection(注射剂),solution(溶

液),odo(u)r(气味),tablets(片剂),derivative(衍生物),liquid(液体),powder(粉末),solid(固体)。

常用形容词:stable(稳定的),odo(u)rless(无臭的),crystalline(结晶的),insoluble(不溶的),tasteless(无味的),colo(u)rless(无色的),sterile(无菌的),soluble(可溶的)。

常见句子结构:sth. occurs as…(为),sth. contains(含有),sth. has/possesses…(具有),sth. is derived from(由……衍生),sth. is prepared from…/sth. is obtained from…(由……制得),sth. is consisted of(由……组成)。

请看以下例句:

(1) Folic acid is a yellowish to orange, crystalline powder; odourless or almost odourless.

译文:叶酸是淡黄色至橙色结晶粉末,无臭或几乎无臭。

(2) It occurs as a white to off-white, crystalline solid, poorly soluble in water, dilute acid and most organic solvents.

译文:本品(炎痛息康)为白色至类白色结晶固体,难溶于水、稀酸及大多数有机溶剂中。

(3) This product is prepared from units of human plasma which have been tested and found nonreactive for hepatitis associated(Australia) antigen.

译文:本品由人血浆制备,此血浆业经检验,并且证明对肝炎(澳大利亚)抗原无反应。

(三) 药理作用

1. 药理表达常见词汇

(1) 常用名词(短语):Pharmacological Action(药理作用),Pharmacological Properties(药理性质),Pharmacology(药理学),Clinical Pharmacology(临床药理),Vitro Experiments(体外实验),Metabolism(药物代谢),Potency(药效),Toxicity(毒性),Actions(作用),Actions and Properties(作用与性质),Clinical Effect(Use)[临床效果(用途)],Mechanism of Action(作用机理),Mode of Action(作用方式),Biological Action(生物活性),Microbiology(微生物学),ability(能力),activity(活性),distribution(分布),excretion(排泄),clearance(廓清率),half life(半衰期),mechanism(机理),serum concentration(血清浓度),tolerance(耐受性)。

(2) 常用动词(短语):absorb(吸收),cause(be caused by)[引起(由……引起)],exert(action on)(起……作用),exhibit(显示),inhibit(抑制),accumulate(积蓄),administrate(投药),excrete(排泄),result in(导致),indicate(表明),maintain(维持),produce(产生),protect(from)[保护(不变)],metabolize(代谢),promote(促进),prevent(阻止,预防),tolerate(耐受)。

(3) 常用形容词(短语):(be) active(effective) against(对……有效的),(be) related to(与……有关的),(be) sensitive to(对……敏感的),resistant to……(有耐药性的),average(平均的),minimum[最低(小)的],maximum[最高(大)的],normal(正常的)。

2. 药理表达常见句型

(1) Mean peak serum concentrations of tobramycin occur between 30 and about 60 minutes after intramuscular administration.

译文：肌注后约 30~60 分钟之间妥布霉素的平均血药浓度达到高峰。

(2) Fenarol has proved to be effective as a striated muscle relaxant.

译文：已证明芬那露是疗效很好的横纹肌松弛药。

(3) Halcion is a potent short-acting hypnotic agent, which produces its hypnotic activity from the first night of administration.

译文：好而睡是一种强力速效催眠药，它从服药后的第一个夜晚开始产生催眠作用。

（四）适应症

1. 常用名词

Indications(适应证)，Indications and Usage(适应证与用途)，Action and Use(作用与用途)，angina pectoris（心绞痛），cancer（癌），diabetes (mellitus)（糖尿病），hypertension(高血压)，Gram-positive bacterium(革兰氏阳性菌)，virus(病毒)，Gram-negative bacterium(革兰氏阴性菌)，E. coli(大肠杆菌)

(2) 常用短语

be active against 对……有效

be administered in... 适用于…

be of value of... 适用于……

be effective in(for, against)... 对……有效

be recommended for 推荐用于……

be employed to... 用于……

be used to(for, as)... 用于……

be helpful in... 有助于

be useful in... 对……有作用

be indicated in(for)... 适用于……

for(in) the treatment(management) of... 用于治疗(控制)

be associated with/in association with 结合

be combined with/in combination with 结合

be compatible with... 可以和……同时使用

in conjunction /concomitant /together with... 与……一起

请看以下例句：

(1) Kanamycin is active both in vitro and vivo against Gram-positive bacterium and Gram-negative bacterium as well as acid-fast bacteria.

译文：卡那霉素在体外及体内对革兰氏阳性菌和革兰氏阴性菌以及耐酸菌都有效。

(2) Benemid is recommended for the treatment of gout and gouty arthritis, and to increase and prolong the plasma concentration of penicillins and cephalosporins during anti-infective therapy.

译文：丙磺舒被推荐用于治疗痛风及痛风关节炎，及在强化抗感染治疗时增加并延长青霉素类及头孢菌素类的血浆浓度。

（3）Information available at present suggests that Oncovin may be useful either alone or in conjunction with other oncolytic drugs for the treatment of acute leukaemia...

译文：据现有资料表明，硫酸长春新碱可单独使用，亦可与其他溶瘤细胞药物合用，以治疗急性白血病……

（4）Adriamycin is frequently used in combination chemotherapy regiments with other cytotoxic drugs.

译文：阿霉素常与其他细胞毒药物合用于化疗方案。

也会出现一些不完全句结构，仅列出疾病或微生物的名称，如：

（5）Angina pectoris, variant angina pectoris, hypertension.

译文：心绞痛，变异型心绞痛，高血压。

（6）The following diseases caused by bacteria including Gram-positive bacterium and Gram-negative bacterium such as Staphylococcus, Streptococcus, Escherichia coli, Klebsiella pneumoniae...

译文：用于治疗由革兰氏阳性菌和革兰氏阴性菌，如葡萄球菌、链球菌、大肠杆菌、肺炎杆菌……引起的下列疾病……

（7）To prevent the formation of urinary calculi, especially in cases where they tend to recur.

译文：预防尿路结石的形成，特别是在易发部位。

（五）禁忌证

1. 高频词

pregnant woman(孕妇), lactation(哺乳期), pregnancy(妊娠期), diabetes(糖尿病), hypertension(高血压), anemia(严重贫血), hypotension(低血压)

2. 高频短语

cardiac(renal) insufficiency 心(肾)功能不全

children under...years of age ……岁以下儿童

the first trimester(3 months) of pregnancy 妊娠期的最初三个月

be allergic(hypersensitive) to... 对……过敏的

allergic(anaphylactic) reaction 过敏反应

allergy(hypersensitivity) to... 对……过敏

cardiac failure 心力衰竭

liver(hepatic) damage 肝损伤

impairment of kidney(renal function) 肾功能损伤

be contraindicated in(for)... 对……禁忌

should not be used(employed) in... 不得用于……

It is advisable to avoid the use of... 建议不用于……

must not be administered(given) to... 对……不得用药
should be used with caution 慎用
be not recommended for... 最好不用于……
none reported 未见报道
not known 不清楚

请看以下例句：

(1) Cefazolin sodium is contraindicated in patients with known hypersensitivity to cephalosporin group of antibiotics.

译文：先锋 5 号禁用于已知对头孢菌素类抗生素过敏的患者。

(2) It is advisable to avoid the use of Aramine with cyclopropane or halothane anesthesia, unless clinical circumstances demand such use.

译文：如果不是临床需要，建议本品不要与环丙烷或氟烷麻醉剂合用。

(3) Children under 5 years of age should not be treated with Antistine.

译文：5 岁以下儿童禁用敌胺。

(4) The use of Alexan in nursing mothers is not recommended.

译文：哺乳期妇女最好不用爱力生。

（六）用量与用法

1. 表达用量用法的词汇

Route of Administration 给药途径（用法）
Administration 用法
Direction for Use 用法
Method of(for) Administration 用法
Application and Dosage 用法与用（剂）量
Mode of Application 用法
Dosage 用（剂）量
How to Use 用法
Posology 剂量学

2. 表示剂量的术语

average dose(平均剂量), minimal(minimum) dose(最小有效量), daily dose[日剂量(一日量)], multiple dose(多剂量), divided dose(分次剂量), overdose(overdose)(过量), fatal(lethal) dose(致死量), single dose(一次剂量), indicated dose(有效剂量), standard dose[标准(合适)剂量], initial(beginning, starting) dose(首次量), suggested (recommended) dose(推荐剂量), maintenance dose(维持量), therapeutic dose(治疗剂量), maximum dose[最大剂量（极量）], usual(normal) dose(常用剂量)

3. 常用剂量单位表示法

g=gram(克), l=liter(litre)(升)
mg=milligram(毫克), ml=milliliter(毫升)
kg=kilogram(千克), c.c.(毫升)

mcg=microgram(微克),I.U.=international unit(国际单位)
ug(微克),body weight(体重)
per square meter of body surface(每平方米体表面积)

4. 给药次数表示法

daily(per day, a day, every day)(每日)
every...hours(每隔……小时)
once(twice) daily(a day)[每日一(二)次]
every other day(每隔一日)
once(twice) a week(weekly)[每周一(二)次]
divided into...doses(分……次)
in two or three divided doses[分为二或三次(个剂量)]

5. 给药方法表示法

locally(局部给药), orally(口服给药), by mouth(OS)(口服), parenterally(肠道外给药), submucously(黏膜下给药), subcutaneously(皮下给药), sublingually(舌下给药), subconjunctivally(结膜下给药), intra-arterially(静脉内给药), intrathecally(鞘内给药), intraperitoneally[腹(膜)腔内给药], intrapleurally[胸(膜)腔内给药], intragluteally(臀肌内给药), intramuscularly(肌内给药), intravenously(静脉内给药), by intramuscular(IM) injection(肌肉注射), by intravenous(IV) injection(静脉注射), by the intra-articatar administration(关节内给药), by the intranasal route(鼻内给药), by the intramuscular administration(route)(肌内给药)

6. 其他表示法

be adjusted(调整), depend on(依据), adapt to(适合,修改), on the basis of(在……基础上), vary from...to...(变化范围由……至……,因……而异), range from...to...(变化范围由……至……), It is advisable to(it is recommended to, it is suggested to)(...建议……)

请看以下例句:

(1) Unless otherwise prescribed by the physician, the average daily dose is 1 capsule 3 times daily.

译文:如果医生不另开处方,平均日剂量为每日三次、每次一粒胶囊。

(2) Children：The usual dose is 50 to 100 mg/kg/day total, given in four equally divided and spaced doses.

译文:儿童:常用总剂量为每日 50—100 mg/kg,均分为四等份,等间隔给药。

(七) 不良反应

本项高频词汇主要有:

fever(发热), flush(潮红), headache(头痛), nausea(恶心), systematic(全身的), pruritus(瘙痒), anorexia(厌食), rash(皮疹), dizziness(眩晕), coma(昏迷), tiredness(疲倦), diarrhea(腹泻), vomiting(呕吐), spasm(痉挛), thirst(口渴);
allergic(hypersensitive, anaphylactic) reaction(s)(过敏反应), local reaction(s)(局

部反应),allergy(hypersensitivity)(过敏),skin reaction(s)(皮肤反应);
abandon(停药),discontinue(discontinuance,discontinuation)[停药,中断(治疗)],cease(cessation)(stop)[停药(停止治疗)],suspend(停药),terminate(停止,结束),withdraw(be withdrawn,withdrawal)(停药)等。

请看以下例句:

(1) When adverse reactions occur, they are usually reversible and disappear when the hormone is discontinued.

译文:当不良反应发生时,它们往往是可逆的,停用激素后副作用即消失。

(2) In some patients nausea, dizziness, and vomiting may occur in the first days of treatment but the treatment need not be discontinued for that. In rare cases a decrease of blood pressure may appear for which a blood pressure check-up is recommended in out-patients before the treatment is initiated. If side-effects persist, lower doses should be administered.

译文:服用本品的头几天,有些病人可能会出现恶心、头晕和呕吐,但不必停药。偶有血压下降的病例,为此,在治疗开始前建议对门诊患者检测血压。若副作用持续不消失,应减少服用剂量。

(3) Side-effects:Loss of appetite and nausea occur in most cases, sometimes with vomiting. These symptoms are usually confined to the first few days of treatment and then tend to disappear.

译文:副作用:多数病例出现食欲减退、恶心,有时呕吐。这些症状通常发生在治疗的最初几天,以后逐渐消失。

(八) 注意事项

本项高频词汇主要有:

blood count(血细胞计数),kidney(renal) function(肾功能),liver(hepatic) function(肝功能),blood picture(hemogram)(血象),blood level(血浓度),serum concentration(血清浓度),blood pressure(血压),serum creatinine test(血清肌酸酐检验),clotting time(凝血时间),urine routine(examination)(尿常规),creatinine clearance(肌酸酐清除率)等。

本项的内容涉及面较广,既有普通词汇,也有大量的专业词汇及缩写词,请看以下例句:

(1) Dosage should be controlled by periodic determinations of prothrombin time (PT) or other suitable coagulation tests.

译文:必须定期检查凝血酶原时间(PT),或做其他相应的凝血试验来控制剂量。

(2) Caution must be exercised in the case of hypersensitivity to iodinated contrast agent, latent hyperthyroidism and bland nodular goiter.

译文:对碘造影剂过敏、隐匿性甲状腺亢进和轻微甲状腺肿的病例,应慎重。

(3) As with all new drugs, patients should be followed carefully so that any side-effects or unusual manifestations of drug idiosyncrasy may be detected. If any allergic

reaction to Keflex occurs, the drug should be discontinued and the patient treated with the usual agents.

译文：像使用所有新药一样，应细心地随访患者，以便观察任何副作用或药物特异反应。如果出现对头孢菌素Ⅳ的过敏反应，应停药，并用常规药物治疗患者。

（九）包装

本项高频词汇主要有：

Packing for Hospital（医院用包装），Method of Supply（包装方式），Package Quantities(Quantity)（包装量），Presentation（包装），Hospital(Size) Packs（医院用包装），Availability（包装），Trade Packs(Packings)（商品包装），Mode(Form)of Issue（包装）；

carton（纸盒），blister pack(package)［铝塑包装（水泡眼包装）］，pack（包），blister strip［铝塑条状包装（水泡眼条状包装）］，strip（条），tube（管），canister（罐），vial（玻璃小瓶）；

aerosol(spray, inhaler)（气雾剂），ampoule（针剂），capsules（胶囊），oral solution（口服液），coated(-)tablets（包衣片），pill（丸剂），cream（乳膏），powder（粉剂），derm TTS（皮肤贴膏），retard capsules(tablets)［缓释胶囊（片）］，dregees（糖衣丸），scored-tablets［刻（划）痕片］，drops（滴剂），solution（溶液剂），emulsion（乳剂），sugar-coated tablets（糖衣片），film-coated tablets（薄膜片），suppositories（栓剂），granule（颗粒），suspension（悬浮剂，混悬剂），liniment（搽剂），syrup（糖浆），liquid（液剂），tablets（片剂），ointment（软膏）等。

本项内容结构简单，多为不完全句，如：

（1）Presentation 30 capsules.

译文：30粒胶囊装。

（2）Also available in Hospital Unit-Dose blister package of 100.

译文：也提供医院用的单位剂量的铝塑包装，（每包）100片装。

（3）Packs Standard packs of 20 dregees. Hospital packs of 100, 500 and 1,000 dregees.

译文：标准包装为20粒糖衣丸。医院用包装为100,500及1 000粒糖衣丸。

（十）贮存

本项的词汇和句式都比较简单，易读易译。本项高频词主要有：

store(keep) in a cool and dry place 存于阴凉干燥处

away from light 避光

away from children 勿让儿童接触

protect from light(heat) 避光（热）

out of(the) reach of children 勿让儿童触及

prevent moisture 防潮

请看以下例句：

（1）Store medicines carefully. Keep away from children.

译文：注意保存。勿让儿童接触。

(2) Storage instructions: Protect from heat and light.

译文:贮存方法:避光及防热贮存。

(3) The solution should be prepared immediately prior to use, but can be stored at 4℃ or up to one week.

译文:药液应在配制后立即使用,但在4℃下可贮存一周。

第四节　口头医学文体

口头医学文体包括会议发言和医学类演讲、医学相关人员的自我介绍等。随着近年来国际交流的日益频繁,此类文体的使用频率明显增多。它既有医学文体的特征,又有口语特征。

1. 学术会议发言

学术会议发言具有一定的学术性,但又有别于书面的学术论文,可带有一定的口语色彩,甚至可以穿插一些修辞和感情色彩,如:

在中华文明的宝库中,闪耀着一颗明珠,那就是中医药。它不仅是中国人民生命与健康的保护神,而且在中华民族几千年的历史绵延和文化传承中,以其独特的理论品质彰显着中国理性与智慧。正如习近平主席所言:"中医药学凝聚着深邃的哲学智慧和中华民族几千年的健康养生理念及实践经验,是中国古代科学的瑰宝,也是打开中华文明宝库的钥匙。"

随着中西文化的交流会通,中医药正在全球范围内被越来越多的人所接受。一方面,"21世纪的医学将从疾病医学向健康医学发展",中医药恰恰契合了这一理念。另一方面,中国学者屠呦呦荣获诺贝尔生理学或医学奖,使得人们确信"中国传统医药能给科学家带来新的启发";应用中医药抗击SARS、埃博拉病毒的良好疗效也一次次地证明中医药适应新的医疗实践、造福人类健康的巨大潜力。但是,在西方医学长期居于主导地位的背景下,中医药的潜力还需要不断地发掘和推广,需要不断促进中医药理论与技术的创造性转化和创新性发展,让世界更多地了解中医药,应用中医药,让中医药更好地与世界对话。

让中医药更好地与世界对话,需要以科学的态度对待中医药。

让中医药更好地与世界对话,需要不断地深入发掘中医药的内在价值。

让中医药更好地与世界对话,需要中医药走出国门,扩大交流。

随着经济"全球化"的不断推进,中西文化的交流会通已经成为当今世界不可避免的历史趋势,中医药的对外交流也呈现出前所未有的良好态势。据统计,截至2015年底,中医药已经传播到183个国家和地区,中国政府与外国政府及国际组织签订了85项中医药合作协议,越来越多的国家通过交流认识和接受了中医药,也通过中医药认识了中国的科学与文化。但这些还远远不够。在中西医文化交流中,在医学模式加速转变的过程中,中医药理论建设还有许多重大问题需要解决。

当前,社会健康观念的变迁使得医学和医学中的人的生存境遇不断发生着变化。我们在促进中医药与世界对话的历史进程中,要全面认识中医药的科学本质和文化内涵,既不能胶柱鼓瑟,浅尝辄止;也不能一味夸大,或盲目否定,应将中医药置于全球视域下,以开放、发展、包容的态度予以对待,自觉地寻求一种更为理性的模式,在与世界的平等对话中,更好地为世界人民的健康服务。

译文: In the treasure house of Chinese civilization, there is a shining pearl—traditional Chinese medicine(TCM). Being the protector of Chinese people's health and life, TCM manifests the logos and wisdom of Chinese people with its unique theoretical essence. Just as President Xi Jinping puts it, "TCM has sophisticated philosophical wisdom, health regimen ideas and practical experience of thousands of years. It is the treasure of Chinese ancient science and the key to Chinese civilization."

In the cultural exchange between China and Western countries, TCM has been increasingly accepted in the global community. On the one hand, "the medicine of 21st Century will evolve from disease-oriented medicine to health-oriented medicine", which concords with the notion of TCM theory. On the other hand, Tu Youyou's winning of the Nobel Prize for physiology or medicine acknowledges "the inspiration from traditional Chinese medicine"; the contribution of TCM in fighting SARS and Ebola reveals the huge potential of TCM in adapting to the new medical condition and benefiting the world. Nevertheless, the potential of TCM needs to be dug out and popularized; its theory and technology need to have creative transformation and development under the background of Western medicine dominating the world. We need to create chances to let the whole world know more about TCM, apply TCM and have dialogue with TCM.

To initiate a better dialogue between TCM and the world, we need to approach it with a scientific attitude;

To initiate a better dialogue between TCM and the world, we need to thoroughly excavate its inner value persistently;

To initiate a better dialogue between TCM and the world, we need to present it to the outside world and promote the international communication.

With the progress of economic globalization, the interaction between the Western culture and the Chinese culture has been the unavoidable historical trend, and TCM has showed a great prospect in its communication with other cultures. According to the statistics, TCM has spread to 183 countries and regions. Chinese government has signed 85 TCM-related cooperative agreements. An increasing number of countries have come to know and accept TCM through communication, and to know Chinese science and culture through TCM. But we are not supposed to stop here. In the cultural communication and process of rapid transferring of medical pattern, there are many important issues in TCM theoretical construction yet to be solved.

Nowadays, the transition of social concept of health has made a great difference in medicine and human being's living condition. In the history process of initiating the dialogue between TCM and the world, we need to recognize its scientific nature and cultural connotation. We should neither stubbornly stick to old ways nor stop after scratching the surface. We should neither exaggerate its power nor blindly deny ourselves. We should approach TCM with an open, progressive, and tolerant attitude in a global view, so that it can make an equal dialogue with the world and better serve the global community in a more reasonable way.

2. 医学演讲

随着健康医疗观念深入人心,为改善医患关系,加强人文管理,医院常常会组织一些医学观念方面的演讲比赛,其中不乏英文的演讲比赛。

演讲是口头表达,所以句子不宜太长,不但要有准确性与流畅性,还要有说服力与感染力(convincing and inspiring)。开头要引人入胜,结尾要余韵悠长。可以适当地加上故事、感情的渲染。看以下例子:

From Patient's Daughter to Doctor—Let's Fight Diseases Together

Good afternoon, ladies and gentlemen! It's my great honour to stand here. I'm Ding Na from Department of Internal Neurology. Today my topic is: **From Patient's Daughter to Doctor—Let's Fight Diseases Together.** Actually that's what I think of "Chronic Disease Management".

Twenty years ago, a little girl was crying, gazing at her father, helpless. Suffering from stroke, her father couldn't move and recognize his only daughter. The little girl was in a daze and kept crying. Under the careful treatment of the doctor, her father could speak and move again. Finally he could recognize his daughter. The little girl thought that the doctor was amazing and at the moment she dreamed to be a doctor. The little girl is me. After graduation, I joined the People's Hospital of Zhengzhou. My dream comes true.

Over the past eight years, more than 2,000 days and nights, I have seen and treated thousands of patients under the guidance of the director Ren Jun. The patients are in all kinds of conditions. Some patients suffered from stroke and were ill in bed. With my treatment, they could stand up again and return to normal life. Some patients were unable to get correct diagnosis. With the joint efforts of our department, we found the cause of the disease and relieve their pain. While looking at the smiling faces of the patients, I found the value as a doctor. But I also have deep concerns behind the success. The professional feature of neurology determines that most patients have several chronic diseases combined. The diseases are like a hanging knife overhead. If you don't care about it, it would be very dangerous, and can even bring the family nothing but misfortune.

How to solve the problem? I thought of WeChat. Since I use WeChat to communicate with my father, I add my patients to friend list. I would give each person a card when they return home from hospital, leaving my telephone number and WeChat ID—to help them keep in touch with me according to their situation. In my view, it's a good way to extend the connections between doctors and patients from the hospital to our daily life. Many of my elder patients often consult me about some health problems through WeChat. For example, "The blood pressure is rising again. Does the drug need to be adjusted?" "What kind of food will affect blood sugar?" I always answer these questions in my spare time patiently.

I still remember that one of my patients was very stubborn. He had suffered from hyperglycemia for many years. Every time he was in hospital, he was able to control his diet and take medicine on time. But after returning home from hospital, he would trust some salesmen and buy the so-called medicine at a high price to seek for a quick fix. His health condition was going from bad to worse. I realized that if we wanted to help him, we must make him realize the great harm of taking the fake medicine clearly. So I decided to add his WeChat. At the beginning, this patient often sent me false research findings that confused me. However, I just read it carefully and found the mistakes in these articles, and then explained to him. Gradually, the patient's mind has changed. Now he uses regular medications, and besides, he has become the volunteer to spread the correct health knowledge to his friends and family. His family are very grateful. There was also a patient who was in very poor health and suffered from various diseases. He needed to take blood tests regularly. However, he was disabled and his only son died several years ago unfortunately. So it was very difficult for him to go to hospital for tests. I was worried about him. And I decided to learn how to draw blood and then took the blood sample to the hospital for testing. I told him the test results to adjust his medication. Now he is in good health.

Every time I put on my white uniform, it reminds me of the moment I made up my mind to be a doctor. I vowed to be a competent doctor, to try my best to serve more people. To simply help a person to manage his health problem and let him know the correct medical knowledge, then he might affect people around him. A little spark can light a great fire.

One of my favorite sentences is "Do your best and God will take care of the rest." In the process of guiding patients, I once felt tired. But every time I think of the patient's heart-felt gratitude, I just feel refreshed again. They treat me as a friend and trust me. In order to live up to their expectation, I encourage myself to keep going. As we all know, the disease can be quite terrible, and it could change the rest of your life. A person's strength is limited. However, I am willing to be your friend and go with you during ups and downs.

虽然演讲稿带有明显的中文思维的痕迹，但是能把枯燥的医学知识、医学管理以生动的语言表述出来，对于医学工作者来说，已属难得。

3. 面试自我介绍

面试自我介绍切忌平铺直叙。很多人喜欢先用汉语写出来，然后逐句进行翻译，结果往往流于中国式表达。最好是基于汉语的自我介绍，按照英语思维和表达习惯重新组织行文，可以在结构和方式上别出心裁，以"巧"取胜。如：

Good morning. I feel greatly honored to have this chance for the interview. First let me have a brief introduction about myself. My name is Li Yang. I graduated from Henan University of Chinese Medicine two years ago, majoring in the Integrated Medicine of Western Medicine and TCM. The major I am applying for is Cardiovascular Ultrasound. I really cherish this opportunity because I've been working in the People's Hospital of Zhengzhou after graduation, and I increasingly realize how I need to improve myself and the desire for further education is so strong that I applied for Zhengzhou University.

My English name is April. I chose this name because this name best interprets my character.

A stands for "active". I am always dynamic and active in whatever I am doing. When I have an urge to do something, I put it into action immediately. No delay. No waste of time.

P stands for "preparing". Though I like to act very quickly after making the decision, I am always well-prepared. I try to equip myself with the knowledge and practice every day so that when opportunity comes, I am ready.

R stands for "responsible". I am always willing to bear the responsibility involved. When my mother passed away, I felt I grew up overnight and I learned to shoulder the responsibility not only in the work, but also in my family.

I stands for "interactive". I like to share my joys and sorrows with my friends. I like to have a lot of interaction with my colleagues and even teachers. No one is living in an isolated island.

L stands for "learning". I believe in life-long learning. Learning is a part of my life, so I will never stop learning until the end of my life.

This is me. I really hope I can get this chance. Give me a green leaf, and I will give you the whole spring.

Thank you.

练 习

Ⅰ. 翻译以下病历片段

(1) 气短,咳嗽伴黄痰 3～4 天。

(2) 咽痛,高烧两天。

(3) 两个月来持续性头痛,伴恶心,呕吐。

(4) 昨晚开始,畏寒发烧。

(5) 发热,右胸痛,咳嗽两周。

(6) 约一周前患者开始感到乏力,食欲不振;两天前开始寒战、发热、咳嗽。体温骤升至 39 ℃,同时感右下胸疼痛,随呼吸和咳嗽加重。之后胸痛变持续性,且剧烈。

(7) 明显的有关病史是 20 年前曾患过十二指肠溃疡,有 15 年多的严重高血压史。无手术史,无结核病史,无其他有关的既往史。

Ⅱ. 翻译以下药品说明

(1) Asverin is an entirely new and patented cough medicine.

(2) Asverin being a non-narcotic, can be used as a common medicine.

(3) Antitussive effect of Asverin is equal to or more powerful than that of codeine.

(4) Asverin is provided with an expectorating action which has never been found in any conventional antitussive agents so far available in the market.

(5) Asverin can be administered safely for a long duration without any side effect.

(6) Methotrexate(MTX) is an antimetabolite of folic acid which has been used for a long time in the chemotherapy of tumours.

(7) Shelf-life: The drug should not be used after the expiry date(=Exp) printed on pack.

(8) Urgenin acts as an anti-inflammatory, reducing the swelling in the prostatic bladder region caused by general obstruction. It also stimulates the blood circulation in this area and the body's natural defence mechanism.

(9) Overdosage may give rise to the following signs and symptoms: tremor, excitation, convulsions, changes in blood pressure, impairment of consciousness, and coma. EEG and ECG changes may also occur. Treatment: Measures to monitor and safeguard vital functions. Administration of diazepam when necessary.

(10) Dormicum can enhance the central sedative effect of neuroleptics, tranquilizers, antidepressants, sleep-inducing drugs, analgesics and anesthetics.

(11) Expiry: 18 months(Expiry date is printed on the vial label.)

第八章　翻译与语境

井蛙不可以语于海者，拘于虚也；夏虫不可以语于冰者，笃于时也。(《庄子·内篇》)
You can't talk about sea with well frogs, for they are confined by their living environment; You can't discuss with summer insects about ice, for they are limited by their time.

词本无意，意由境生。
A word itself has no meaning, but the context just vitalizes it.

翻译和语境的关系非常密切，但对语境的研究并非一开始就有的。传统语言学认为语言的意义是内在的、固有的，对词义的研究与语言实际运用相脱节。1930—1960年，语言学家们逐渐意识到语义对语境的依赖性——如果不考虑语境就无法确切描述或理解语义，翻译更无从谈起——由此开启了由语义逻辑结构的分析向语言使用研究的转化。

语境论认为语义并非由语言本身决定，还受到语境的限制和影响，正如张维友所言："Context is of paramount importance for the understanding of word-meaning because the meaning is influenced immediately by the linguistic environment, and in many cases by the whole speech situation as well."。

比如下面这句话："But when I looked over at my son, I lost it."，我们可以翻译为："当我看着儿子的时候，我失去了它。"很显然不知所云，但联系上下文意思就会很明了：

There were a flurry of calls made. And at the end of our appointment, Dr. Li said she wanted to get a second opinion to make sure Luke was stable enough to begin treatment. The next morning we saw Dr. Ehrlich. We arrived early. I hadn't really cried in a long time. But when I looked over at my son, I lost it.

译文：打了一连串的电话。临近结束时，李医生说她想再听听别的意见，以确保卢克的情况足够稳定，可以开始治疗。第二天早上我们见到了埃利希医生。我们来得很早，我好久没哭了。但当我看着我儿子的时候，我忍不住哭了。

第一节 一般语境和具体语境

没有任何一个词是一座独立的孤岛,它总是和其他词语处于千丝万缕的联系之中,而且,总是在一定的语言环境、背景中出现的。从广义上说,文本的写作年代、历史背景、作者的身份、写作的目的、上下文、词的搭配都属于语境的范畴。语境可以帮助读者理解某个词的意思,也帮助限定该词的意思(尤其对于多义词)。

语境可以分为一般语境和具体语境。一般语境包括世界知识(world knowledge)、常识(common sense)以及说话人所处的文化背景等。具体语境即上下文和词语的搭配,即文本中的信息。语境决定了说话人对语言的使用和听话人对话语的理解。

1. 一般语境

一般语境始终作用于听话人或者读者对文本的理解。因为对语言的理解在相当大的程度上依赖于个人相关的世界知识。比如一个从来没有接触过棒球的人往往很难理解解说员对棒球比赛的介绍,而丝毫不懂艺术的人听别人讲印象派也会感到晦涩难懂。医学领域的文本更是如此,比如对中医术语的理解就有赖于对文言文以及对中国哲学背景的认识。每个人对话语的理解都不可避免地受到其知识和阅历的影响,所以庄子说:"井蛙不可以语于海者,拘于虚也;夏虫不可以语于冰者,笃于时也"。

脱离了语境,很多笑话、典故便无法理解,请看下面的例子:

(1) Old math teachers never die, they just become irrational. (老的数学教师永远不死,他们只是变成了无理数。)

典自西点军校的军歌:"Old soldiers never die, they just fade away."。(老兵永远不死,只会慢慢凋零。)

(2) 为什么我嘴里常叼着玉米,因为我对母校爱得深沉。(美国伊利诺伊大学香槟分校的中国留学生自嘲学校周围都是玉米地。)

出自艾青的诗:为什么我的眼里常含泪水?因为我对这土地爱得深沉。(艾青《我爱这土地》)

(3) I come. I learn. I enjoy. (我来了,我学习,我享受。)

出自Julius Caesar(恺撒大帝)在公元前46年说过的一句话"Veni, vidi, vici",译成英语是"I come. I see. I conquer."。

这种一个文本与一种文化中其他相关文本之间的关系被语言学家称为"互文性"(intertextuality)。语篇学家们把"互文性"这一概念引入语篇分析,用来指一个语篇的产生和理解有赖于读者、听众对其他语篇的了解这样一种语言现象。就像哈利迪(Halliday)和哈森(Hason)所指出的:"事实上,语篇和语境是一种辩证的关系——语境创造语篇,语篇也创造语境……任何语篇都有一部分是由以前的语篇构成的,那些语篇被认为是所有参与者理所当然所共有的。"(刘承宇,2002)

有些医学论文中会出现一些机构的名称,对其翻译得正确得体与否往往取决于译者对一般语境的了解。如:

UK Department of Health，NHS City and Hackney 英国卫生部 国民卫生服务体系 受托基金机构 City & Hackney

这里提到的资助单位 NHS，据查全称为"National Health Service trusts，including NHS City & Hackney，NHS South West Essex，NHS Wigan，NHS Oxfordshire."。(http：//en.wikipedia.org/wiki/Event_Marketing_Solutions)

据此，采用增译法在译文中补充必要信息"受托基金机构"。

对中医术语的翻译首先建立在理解的基础上，而对其一般语境及中医理念的认识在很大程度上可以帮助正确理解和翻译，如中医的"阴阳"一词源于《易经》，乃中医学说的基本概念之一。

中医理论关于阴阳的术语非常多。如：阴阳对立(opposition of yin-yang)，阴阳互根(mutual rooting of yin-yang)，阴阳消长(waning and waxing of yin-yang)，阴阳转化(mutual convertibility of yin-yang)等。

但"阴阳"的含义远不止于此，对其具体含义的理解有赖于上下文，如《黄帝内经·素问·上古天真论》"丈夫八岁，肾气实，发长齿更；二八，肾气盛，天癸至，精气溢泻，阴阳和，故能有子"中的"阴阳"指的是男女，故译为"the male and female unite in harmony"。《黄帝内经·灵枢·口问》"夫百病之始生也，皆生于风雨寒暑，阴阳喜怒，饮食居处"中"阴阳"的意思是"性生活过度"，应译为"intemperance in sexual life"。此外，阴阳还可以表示"阴阳经脉""男女生殖器""阴气和阳气"等(兰凤利，2007：70-71)。

对常用术语的翻译也不能想当然，既要考虑一般语境，即对整个中医理念的理解和认知，又要看具体语境，如《素问·四气调神大论》中有"春夏养阳，秋冬养阴"一说，此句看似简单，很多文献对这句话的解释为：春夏养阳，以养阳之生长；秋冬养阴，以养阴之收藏。然而历代医家对此认识不一。主要观点有四：一是以马莳、高世栻为代表，认为春夏顺其生长之气即养阳，秋冬顺其收藏之气即养阴。二是以王冰为代表，认为养即制也，春夏阳盛，故宜食寒凉以制其亢阳；秋冬阴盛，故宜食温热以抑其盛阴。三是以张介宾为代表，认为阳为阴之根，养春夏之阳是为了养秋冬之阴；阴为阳之基，养秋冬之阴是为了养春夏之阳。四是以张志聪为代表，认为春夏阳盛于外而虚于内，故当养其内虚之阳；秋冬阴盛于外而虚于内，故当养其内虚之阴。

但根据《内经》的理论体系和语言特点这一具体语境，"春夏养阳，秋冬养阴"是一个互文。上文言春夏，下文说秋冬，春夏秋冬皆备；上文言养阳，下文说养阴，养阳养阴皆备，与《木兰辞》中"东市买骏马，西市买鞍鞯，南市买辔头，北市买长鞭"和"开我东阁门，坐我西阁床"是同样的手法，并非春夏养阳不养阴，秋冬养阴不养阳。把春夏强并，秋冬强合，把春夏与秋冬割裂或对立的理解，都是错误的。这句话就是说，春养生，夏养长，秋养收，冬养藏，更具体一点："春三月……夜卧早起，广步于庭，……养生之道也""夏三月……夜卧早起，无厌于日，……养长之道也""秋三月……早卧早起，与鸡俱兴，……养收之道也""冬三月……早卧晚起，必待日光，……养藏之道也"。简言之，"圣人春夏养阳，秋冬养阴"就是说，圣人根据四时调理阴阳！正如《灵枢·本神论》所言："故智者之养生也，必顺四时而适寒暑，和喜怒而安居处，节阴阳而调刚柔"。

但是，春夏季节养阳，秋冬季节养阴也有一定的道理和适用范围，故斟酌后将此句译为:"People cultivate Yang in spring and summer while nourish Yin in autumn and winter"。

2. 具体语境

语篇所起的作用就是具体语境的作用,影响读者对句子和单词层面的解读。没有语境,常常会使人们对句子的理解产生歧义,或者难以分清词汇的字面意义和修辞含义。

语境常被理解为文本的环境,包括解读者为了理解文本的表层含义和深层含义所使用的一切信息。语境定义着文本的意义和使用,可以说,没有语境就没有意义。正如张维友所言:"Without context, there is no way to determine the meaning that the speaker intends to convey, whereas with context there is generally no danger of misinterpretation, for meaning lives in context and the context throws light on meaning."。

中医文本中的"神"在不同语境下要采用不同的译法:

(1) 精神内守,病安从来?

译文:Keeping a sound mind can prevent occurring of any disease.

此处的"神"指"人的思想和注意力",故译作"mind"(person's thoughts or attention)。这里的"神"不宜译作"spirit"。

(2) 脑为元神之府。

译文:The brain is the seat of mental activities.

"元神"出自《脉望》,指"脑神",在《养生秘录·玉溪子丹房语录》中,指"意识思维活动",故译为"mental activities"。

(3) 神呆少言为失神之证。

译文:A blank expression and taciturnity indicate loss of vitality.

"神呆"指精神呆板或表情茫然,可以译成"a blank expression";"失神"出自《素问·移精变气论》,指神气丧失,故译作"loss of vitality"。

再看"窍"在不同语境中的译法:

(1) 目为肝之窍。

译文:The eye is the window of the liver.

"目为肝之窍"又称"肝开窍于目","窍"是"孔"的意思,直译的话,便是"The eye is the orifice of the liver",令人费解。这里用了"window",与原意接近多了。

(2) 热病谵妄应当清心开窍。

译文:Febrile delirium is dealt with by clearing heart-fire to induce resuscitation.

"开窍"指"治疗神志不清或昏迷的方法",故译作"inducing resuscitation"。

再看"从"字在不同语境中的译法:

(1) 脉从四时。

译文:A pulse agrees with seasonal variations.

此处的"从"指的是"和……相一致",即"agree with"或"be consistent with"。"脉从四时"是指脉象随着四时气候的变化而变化的生理现象,亦称"脉应四时",所以译成"A pulse agrees with seasonal variations."。

(2) 黄家所得，从湿得之。

译文：Jaundice is usually caused by the dampness.

此处的"黄家"指的是"黄疸病"，"从"指的是"由……引起"。

(3) 善用针者，从阴引阳，从阳引阴，以右治左，以左治右。(《素问·阴阳应象大论》)

译文：Those who are excellent in acupuncture are often trying to draw yang from yin, draw yin from yang, needle the acupoints located on the right side to treat diseases on the left side and needle the acupoints located on the left side to treat diseases on the right side.

"从阴引阳，从阳引阴"中的"从"意为"从……中"，即"from"。

第二节　语境与文本翻译

（一）根据语境来确定语义

没有语境，就没有意义，任何语义的确定都需要紧密联系语境。

1. 医学英语翻译中的语境

很多词在普通语境和医学语境中语义不同，需要酌情翻译。如：

(1) On Feb. 5, in the first live broadcast by Li Jiaqi, a Chinese male beauty blogger who had gone viral online thanks to his lipstick reviews, there were only three cosmetics among the 19 recommended products: one for eye makeup and two for foundation. There were no traces of lipstick.

译文：2月5日，中国男性美妆博主李佳琦（因对口红产品有独到见解而迅速走红网络）进行了第一次直播。其所推荐的19种产品中只有三种化妆品：一件是眼妆，两件是粉底，完全没有口红的踪影。

此处的"go viral"意思是像病毒一样传播开来，联系语境可译为"迅速走红"，而foundation本来指"地基；基础"，此处结合语境译为"粉底"。

(2) We therefore recommend implementation of HIV screening in general practices in areas with high HIV prevalence.

如果不考虑语境，可译为：

——因此，我们建议在艾滋病毒流行率高的地区以常规方式实施艾滋病毒筛查。

但是，根据语境，尤其是直接语境"Promotion of opt-out rapid testing in general practice led to increased rate of diagnosis, and might increase early detection of HIV. (在全科诊疗中推广常规HIV快速检测不仅增加诊断率，还可促使HIV的早期发现。)"可知此处的 in general practices 指的是全科诊疗，而非"以常规方式"。另外，"screening"也可以根据语境判断出是"筛查"，而非"屏蔽"。据此，上句可以改译为：

——因此，我们建议在HIV高流行地区的全科诊疗中实施HIV筛查。

有时候，原文中省略的信息根据上下文可以在目的语中增补出来，以帮助读者理解。

如：

(3) <u>28％ versus 46％</u> had CD4 count less than 200 cells per μL(0.60，0.32 to 1.13). All patients diagnosed by rapid testing were successfully transferred into specialist care. No adverse events occurred.

译文：CD4 细胞计数低于 200 个/μL 的患者<u>在干预组中和对照组中分别为 28 ％及 46 ％</u>(0.60,0.32～1.13)。所有快速检测诊断出的患者均顺利转入专科治疗。无不良事件发生。

2. 中医术语翻译中的语境

在中医四字术语中,同一字的翻译也要根据上下文判断语义,做出正确的翻译。

1) "不"字的翻译

(1) 可译为：fail,failure,表示"未能达成,未能做到"。如：

孤阴不生 <u>failure</u> of solitary yin to exist alone

气不摄血 qi <u>failing</u> to control blood

肺气不宣 <u>failure</u> of lung qi in dispersion

肾不纳气 deficiency of kidney qi <u>failing</u> to control respiring qi

水不涵木 water <u>failing</u> to nourish wood；kidney <u>failing</u> to nourish liver

(2) 可译为：insufficiency,表示"不足"。如：

禀赋不足 <u>insufficiency</u> of natural endowment

肾精不足 <u>insufficiency</u> of kidney essence

心阴不足 <u>insufficiency</u> of heart yin

肝阴不足 <u>insufficiency</u> of liver yin

补其不足 supplementing the <u>insufficiency</u>

(3) 可译为：disharmony,表示"不和,不调,不交"。如：

营卫不和 <u>disharmony</u> between nutrient qi and defensive qi

冲任不调 <u>disharmony</u> of Chong and Conception Channels

心肾不交 <u>disharmony</u> between heart and kidney

(4) 可译为：non-consolidation,表示"不固"。如：

肾气不固 <u>non-consolidation</u> of kidney qi

(5) 可译为：not functioning normally,表示不能正常运行。如：

金破不鸣 damaged lung <u>not functioning normally</u>

金实不鸣 obstructed lung <u>not functioning normally</u>

(6) 其他翻译。如：

半身不遂 hemiplegia

月经不调 menstrual disorders

胎动不安 threatened abortion

乳汁不通 agalactia

不内外因 non-endo-non-exogenous cause

心阳不振 devitalization of heart yang

2)"上"字的翻译

肝火上炎 liver fire flaring up

虚火上炎 flaring up of deficient fire

心火上炎 flaring up of heart fire

胃气上逆 adverse rising of stomach qi

3)"下"字的翻译

下焦湿热 dampness-heat in lower jiao

中气下陷 sinking of middle qi

恐则气下 fear leading to qi sinking

水曰润下 water characterized by moistening and descending

胞衣不下 retention of placenta

恶露不下 lochioschesis

泻下不爽 non-smooth diarrhea

上热下寒 upper heat and lower cold

赤膜下垂 dropping pannus

上睑下垂 blepharoptosis

4)"利"字的翻译

咽喉不利 discomfort in throat

小便不利 dysuria

气机不利 disorder of qi movement

利水消肿 inducing diuresis for removing edema

3. 中医文献翻译中的语境

翻译古代文献时还需要联系文章第一读者所处的时代语境,这往往意味着追溯至文本当时的语义环境。如下文的翻译:

《史记·扁鹊仓公列传》是中国医学史上第一篇医家传记。其中有这样一段关于扁鹊"六不治"的记载:"人之所病,病疾多;而医之所病,病道少。故病有六不治:骄恣不论于理,一不治也;轻身重财,二不治也;衣食不能适,三不治也;阴阳并,藏气不定,四不治也;形羸不能服药,五不治也;信巫不信医,六不治也。有此一者,则重难治也"。

扁鹊"六不治"的思想,对后世医学的影响很大,其中涉及医学心理学、预防医学、医学社会学等学科,与医患关系、社会、自然等都密切相关。

根据大多数医古文对此文的注释,编者将这篇文章译为:

The common people are troubled by too many types of diseases (out there), whereas doctors are concerned with too few effective treatments. For six types of patients, no treatment is good enough: those who are too self-indulgent and unreasonable; those who value wealth above health; those who fail to adjust diet and clothing accordingly; those whose qi and blood are disordered and visceral-qi disturbed; those who are too weak for medication, and those who trust sorcery instead of medicine. If one falls into any of these categories, there is hardly any cure for him.

然而,对其中"阴阳并"三字的含义,《史记》注家历来存疑,迄今仍无定论。许敬生(2011:9)在《医林掌故》一书中对"阴阳并"一词的注释是:"谓阴阳偏亢,血气错乱"。这也是一种比较普遍的理解,大部分医古文教材将之译为"阴阳混淆""阴阳错乱""阴阳偏盛""血气紊乱"。但对这一解释提出质疑者颇多。

从具体语境看,《史记》此句与其他五种情况并列,意思很明显,即病势已重,很难医治。但"阴阳混淆"和"阴阳错乱"均非中医术语,含义难明,而"阴阳偏胜""阴阳偏亢"是否能说得通呢?

从一般语境看,《内经》断定万事万物都具有阴阳矛盾,人体的阴阳之间不断处于此消彼长、此盛彼衰、生生化化、不断变动之中,错综复杂的临床病理均与阴阳失调相关,所以"阴阳偏盛""阴阳失调"均属正常的病理现象,非不治之症,不适合此句的解释。

再看"血气错乱"或"血气紊乱"。血与气是维持人体生命活动最基本的物质。血属阴,气属阳。气血阴阳之间的协调平衡,是健康的标志。反之,"血气不和,百病乃变化而生"(《素问·调经论》),而治病的重要法则即"疏其血气,令其调达,而致和平"(《素问·至真要大论》)。所以,"血气错乱"或"血气紊乱"均属正常病理,非不治之疾。

陈立中(1980:46-47)认为,"阴阳并"本于《内经》,而《内经》述及阴、阳、气、血、精、邪的"并"而病的有多处,《素问·调经论》在五次重复"血气未并,五藏安定"后说:"气血以并,阴阳相倾,气乱于卫,血逆于经,血气离居,一实一虚。……故气并则无血,血并则无气,今血与气相失,故为虚焉。……血与气并,则为实焉。血之与气并走于上,则为大厥,厥则暴死,气复反则生,不反则死"。从而可知:"阴阳并"就是"血气离居""阴阳离决"。"阴阳离决"是体内的阴液或阳气突然大量地亡失,导致生命垂危的一种病理状态。

但问题是,"并"字是否有"离决"之意?这需要了解"并"字在不同语境中的含义。

宁越(1988)从训诂学的角度对"阴阳并"的含义做了考证,发现"并"和"竝"在历史上曾经通用。《说文解字》云:"竝,从二立";朱骏声《说文通训定声》中云:"相合为'并',相对为'竝'";旧《词源》中有"两人相竝曰离"的解释。《后汉书·后纪第十》中有"其衣有与阴后同色者,即时解易。若并时进见,则不敢正坐离立,行得偻身自卑"。由此推定,"阴阳并(竝)"意为"阴阳相离"。按中医病机,"阴阳离决,精气乃绝"。阴阳对立即为死证。

刘百闵(1970:483)指出:"汉人治经凡三:以字解经,以经解经,以师说解经。以字解经,文之事也,以经解经,以师说解经,则皆义之事也。以字解经,则训诂之学之所由出也。以义解经,则义理之学所由起也。"可见,以字解经,以义解经,是历来阐释经典的方式。无论是陈立中的以义解经,还是宁越的以字解经,均离不开对语境的依赖。

至此,"阴阳并"的含义渐明,该句的翻译也应改为:"those whose yin and yang are separated and visceral-qi disturbed"。

2. 根据语境来确定翻译风格

语言所处的文化语境规定并制约着语言的风格。如:新冠肺炎在中国境内蔓延期间,许多媒体习惯称之为一场"战役","役"与"疫"同音,这一隐喻显得自然而恰当。但当译入英语文化语境时,不一定要将战争的意味译出来。如下文:

(1) 中国庞大的国土成为战疫的第一挑战。中国乃泱泱大国，而此次疫情直击其腹地要害。疫情爆发于 1 600 万人口的中部大都市武汉。屋漏偏逢连夜雨，武汉周围城市众多，人口皆以百万计。武汉乃交通枢纽，疫情大有扩散至周边城市之势。疆土广阔反倒成为战疫的重大阻碍。

译文：The challenge lies in the country's size. China is a big country with a large span, and the virus hit the center, literally. The epicenter is a metropolis of 16 million people in the middle of the country. To make matters worse, it is surrounded by many cities, also with millions of inhabitants. Wuhan is a transport hub, and the virus is threatening to infect the whole surrounding area. The size of the country is a significant obstacle.

(2) 但凡事有弊也有利。由于中国疆土广阔，不同地区得以相互接济。武汉告急之时，四面八方来援。此时此刻，全国十分之一的重症监护医生正奋战于武汉。4 万余名医务人员应急响应，火速奔赴抗疫前线。中国火力全开，应对疫情。

译文：But that's only half the story. Because of its continental size, all the parts feed off each other. When Wuhan fell, the other provinces came to its aid. As we speak, one tenth of the intensive-care doctors of the entire country is in Wuhan. A total of 40,000 medical staff moved to the center in a wartime fashion. China plans to take the virus full on.　　——选自 CGTN《悦辩悦明》栏目，2020 年 3 月

比较原文和译文，虽然译文中也有 fall, wartime fashion 此类的字样，但相比于原文的"直击其腹地要害""火速奔赴抗疫前线""火力全开"等字眼，火药味明显淡了很多。

文本的使用场合也是语境的一个方面，比如学术会议的发言一般是比较严肃正式的，用语规范、严谨客观，忌讳过于情感化的表达。然而下面的这段叙述是医学学术会议上一位患者家属的发言，与学术语言形成了鲜明的对比，在翻译的时候要考虑其具体语境，译出风格相宜的汉语。如：

Good afternoon, my name is Tiffany Watson. I am honored to be here today. I was invited today to share with you the journey of my son Lucas and the role that Dr. Li and traditional Chinese medicine has played.

下午好，我叫蒂芙尼·沃森。我很荣幸今天能来这里。今天我受邀与大家分享我儿子卢卡斯所经历的治疗过程，以及李医生和中医药所起到的作用。

This picture was taken 11 months ago on the morning of our first appointment with Dr. Li. As you can see, my child was suffering. To better understand how we got here, I have to take you back to where it all began: his birth.

这张照片是 11 个月前我们第一次见李医生的那个早晨拍摄的。大家能看出来我的孩子很痛苦。为了让大家更好地理解我们是如何来到这里的，我必须从他的出生讲起。

Shortly after Lucas was born in 2008, I noticed his skin seemed unstable. Through appointments with our pediatrician, we learned my son had eczema, a condition he would most likely outgrow. I nursed Lucas and was told to try avoiding certain foods to see if it would help. As the months went on, his condition worsened. Eczema settled into the bends of his arms, legs, feet, and the crease in his neck. When he was around six months old, we were given topical steroids to apply.

2008年卢卡斯出生后不久,我注意到他的皮肤似乎不太正常。看过儿科医生后我们得知,儿子患有湿疹,这种情况很可能会渐渐消失。我照顾卢卡斯,遵照医嘱尽量避免吃某些食物,看看是否有帮助。几个月过去了,他的病情愈发恶化。湿疹在他的胳膊、腿、脚和脖子的折痕处沉淀下来。当他六个月大时,医生让我们给他局部注射类固醇。

Although the eczema never went away, it was manageable. Over the years, we continued to search for cures or remedies. Through testing, there was some confusion of possible food allergies. After some back and forth, we were told to just stay away from peanuts. Years went on with flares and breakouts and, of course, the intense itching. Topical steroids became less and less effective. It was at this point we were introduced to the world of oral steroids.

尽管湿疹从未消失过,但还是可以控制的。多年来,我们继续寻找治疗方法或补救措施。通过测试,我们有点困惑他是否有食物过敏的可能。几番来回后,医生说他必须远离花生。年复一年,伴随着急性期和爆发期,当然还有强烈的瘙痒。局部类固醇的效果越来越差。正是在这个时间,我们接受建议,开始尝试口服类固醇。

Fast forward to kindergarten, which proved to be a turning point in his condition. Nights became unbearable. Anyone who is familiar with the condition knows that nights bring an intense itch. Every night, he would shed a pile of dead skin. Over the next year, the only relief we would see was from rounds of oral steroids. The year leading up to our appointment with Dr. Li was the hardest year of my life. My son's quality life had deteriorated to the point where he was pulled from school, and Lucas loves school. His nonstop flares had become so painful that he spent most of his time under a blanket with his iPad. You see, even the air hurt, but under his blanket he could create a warm, humid environment. We saw countless specialists and took him to the hospital in desperation several times.

很快就到了幼儿园,这证明是他身体状况的一个转折点。夜晚变得难以忍受。任何熟悉这种情况的人都知道夜晚会带来强烈的瘙痒。每天晚上,他都会掉一堆死皮。在接下来的一年里,我们能看到的唯一的缓解是口服类固醇。在我们和李医生预约之前的一年是我生命中最艰难的一年。我儿子的生活质量恶化到了他必须辍学的地步,卢卡斯热爱学校。不间断的急性发作使他痛苦难耐,以至于他大部分时间都躲在毯子下玩iPad。你看,即使空气也使他感觉到痛,但在他的毯子下,他可以创造一个温暖、潮湿的环境。我们去看了无数专家,一次次绝望地带他去医院。

Doctors began to question if I was truly doing what they had prescribed. They began to suspect neglect.

医生开始质疑我是否真的按照他们的处方做了,他们开始怀疑我们太轻视了。

In the end, no one knew what to do except the old faithful round of oral steroids. Through more testing we were told that Lucas did have multiple food allergies as well as environmental allergies. One of the hardest blows to the family was when we found out my son had a Class 6 allergy to dogs. My already sick and depressed son had to say goodbye to his dog, his companion. During the holidays that year, Luke had an intense flare. I took him to Children's Healthcare of Atlanta, begging and pleading for help. They told us he had the most impressive case of eczema they had seen, but released us only saying to follow up with the allergist. So, I did. I went straight from the hospital to his allergist over an hour away.

最后,除了忠实服用口服类固醇,没人知道该怎么办。通过更多的测试,我们得知卢卡斯确实有多种食物过敏和环境过敏。对这个家庭最沉重的打击之一是我们发现我儿子对狗有六级过敏。本来因为生病而非常沮丧的儿子不得不和他的狗、他的同伴告别。那一年假期,卢克有一次强烈的急性发作。我带他去了亚特兰大儿童保健中心,乞求帮助。他们说这是他们见过的最严重的湿疹,但只说要我们去找治疗过敏症的医生就把我们打发了。所以,我从医院出来后,直接去了一小时车程以外的过敏医生那里。

With his hospital bracelets still on, I burst into the waiting room demanding to see the allergist. Within minutes, they had me back to see Dr. Walker. Holding my 7-year-old son in my arms, Dr. Walker pulled up a chair and said the words that changed our lives: "How open are you to other forms of treatment?" He began to tell me of patients who had great success with traditional Chinese medicine. He explained it is expensive but is proving to be very effective. He immediately put me in contact with a mother who had a child in treatment with Dr. Li. She called me as I left his office, and from that moment on my hope was renewed.

他手上还戴着医院的手环,我就冲进候诊室,说要见过敏症医生。几分钟后,他们让我去见沃克医生。沃克医生抱着我七岁的孩子,把椅子拉过来,说了一句改变我们人生的话:"你愿意尝试其他形式的治疗吗?"他开始告诉我那些靠中医成功获治的病人。他解释说这很贵,但事实证明非常有效。他立刻让我和一位母亲联系,她有一个孩子正在接受李医生的治疗。我离开他的办公室时,她就打电话给我,从那时起,我的希望再一次被点燃了。

We had our appointment set for June 1, 2016. But, a few days before Luke became very ill. He broke out in these tiny bumps, and his skin was shedding at an alarming rate. I took him to a walk in clinic and two hospitals. At this point I was just asking them to make him stable enough to make it to New York.

我们预约了2016年6月1日。但是,在临行的前几天,卢克忽然病得很重,身上出现一些小肿块,以惊人的速度掉皮。我带他去了免约诊所和两家医院。此时,我只求他们让他的状况足够稳定,可以去纽约。

They told us more than likely we wouldn't be allowed on a flight due to his startling appearance. So instead, we immediately drove from Georgia to New York.

他们告诉我们说,由于他的样子很吓人,极有可能不允许搭乘飞机。因此,我们立即从佐治亚州开车到纽约。

Here we are, the day of the appointment, the day this picture was taken. When Luke woke up that morning, he called out for us because he couldn't see. He also couldn't walk. When we arrived to Dr. Li's office, we carried him in. Our trip to New York reminded me somehow of *The Wizard of OZ*. We had come to see the great wizard. But, this wizard proved to be real.

就这样,预约当天,我们拍了这张照片。那天早上卢克醒来时,他大声喊我们,因为他看不见了,也不能走路。到李医生办公室时,我们是抱着他进来的。此次纽约之行让我想起了《绿野仙踪》,我们是来拜见大巫师的,事实证明这个巫师是真实的。

There were a flurry of calls made. And at the end of our appointment, Dr. Li said she wanted to get a second opinion to make sure Luke was stable enough to begin treatment. The next morning we saw Dr. Ehrlich. We arrived early. I hadn't really cried in a long time. But when I looked over at my son, I lost it.

打了一连串的电话。临近结束时,李医生说她想再听听别的意见,以确保卢克足够稳定,可以开始治疗。第二天早上我们见到了埃利希医生。我们来得很早,我好久没哭了。但当我看着我儿子的时候,我实在忍不住了。

One of the ladies came over and said, "Breathe, Mommy, you are at the best in the world now." I cried tears of relief in that office. When Dr. Ehrlich arrived, he immediately began evaluating him. After going back and forth and getting some results back from Children's Healthcare of Atlanta, he decided that if we could keep him hydrated that he believed we could begin treatment with Dr. Li. He asked us to stay for several hours and be certain he was drinking and urinating. The last thing I wanted was to be sent to the hospital for a third time with no results. I knew we needed a different approach.

一位女士走过来说:"放心,妈妈,这里的医生可是全世界最好的。"我在办公室里释然地哭了。埃利希医生来的时候,他立即开始对他进行评估。经反复斟酌,又从亚特兰大儿童保健中心获得检查结果后,他决定,如果我们能让他充分饮水,他相信我们可以开始李医生的治疗。他让我们待几个小时,确定他充分喝水和小便。我最不希望得到的回应是第三次被送到医院,却毫无结果。我知道我们需要一种不同的方法。

Hours went by, and we were able to hydrate Luke. Dr. Ehrlich said he wanted to have another doctor come in to evaluate. A few minutes later, Dr. Rigel entered the room. We have seen so many doctors over the years, and I can tell you what sets apart the great ones is kindness. I heard Dr. Rigel ask who would be the lead doctor on this case. When Dr. Ehrlich said Dr. Li, he shook his head in agreement and said, that's who he needs. Lucas's body was covered head to toe with impetigo and staph. Dr. Rigel adjusted his antibiotic and told us a story of how he became a dermatologist. Small worlds collided when he told us that he lived in Georgia when he was around Luke's age. He had been away at a summer camp just minutes from our house when he was plagued with head to toe impetigo just like Luke. As we left Dr. Ehrlich's office,

I asked him what his advice would be going forward. The advice he gave me was to do EXACTLY what Dr. Li says. I was certain this advice would be the key to our extraordinary success.

几个小时过去了,我们可以给卢克补充水分。埃利希医生说他想请另一位医生来做评估。几分钟后,里格尔医生进了房间。多年来,我们见过这么多医生,我可以告诉你,善良是好医生区别于其他医生的特质。我听到里格尔医生问谁是这个病例的主治医生。当埃利希博士说是李医生时,他点点头表示同意。说,这正是他需要的人。卢卡斯的身体从头到脚都被脓疱和葡萄球菌覆盖着。里格尔医生为他调整了抗生素的使用,告诉我们他是如何成为皮肤科医生的。世界真小! 他告诉我们他在卢克这么大的时候住在佐治亚州,一次在距离我们家几分钟的地方参加夏令营,也像卢克一样从头到脚长满了脓疱。当我们离开埃利希医生的办公室时,我问他对我们今后的建议是什么。他说严格照李医生说的去做。我确信这一建议将是治疗成功的关键。

Once Dr. Li was given the go ahead, she explained in detail the protocol of baths, creams, and herbs. We were asked to stay in New York for a few weeks until Luke was more stable. We immediately began the herbal baths, and after the first bath, we saw rapid healing.

李医生一得到可以施治的评估结果,就详细对我们解释了药浴、外敷和中药相结合的治疗方案。我们需要在纽约待几周,直到卢克更加稳定。我们立即开始对他进行药浴,第一次药浴后,我们看到情况在迅速好转。

Here is a photo before his first bath and another photo 12 hours after his first bath. A few days later we received the creams and pills. Lucas slept like he had never slept in his life. The healing was incredible to witness. Within days we were on the subway headed to Times Square. He was building forts with his aunt and uncle. He was starting to LIVE again! After two weeks, we went back to see Dr. Li and Dr. Ehrlich. They were extremely pleased with his progress and gave us the go ahead to return home. The only way I can show you the incredible healing over the past 11 months is through these photos.

这是他第一次药浴前的照片和他第一次药浴12小时后的另一张照片。几天后,我们收到了药膏和药丸。卢卡斯睡得像他一生中从未睡过一样。康复的过程令人难以置信。几天后,我们坐地铁去了时代广场。他正在和叔叔阿姨一起建堡垒。他重获新生了! 两周后,我们又去看李医生和埃利希医生。他们对他的情况非常满意,并同意我们回家。我只能通过这些照片让大家看到过去11个月里发生了如何令人难以置信的愈合。

Thank you everyone for your time and having the opportunity share the incredible healing that has taken place with Dr. Li and her dream team, as I like to call them. Lucas is incredibly happy and enjoying life.

感谢大家,感谢给我机会分享李博士和她的梦之队(我喜欢这么称呼他们)带来的奇妙医治。卢卡斯现在非常快乐,在尽情享受生活。

这段文本是一位母亲在一个国际医学会议上所作的见证,笔者负责进行会议翻译的这段文字充满了感性的描述和生活化的语言,但是其中提到的一些药物、疗法等又相对具有专业化的色彩。翻译时要灵活把握,充分考虑文本所处的语境,包括与会听众的理解能力等,这样才能将整个语篇的风格把握得恰到好处。

练 习

Ⅰ. 将以下段落译成英语

(1) 食疗既是治疗手段又是营养文化,有病治病,无病防病。中国民间传承下来的关于"药补不如食补"和食疗、保健的谚语有很多,比如"冬吃萝卜夏吃姜,不劳医生开药方""萝卜杏仁干姜梨,治咳有效不求医""家中一碗绿豆汤,清热解毒赛神方""黄瓜丝瓜加番茄,美容不找郎中爷""只要三瓣蒜,痢疾好一半""常吃大枣,抗癌防老"……这些医谚顺口精练、通俗易懂、便于记忆,在生活中教会人们食疗养生、防病治病。

(2) 但是保持平衡实非易事。每个决定的背后都有取舍,它会影响百姓生计,甚至攸关生死。我们需要减缓疫情传播速度。中国许多地区都在执行严格的检疫隔离。建立广泛的检疫隔离网络,减少违规行为固然是个好办法,问题是我们仍然不知道确切的疫情扩散范围。在不侵犯人们的权利和尊严的情况下有效隔离感染者困难重重。

(3) 经济发展依赖于人与人的交往,但疫情防控要求人与人保持距离。我们需要保持一定距离,但我们也需要携手合作。那么,我们如何在挽救生命和挽救经济之间取得平衡? 每个决策都艰难无比。

Ⅱ. 将以下句子或段落译成汉语

(1) Coronaviruses are a large family of viruses found in both animals and humans. Some infect people and are known to cause illness ranging from the common cold to more severe diseases such as Middle East Respiratory Syndrome(MERS) and Severe Acute Respiratory Syndrome(SARS).

(2) A novel coronavirus(CoV) is a new strain of coronavirus that has not been previously identified in humans. The new, or "novel" coronavirus, now called 2019-nCoV, had not previously detected before the outbreak was reported in Wuhan, China in December 2019.

(3) As with other respiratory illnesses, infection with 2019-nCoV can cause mild symptoms including a runny nose, sore throat, cough, and fever. It can be more severe for some persons and can lead to pneumonia or breathing difficulties. More rarely, the disease can be fatal. Older people, and people with pre-existing medical conditions (such as, diabetes and heart disease) appear to be more vulnerable to becoming severely ill with the virus.

(4) The incubation period is the time between infection and the onset of clinical symptoms of disease. Current estimates of the incubation period range from 1–12.5

days with median estimates of 5-6 days. These estimates will be refined as more data become available. Based on information from other coronavirus diseases, such as MERS and SARS, the incubation period of 2019-nCoV could be up to 14 days. WHO recommends that the follow-up of contacts of confirmed cases is 14 days.

(5) Avoid consumption of raw or undercooked animal products: Handle raw meat, milk or animal organs with care, to avoid cross-contamination with uncooked foods, as per good food safety practices.

（以上文献选自 WHO 官网）

参考答案

第一章练习答案

Ⅰ.翻译下列短语(英译汉)
(1) 老于世故的人
(2) 老练的专栏作家
(3) 高度精密的电子仪器
(4) 尖端武器
(5) 软骨病
(6) 明升暗降
(7) 嗜杀成性的
(8) 思乡的
(9) 脾气暴躁的
(10) 喂饲;以少量点滴给予
(11) 健康申报
(12) 集中观察
(13) 防范疫情跨境传播
(14) 出入境防疫
(15) 零散病例

Ⅱ.翻译下列句子(英汉互译)
(1) 翻译是两种文化之间的交流。对于真正成功的翻译而言,了解两种文化比掌握两种语言更为重要,因为词汇只有在它有效的文化背景下才有意义。(尤金·奈达)

(2) 译文应完全复写出原作的思想。译文的风格和笔调应与原文的性质相同。译文应和原作同样流畅。(亚历山大·泰特勒)

(3) 翻译,就是像原作者把思想变成文字那样,把一个文本的意思译成另一种语言。常识告诉我们,这应该是一件很简单的事,就如一个人能够用一种语言自如表达,也应该能够用另一种语言自如表达一样。但从另一方面来说,你会看到翻译是复杂的、做作的、虚假的,因为在使用另一种语言的时候,你实际上是在假装成另一个人。翻译不可能是简单的复制,也不可能是如出一辙的原本。既然如此,译者的首要任务就是翻译。(彼得·纽马克)

(4) 一些职业翻译工作者相当得意地称他们没有翻译理论——他们只顾埋头翻译。然而,事实上,所有从事翻译这项复杂工作的人都具有或隐或掩的理论,尽管这种理论尚处在萌芽状态,或者被轻描淡写地说成"忠实于作者想要说的"。(尤金·奈达)

(5) 好的翻译应该是把原作的长处完全地移注到另一种语言,以使入语所属国家的本地人能明

白地领悟、强烈地感受,如同使用原作语言的人所领悟、所感受的一样。(亚历山大·泰特勒)

(6) Most people like Chinese food. In China, cooking is considered as not only a skill but also an art. Since food is crucial to health, a good chef is insistently trying to seek balance between cereal, meat and vegetable, and accordingly Chinese food is delicious as well as healthy.

(7) The world-renowned Silk Road is a series of routes connecting the East and the West. The Silk Road represents the ancient Chinese silk trade. Nowadays, tea is one of the most popular beverage in the world, and it is not only the treasure of China but also an important part of Chinese tradition and culture.

Ⅲ. 审阅并修改下列译文

(1) 改译:This theory <u>has</u> guiding significance for health preserving and disease prevention.

(2) 改译:The relationship of them manifests in the <u>commutative dependence of</u> containing and transporting foodstuff, <u>the coordination of</u> ascending and descending qi, <u>mutual supplementing between</u> yin, yang, dryness, and moisture.

(3) 改译:The essence stored in the kidney has two main sources: <u>the one from the</u> parental reproductive essence is called the "congenital essence"; <u>the nutrient acquired</u> from diet after birth and subtle substance metabolized by viscera, is called "acquired essence".

(4) 改译:But I was drenched from head to toe like a drowned rat.

(5) 改译:库卡索岛上的实验取得了巨大的成功,引起了佛罗里达州牲畜养殖者的兴趣,他们要用相似的办法来缓解螺旋锥蝇这一祸害。

第二章练习答案

Ⅰ. 段落翻译(汉译英)

(1) China is a densely populated country with vast territory and rich natural resources, and its various land-form as well as climates breeds all kinds of animals and plants. Since long ago, ancient Chinese have been coping with diseases under the help of medicine from natural resources. Traditional Chinese Medicine is a theoretical system accumulated and developed through long-term medical practice.

(2) The name TCM(Zhong Yi) is short for Traditional Chinese Medicine, which started in West Han dynasty and means "neutralized medicine". Theoretically based on Yin-yang and Wuxing (five elements: metal, wood, water, fire and earth) system, it takes the human body as the whole cycle of qi, shape and spirit, so neutralization and balance is the key to health. Based on humans and aiming at the cures, TCM emphasizes the unity between humans and nature. An outstanding TCM doctor shall acquire profound traditional culture apart from professional medical knowledge and rich clinical experience.

(3) One major treatment method is Chinese herbal medicine. Most of the Chinese medicines are made up of herbs, and are put into different cabinets in pharmacy or drug stores, which are divided into several cases and then are further divided into several smaller cells. One herb in one cell. Pharmacists take and weigh the herbal medicine based on the prescription. Customers can pay the pharmacy or the drug store to have the prescribed medicine decocted or to do it themselves at home.

(4) In the first-aid kit of Chinese, there are frequently-used OTC medicines for emergency like Wangshi Baochi Pill for infantile malnutrition, Quick Acting Heart Reliever Pill for stenocardia,

Yunnan Baiyao for inflammation-relieving and hemostatic, Chuanbei Pipa Syrup for diffusing the lung and suppressing coughing, Safflower Oil for relieving muscle pain, Radix Isatidis granules for clearing heat and removing toxicity, Rendan mini-pills and cooling oil for sunstroke prevention and refreshment, etc. These Chinese patent medicines have various forms like pill, powder, plaster, and pellet. Passed down from generation to generation, they are effective in treatment, easy for self-aid, and convenient to carry.

Ⅱ. 段落翻译(英译汉)

在西太平洋地区,起源于古代中国的传统医学主要体系仍在继续发展,不仅是在中国,而且在周边国家和地区亦是如此,特别是日本、韩国和越南。但因各国的生存条件不同而呈现出一些差异,如自然资源的可利用性、本土文化和政治氛围等。传统医学在各国的发展中也被赋予不同的名称。如:东方医学、中医学、韩医学、日本汉方医学、越南传统医学。在西太平洋地区,则统称为传统医学(TRM)。

传统医学是一个综合医学体系,具有独立的理论基础和实践经验,它包括草药、针刺和其他非药物疗法。因其范式独特、疗效显著且副作用小,该体系的国际关注度与日俱增。鉴于近年来越来越多的国家使用传统医学(TRM)治疗疾病,迫切需要用统一的语言对该领域的术语进行规范,即国际标准术语。

1981 年,世卫组织西太区办事处(WPRO)组建了针灸命名标准化工作组。经过 10 年的努力,该工作组最终与位于日内瓦的世卫组织科技组达成共识,批准通过针灸术语国际标准。1991 年,世卫组织在日内瓦出版了《针灸穴名国际标准》(*A Proposed Standard International Acupuncture Nomenclature*),西太区办事处在马尼拉也出版了《标准针灸名词》(*Standard Acupuncture Nomenclature*)(第一部分和第二部分修订版)。实践证明,世卫组织出版的这些针灸标准对促进国际针灸信息交流发挥了巨大作用。然而,这些标准仍然十分有限,仅包括十四经脉、361 个传统穴位、奇经八脉、48 个经外奇穴、14 个头针穴区以及与针灸针有关的术语。此外,为满足日益增长的实践、教育、科研和交流需求,迫切需要为整个传统医学(TRM)开展术语标准化工作。

……

英语表达的选择原则

1. 准确再现中文术语的原始概念

在此语境下,应该强调的是每个术语都是一个意义单位,但这并不等同于构成该术语的各个汉字意义的总和。根据汉语言文字学,一个汉字通常有若干种不同的意义,在某种程度上很像英语的音节。通常情况下,由两个或两个以上字符构成的复合词能够表达特定的含义。但是,复合词的含义也不等同于其组成成分各自的含义。此外,英语对等成分的恰当与否应主要依据其是否准确反映汉语医学概念来判断。

2. 避免创造新词

本文件所有英译术语在全球公认的英语字典中均有收录。如有例外,则是从现有的英语词汇经过语法修改衍生而来。

3. 避免拼音(罗马化的汉字)的使用

对于某些传统医学术语,确定英语对等词极其困难,许多出版物采用拼音方式处理。然而,应该强调的是,罗马化的汉字仍然是汉语,拼音并不是真正意义上的翻译。此外,汉语、日语和韩语中的汉字非常相似,但发音差异较大。古典文献的标题和作者名称都是用最初的发音来描述的。

4. 与 WHO 发布的《标准针灸名词》保持一致

特别是针灸术语的翻译,《国际术语标准》(International Standard Terminologies, IST)遵循 1991 年世卫组织西太区办事处发布的《标准针灸名词》(第一部分和第二部分修订版)的英译版本。

西方医学术语的应用

传统医学和现代医学都致力于保健和治疗疾病,因此,这两种医药体系在概念和术语上必有重叠之处。在这种情况下,唯一的区别就是用词。当汉语中的中医术语有相应的表达相同概念的西医术语时,使用西医术语不仅合理且非常有必要。否则,创建一个新的英语术语会引起混淆。另一方面,西医术语的使用不当具有误导性,因此本文件竭力避免此种现象。

标准术语和直译

在本文件中,大多数英译术语与中文原始译文完全一致,但也有例外。

由于历史背景的原因,许多术语都有其他名称。甚至在中国政府颁布的国家标准中,也保留了一些替代名称,因为替代名称在许多中国经典作品中多有出现,所以替代名称的保留仍然具有现实意义。翻译这些术语,特别是采用直译法时,每一个替代名称都应被翻译出来。结果,一个概念可能有多个英文表达。事实上,这种英语表达的多样化并没有任何技术意义。

由于中国的构词习惯,添加或删除一些字符只是为了语言或修辞目的。既然添加或删除字符不具有技术意义,就没有必要在国际标准术语中体现这种用词的变化。

由于传统医学术语的演变,一些传统医学术语的原始概念发生了变化,抑或目前所使用的中医术语中仅采用多种概念中的一种概念。在这种情况下,术语当代意义的英文表达应该被视为标准。

(编者译)

简言之,国际标准术语与恰当的翻译密切相关,但绝不是简单的翻译转换。

Ⅲ. **下列英译文均来自中国古代典籍作品,将其回译为汉语**

(1) 知我者,谓我心忧;不知我者,谓我何求。

(2) 知者乐水,仁者乐山;知者动,仁者静;知者乐,仁者寿。

(3) 知者不惑,仁者不忧,勇者不惧。

(4) 君子坦荡荡,小人长戚戚。

(5) 结庐在人境,而无车马喧。问君何能尔?心远地自偏。采菊东篱下,悠然见南山。山气日夕佳,飞鸟相与还。此中有真意,欲辨已忘言。

(6) 人之初,性本善。性相近,习相远。苟不教,性乃迁。教之道,贵以专。昔孟母,择邻处。子不学,断机杼。

(7) 希言自然。故飘风不终朝,骤雨不终日。

(8) 企者不立;跨者不行;自见者不明;自是者不彰;自伐者无功;自矜者不长。

(9) 为学日益,为道日损。损之又损,以至于无为。无为而无不为。取天下常以无事,及其有事,不足以取天下。

(10) 祸兮福之所倚,福兮祸之所伏。

第三章练习答案

Ⅰ. **翻译下列养生谚语(英译汉)**

(1) 一睡解千愁。

(2) 气大伤身。

(3) 愤怒以愚蠢开始,以后悔告终。

(4) 只工作,不玩耍,聪明小孩也变傻。

(5) 忧郁催人老。

(6) 生病不忧虑,节省医药费。

(7) 问心无愧,高枕无忧。(不做亏心事,不怕鬼敲门。)

(8) 伤风宜吃,发热宜饿。

(9) 忧虑伤身。

(10) 节食、静心和快乐才是最好的医生。

(11) 一个小丑进城,胜过一打医生。

(12) 一天一苹果,医生远离我。

(13) 饭吃七分饱,胃口才能好。

(14) 早睡早起。

(15) 病从口入,祸从口出。

Ⅱ. 翻译下列缩略语

(1) n. p. o←nos per os(nothing by mouth) 禁食

(2) p. o.←per os(by mouth) 口服

(3) baso←basophils 嗜碱性粒细胞

(4) gtt←gutta; guttae(drop; drops) 点滴;滴剂

(5) chemo←chemotherapy 化疗

(6) chol←cholesterol 胆固醇

(7) postop←postoperative 术后

(8) primip←primipara 初产妇

(9) pulv←pulvis 粉剂

(10) cath←catheter; catheterization 导管(检查)

Ⅲ. 翻译下列术语

(1) 传染性细菌或病毒

(2) 适应性免疫系统

(3) 神经过载

(4) 恶性肿瘤

(5) 肌束

(6) 脂肪肝

(7) 紫外线

(8) 脾窦腔

(9) 10 年的跟踪研究

(10) 防孩子打开的盖子

Ⅳ. 借助词根及词缀翻译下列术语

(1) 经量减少,月经过少

(2) 月经过多

(3) 月经不调,闭经

(4) 痛经

(5) 红血细胞

(6) 白细胞

(7) 血细胞

(8) 杀菌剂

(9) 结肠造口术

(10) 心穿刺术

Ⅴ. 翻译以下段落，注意词语的选择

（1）疫苗可预防的疾病产生严重危害的概率要远大于疫苗产生危害的概率。例如，脊灰能导致瘫痪，麻疹能导致脑炎和盲症，一些疫苗可预防的疾病甚至能导致死亡。疫苗不但几乎不会导致任何严重伤害或死亡，它所带来的益处也远远大于其风险。没有疫苗，会出现更多的伤害和死亡。

（2）患者一天或一周内可多次出现症状。对某些人而言，在体力活动期间或在夜间症状变得更为严重。缺乏认识和不能避免造成气道狭窄的诱因可威胁生命，并且可导致哮喘发作、呼吸窘迫甚至死亡。

（3）哮喘诱因可包括冷空气，极端情绪激发，例如愤怒或恐惧，以及体育锻炼。

（4）通常对哮喘的诊断和治疗不足，对个人和家庭造成相当大的负担，并且可能终生限制个人的活动。

（5）罹患哮喘的最大危险因素是接触室内过敏原，例如床上用品、地毯和填充家具中的尘螨、污染和宠物皮屑；室外过敏原，例如花粉和霉菌；烟草烟雾以及工作场所的化学刺激物。

Ⅵ. 短文翻译

什么样的食物最增肥？

肥胖研究中一个基本且尚未解决的问题是什么样的食物最导致肥胖。专家们提出的原因各不相同，例如含脂肪或糖的食物或缺乏蛋白质的食物，因其可能会在不知不觉中使我们饮食过量。

今年夏天在《细胞代谢》(*Cell Metabolism*)杂志发表的一项饮食研究中，研究人员从29种饮食中随机抽取一种分配给数百只成年雄性小鼠（科学家希望在之后的实验中纳入雌性小鼠）。有些食物以饱和及不饱和脂肪的形式提供最多达80％的卡路里，碳水化合物则很少；另一些则脂肪很少，大部分由主要来自谷物和玉米糖浆的精制碳水化合物组成，尽管其中有些碳水化合物来自食糖。而另一种饮食的特征是含有极高或极低百分比的蛋白质。这些小鼠保持相同的饮食三个月——估计大约相当于人类的九年——同时允许它们随意进食、在笼子里走动。然后研究人员测量小鼠的体重和身体组成，并检查其脑组织是否存在基因活动被改变的证据。

只有部分小鼠变得肥胖——几乎全是接受高脂肪饮食的小鼠。这些小鼠也显示出某些基因活动被改变的迹象，且出现的大脑区域与处理奖励相关；显然，高脂肪粗粒食物让它们开心。其他饮食，包括那些富含食糖的饮食，都没有导致显著的体重增加或相同方式的基因表达改变。即使是含有超过60％脂肪的超高脂肪饮食，也不能显著增加体重，而且这种饮食中的小鼠比其他同类吃的食物少，可能是因为它们根本无法吃下如此多的脂肪。

负责该项研究的北京中国科学院及苏格兰阿伯丁大学教授约翰·斯皮克曼（John Speakman）说："看起来，如果你是一只小鼠，吃高脂肪但非极度高脂肪饮食的话，会导致你体重增加。"斯皮克曼和他的合著者认为，含脂肪膳食刺激并改变了大脑的某些区域，导致小鼠非常想吃含脂肪食物，以至于忽略了其他身体信号，正是这些信号在提示它们已经摄入了足够的能量。

第四章练习答案

Ⅰ. 翻译以下带数字的中医术语

（1）五行学说 five-phase/element theory

（2）三因学说 theory of three types of disease causes

（3）奇经八脉 eight extraordinary meridians

（4）十五别络 fifteen divergent collaterals

（5）十二皮部 twelve cutaneous regions

(6) 十二经筋 twelve musculature zones

(7) 十五络脉 fifteen collateral vessels

(8) 六淫 six climatic exopathogens

(9) 五邪 five pathogens

(10) 一指禅推法 pushing manipulation with one finger meditation

(11) 五志化火 five minds transforming into fire

(12) 五腧穴 five acupoints

(13) 八脉交会穴 eight confluence point

(14) 足三阳经 three yang meridians of the foot

(15) 八会穴 eight influential point

Ⅱ. 翻译下列四字中医术语，并根据其语法关系进行归类

(1) 补中益气 invigorating spleen-stomach and replenishing qi

(2) 阴阳转化 mutual convertibility of yin-yang

(3) 阳盛阴衰 yin deficiency due to yang excess

(4) 阴盛阳衰 yang deficiency due to yin excess

(5) 阴阳偏盛 excess of either yin or yang

(6) 阴阳偏衰 deficiency of either yin or yang

(7) 阳盛格阴 exuberant yang repelling yin

(8) 精血同源 homogeny of essence and blood

(9) 潜阳熄风 subduing yang and extinguishing wind

(10) 养阴清热 nourishing yin and clearing heat

(11) 祛风散寒 dispelling wind and dispersing cold

(12) 绝对偏盛 absolute predominance

(13) 藏而不泻 store essence but not excrete it

(14) 泻而不藏 transform food into essence but not store it

(15) 上焦如雾 upper/energizer being organ of fogging

(16) 中焦如沤 middle/energizer being organ of soaking

(17) 下焦如渎 lower/energizer being organ of draining

(18) 健脾化湿 invigorating spleen for eliminating dampness

(19) 健脾和胃 invigorating spleen and harmonizing stomach

(20) 坚者削之 removing hardness

Ⅲ. 翻译下列书名

(1)《丹溪心法》*Danxi's Experiential Therapy*

(2)《景岳全书》*A Comprehensive Medical Book by Zhang Jingyue*

(3)《马王堆汉墓医》*Mawangdui Han Dynasty Medical Books*

(4)《难经》*Classic of Difficult Issues*

(5)《千金要方》*Prescriptions Worth Thousand Gold for Emergencies*

(6)《千金翼方》*Supplement to Prescriptions Worth Thousand Gold for Emergencies*

(7)《伤寒论》*Treatise on Febrile Diseases*

(8)《神农本草经》*King Shen Nong's Classics of Herbal Medicine*

(9)《药性论》*Theory of Medicinal Property*

(10)《医经溯洄集》*A Historiographic Account of Medical Theories*

Ⅳ. 回译下列中医药术语

(1) 邻近取穴

(2) 留针

(3) 痰厥

(4) 伤寒

(5) 消渴

(6) 砭石

(7) 阳黄

(8) 风邪

(9) 湿热内阻

(10) 二便失调

Ⅴ. 下列译文选自李照国所译《黄帝内经》英文版,试将其回译为汉语,然后对照原文

(1) 上古之人,其知道者,法于阴阳,和于术数,食饮有节,起居有常,不妄作劳,故能形与神俱,而尽终其天年,度百岁乃去。

(2) 夫上古圣人之教下也,皆谓之虚邪贼风,避之有时,恬淡虚无,真气从之,精神内守,病安从来。

(3) 是以志闲而少欲,心安而不惧,形劳而不倦,气从以顺,各从其欲,皆得所愿。故美其食,任其服,乐其俗,高下不相慕,其民故曰朴。是以嗜欲不能劳其目,淫邪不能惑其心。

(4) 外不劳形于事,内无思想之患,以恬愉为务,以自得为功。

(5) 从阴阳则生。逆之则死,从之则治,逆之则乱。

第五章练习答案

Ⅰ. 翻译句子(英译汉)

(1) 进入肺泡的微小有害物质被第四道防线——巨噬细胞清除了。

(2) 直接喉镜检查可以做出诊断,脱出的喉室可用喉镜刀或钳进行复原。

(3) 本部分的重点在于病理学家可见的炎症过程的形态学方面,而不在于药理和生化方面。

(4) 因此,当消化性溃疡处于出现症状的阶段时,溃疡直接接触盐酸通常会引起典型的溃疡疼痛,这一点似乎是没有疑问的。

(5) 在美国,通过国家公共卫生体系,目前至少有 160 698 例冠状病毒病例已得到确诊和检测。

(6) 目前,一系列包括如血液制品、免疫疗法以及药物疗法等潜在的治疗方法正在进行检验。

(7) 对于患有潜在疾病或免疫功能低下的老年病人或其他人来说,其在表现出轻微症状时即应尽早联系医生进行诊治。

(8) 有效的治疗办法应该会比疫苗早出现。理想的情况下,这将减少需要采用呼吸机等措施的重症监护病例。

Ⅱ. 翻译下列含有被动句的句子(英译汉)

(1) 2016 年,在由于"第一种疾病类型"而导致的全球死亡病例中,有超过一半都来自低等收入国家。这一类疾病类型包括传染性疾病、母婴传播类疾病、怀孕和分娩期间可能引发的疾病以及营养不良等。

(2) 公共卫生专家已提出美国将有可能成为"下一个意大利"的警示。因为在这里,那些在挤满了感染新型冠状病毒肺炎病人的医院里工作的医生,不得不采取定量分配护理的措施来决定谁有机会使用呼吸机。

(3) 病毒是通过野生动物而传播给人类,然后再通过接触被感染者的血液、排泄物、器官等而在人群中散播开来。

Ⅲ. 翻译下列含有动词不定式的句子(英译汉)

(1) 为了尽可能地减少损失,信任以及信息流通至关重要。

(2) 听从医护人员、当地公共卫生机构及公司老板所提出的,关于新型冠状病毒肺炎防护相关建议举措。

(3) 官方指南建议人们保持卫生、勤洗手,如果需要可以囤两周的食物和水,以及其他日用品。

Ⅳ. 翻译下列含有状语从句的句子(英译汉)

(1) 若感身体不适,或出现轻微头疼、流涕症状,请待在家中避免外出,直至身体康复。

(2) 最主要的就是采取刚才我提到的"闭关"措施,让你的社区感染率迅速下降,然后让我们的生活尽快回归正轨。

(3) 谭德塞还强调,除了调动政府各部门的力量外,还必须调动全社会和全体人民的力量,使各国在防疫行动中取得进展。

Ⅴ. 英汉段落互译

(1) Immunization has also dramatically reduced other vaccine-preventable diseases in China, including rubella, Japanese encephalitis, meningitis and hepatitis B among children. Between 1992 and 2014, an estimated 120 million hepatitis B virus infections and 28 million chronic infections were averted by the use of hepatitis B vaccine. Thanks to immunization, today's generation of Chinese children are virtually hepatitis B free—meaning their risk of developing nasty diseases such as cirrhosis of the liver and liver cancer in the future are drastically reduced.

(2) 多年来辣椒一直因其食疗特性而受到赞誉,如今研究人员发现,定期吃辣椒可以降低死于心脏病和中风的风险。这项研究在意大利开展,在那里辣椒是一种很常用的调味料。该研究比较了2.3万人的死亡风险,其中一部分人吃辣椒,而另一部分人不吃辣椒。

第六章练习答案

Ⅰ. 翻译下列论文标题(汉译英)

(1) Comparison of English References from Journals of Different Medical Colleges and Universities

(2) Fatality Case Analysis in the Pediatric Unit of Chengdu First People's Hospital from 2007 to 2016

(3) Pediatric Residents: Professional Situation and Talent Drain

(4) Detection, cloning and sequencing of a new gene related to diabetic nephropathy

Ⅱ. 翻译下列发言人简介(英译汉)

Scott N. Smith,医学博士,Elliot and Roslyn Jaffe 的儿科学和过敏与免疫学教授,儿科过敏和免疫科主任。他是临床研究中心的医学主任,该中心是西奈山伊坎医学院转化科学所的下属单位。Smith 博士是西奈山谢斐食物过敏研究所的临床医生和临床研究员。他的临床研究资金部分来自国家卫生和食物过敏研究和教育研究所,研究方向包括:食物过敏的临床表现,由特异性食物(如花生、坚果、海鲜和牛奶)引起的过敏性疾病,食物过敏的自然史,食物过敏的环境危险因素,食物过敏的诊断,食物过敏的流行病学,食物过敏相关的社会心理问题,食物过敏的遗传流行病学研究,以及针对卫生保健提供者和家长的有关食物过敏的教育材料的开发。

Ⅲ. 将下列短文译成汉语

关节炎

关节炎这个词通常用来形容影响关节正常活动的症状。通常的症状包括关节疼痛和关节僵化。其他的症状包括发红、发热、肿大以及受伤关节可活动范围的减少。部分类型中,其他器官也会受到损害。有逐渐加剧的,也有突发的。

关节炎有一百多种,最为普遍的是骨关节炎(一种退行性关节疾病)和类风湿性关节炎。骨关节炎通常随着年龄的增长而发生并会损害人们的手指、膝盖和臀部。类风湿性关节炎是一种自身免疫性疾病,通常会损害人们的手和脚。其他类型的关节炎包括痛风、系统性红斑狼疮、纤维肌痛和化脓性关节炎。它们都属于类风湿性关节炎。

治疗的方法包括放松关节以及交替进行冰敷和热敷。减肥和锻炼也会有帮助。可能要用到减轻疼痛的药物如布洛芬和对乙酰氨基酚。关节置换术某些情况可用。

骨关节炎的发生率大于 3.8%,而类风湿性关节炎的发生率大约为 0.24%。在西方国家,大约 1%~2% 的人在一生中的某个阶段会受到痛风的影响。澳大利亚大约有 15% 的人会患关节炎,而在美国超过 20% 的人会患有一种关节炎。总的来说,这种疾病会随着年龄增大而变得普遍。关节炎常使人不能上班,导致人们生活质量下降。这个单词来源于希腊,arthro-意思是关节,-itis 意思是炎症。(编者译)

Ⅳ. 翻译下列片段(汉译英)

Humanity has created a colorful global civilization in the long course of its development, and the civilization of China is an important component of the world civilization harboring great diversity. As a representative feature of Chinese civilization, traditional Chinese medicine(TCM) is a medical science that was formed and developed in the daily life of the people and in the process of their fight against diseases over thousands of years. It has made a great contribution to the nation's procreation and the country's prosperity, in addition to producing a positive impact on the progress of human civilization.

TCM has created unique views on life, on fitness, on diseases and on the prevention and treatment of diseases during its long history of absorption and innovation. It represents a combination of natural sciences and humanities, embracing profound philosophical ideas of the Chinese nation. As ideas on fitness and medical models change and evolve, traditional Chinese medicine has come to underline a more and more profound value.

Since the founding of the People's Republic of China in 1949, the Chinese government has set great store by TCM and rendered vigorous support to its development. TCM and Western medicine have their different strengths. They work together in China to protect people from diseases and improve public health. This has turned out to be one of the important features and notable strengths of medicine with Chinese characteristics.

第七章练习答案

Ⅰ. 翻译以下病历片段

(1) Shortness of breath, cough, associated with yellowish sputum for 3 – 4 days.

(2) Sore throat, high fever for 2 days.

(3) Continuous/ persistent headache, associated with nausea and vomiting for 2 months.

(4) Chills and fever from/ since last night.

(5) Fever, right chest pain and cough for two weeks.

(6) About one week ago, the patient began to have weakness and poor appetite; about two days ago, the patient began to have chills, fever and cough. The temperature increased to 39℃ promptly. And he noticed some pain in the lower part of the right chest, aggravating with breathing and coughing. Later on, the chest pain became persistent and sharp.

(7) Significant/ notable history was duodenal ulcer 20 years ago. He has suffered from severe hypertension for over(more than) 15 years. No surgical procedures, no history of tuberculosis, and no other pertinent past history.

Ⅱ. 翻译以下药品说明

(1) 安嗽灵是一种全新的、获得专利的镇咳药。

(2) 安嗽灵属非麻醉药,可作为常用药使用。

(3) 安嗽灵的镇咳作用相当于或强于可待因。

(4) 安嗽灵的祛痰作用是迄今市场上可买到的常用镇咳药中前所未有的。

(5) 安嗽灵可长期服用,既安全又无副作用。

(6) 氨甲叶酸(简称 MTX)为甲酰四氢叶酸的抗代谢物,长期以来一直用作治疗肿瘤的化疗药物。

(7) 本品超过包装上印刷的有效期后不得使用。

(8) 护前列腺素具有抗炎作用,能减轻前列腺膀胱区因一般性梗阻引起的肿胀,本品能刺激上述部位的血液循环,并增加机体的自然防御机制。

(9) 超剂量可能引起下列体征和症状:震颤、兴奋、痉挛、血压改变、意识损害及昏迷。心电图和脑电图也可能发生改变。治疗:采取措施监护重要器官的功能。必要时给予安定。

(10) 速眠安能增强神经抑制剂、安定剂、抗抑郁剂、催眠药、镇静剂和麻醉剂的中枢神经镇静作用。

(11) 有效期:18 个月(失效日期印在瓶签上)。

第八章练习答案

Ⅰ. 将以下段落译成英语

(1) Dietary therapy involves both treatment methods and nutrition culture. It can cure you of your diseases when you are sick and protect you against diseases when you are healthy. A lot of Chinese proverbs and sayings are about dietary therapy and health care, such as "Turnips in winter and ginger in summer, keep you from needing a doctor." "Turnips, almond, ginger and pears keep you from coughing and doctors". "A bowl of mung bean soup can clear heat and detoxify you better than any magical prescriptions". "Cucumbers, towel gourd, and tomatoes make you beautiful/better than a doctor's prescription.". "Three slices of garlic can cure half your dysentery.""Chinese dates keep away cancer and aging". The Chinese renderings of these proverbs are simple and melodic, easy to understand and remember, and serve as guides to health care, dietary therapy, prevention and treatment of diseases.

(2) But keeping the balance is hard. Every decision is a tradeoff when it affects the lives of thousands and the livelihoods of millions. We need to slow the spread. Draconian quarantines are being enforced in many parts of the country. Maintaining a large network of isolation and a low rate of rogue behavior is the answer; the question is: we still don't know the exact extent of the infection. Isolating

the infected while not infringing on people's rights and decency is not an easy task.

(3) Our economy relies on human transaction, but epidemic control depends on social distancing. We need to keep a distance, and yet we need to work together. So how do we balance saving lives and saving economy? This is an issue that requires hard decision-making.

Ⅱ. 将以下句子或段落译成汉语

(1) 冠状病毒是在动物和人类身上发现的一个大类病毒。有些会感染人类并导致疾病,从普通感冒到更严重的疾病,就像中东呼吸综合征(MERS)和严重急性呼吸综合征(SARS)。

(2) 新型冠状病毒(CoV)是先前在人类中尚未发现的一种新型冠状病毒株。新的或者"新型"冠状病毒,现在称为2019-nCoV,在2019年12月中国武汉报道爆发之前没有检测到。

(3) 与其他的呼吸性疾病一样,感染2019-nCoV会导致流鼻涕、喉咙痛、咳嗽和发热这些轻度症状。对一些人来说会更严重,可以导致肺炎和呼吸困难。该病很少致命。老人和有过往病史的人们(例如糖尿病和心脏病)似乎更容易感染该病毒。

(4) 潜伏期是感染和疾病临床症状发作之间的时期。目前潜伏期的范围估计为1~12.5天,中位数估计为5~6天。随着更多可用数据的获得,这些估算会更精确。在其他冠状病毒,像中东呼吸综合征和严重急性呼吸综合征的信息基础上,2019-nCoV的潜伏期会高达14天。世界卫生组织建议,确诊病例的接触者应跟踪14天。

(5) 避免食用生的或者未煮熟的动物产品:按照完善的食品安全规范,要妥善处理生肉、牛奶或者动物器官,避免与未煮熟的食物发生交叉污染。

参考文献

1. Bellos D, 2011. Is that a fish in your ear: Translation and the meaning of everything[M]. London: Penguin Books Ltd.
2. Namit B, 1992. The Oxford companion to the English Language[M]. USA: Oxford University Press.
3. Nida E A, Taber C R,1982. The theory and practice of translation[M]. Leiden: E. J. Brill: 33-173.
4. Robinson D, 2006. Western translation theory: from Herodotus to Nietzsche[M]. Beijing: Foreign Language Teaching and Research Press.
5. Waley A,1999. 论语[M]. 长沙:湖南人民出版社.
6. World Health Organization Western Pacific Region, 2007. International standard terminologies on traditional medicine in the Western Pacific Region [Z]. Manila, Philippines: WHO.
7. 埃斯皮卡,1987. 文学社会学[M]. 王美华,于沛,译. 合肥:安徽文艺出版社:137.
8. 柴可夫,2010. 中医基础理论(双语教材)[M]. 张庆荣,译. 北京:人民卫生出版社.
9. 陈立中,1980. 对《医古文》一书文选注释的意见[J]. 上海中医药杂志(2):46-47.
10. 陈晓华,施蕴中,2008. 从翻译目的论看 Nigel Wiseman 的中医英译翻译思想[J]. 辽宁中医药大学学报(5):182-184.
11. 程卫强,丁年青,2012. 中医翻译的文化因素处理方法:归化与异化[J]. 上海中医药大学学报,26(5):13-15.
12. 冯庆华,2010. 实用翻译教程(英汉互译)[M]. 3 版. 上海:上海外语教育出版社.
13. 国务院,2016.《中国的中医药》白皮书[G]. 北京:国务院新闻办公室.
14. 胡庚申,2008. 从术语看译论:翻译适应选择论概观 [J]. 上海翻译(2):1-5.
15. 季佩英,孙庆祥,2012. 学术英语 医学[M]. 北京:外语教学与研究出版社.
16. 孔兵,2010. 论语选萃[M]. 付雅丽,译. 北京:中国对外翻译出版公司.
17. 兰凤利,2007. 中医古典文献中"阴阳"的源流与翻译[J]. 中国翻译(4):69-72.
18. 李照国,2005. 黄帝内经(汉英对照)[M]. 西安:世界图书出版公司.
19. 刘承宇,2002. 英汉语篇互文性对比研究[C]//认知•语用•功能 英汉宏观对比研究. 上海:上海外语教育出版社:143-151.
20. 宁越,1988. 释"阴阳并"[J]. 甘肃中医学院学报(1):8-11.
21. 牛喘月,2004. 名不顺则言不顺,言不顺则事不成:谈谈中医名词术语英译的原则问题[J]. 中西医结合学报,2(6):474-476.
22. 孙俊芳,2016. 对中医药古籍书名的辨证论译[J]. 中国中医基础医学杂志(11):1538-1541.
23. 谭载喜,2004. 西方翻译简史(增订版)[M]. 北京:商务印书馆.
24. 王洁华. 2010. 中医"数量"表达的分类、特征及英译[J]. 中国中西医结合杂志 30(5):546-548.
25. 王燕,2016. 医学论文英文摘要的句法研究[M]. 青岛:中国海洋大学出版社.

26. 魏迺杰,1995.汉英·英汉中医词典[M].长沙:湖南科学技术出版社.

27. 谢竹藩,2005.评魏迺杰先生的《实用英文中医辞典》:论魏氏直译法[J].中国中西医结合杂志(10):937-940.

28. 许敬生,2011.医林掌故[M].北京:人民卫生出版社.2011.

29. 许钧,1989.论文学翻译再创造的度[J].外语研究(4):8.

30. 宇文所安,2003.中国文论:英译与评论[M].王柏华,陶庆梅,译.上海:上海社会科学出版社.

31. 张维友,2004.英语词汇学教程[M].武汉:华中师范大学出版社.

32. 《中国翻译》编辑部,2010.名家评点翻译佳作:"韩素音青年翻译奖"竞赛作品与评析[M].南京:译林出版社:183.

33. 《中国翻译》编辑部,2010.名家评点翻译佳作:"韩素音青年翻译奖"竞赛作品与评析[M].南京:译林出版社:183.

34. 朱明炬,谢少华,吴万伟,2010. 英汉名篇名译[M].南京:译林出版社.

35. 邹德芳,2016.基于中医英语语料库的中医英语翻译研究[M]. 长春:吉林大学出版社:117.

36. 左飙,2009.论文化的可译性[M]//罗选民.结构·解构·建构 翻译理论研究.上海:上海外语教育出版社:23-41.

附录 中医常用四字术语对照

1. 基础理论类

    整体观念 holism
    辨证论治 treatment based on syndrome differentiation
    阴阳学说 yin-yang theory
    阴阳对立 opposition of yin and yang
    阴阳互根 mutual rooting of yin and yang
    阴阳消长 waxing and waning of yin and yang
    阴阳平衡 yin-yang balance
    阴极似阳 extreme yin with yang manifestation
    相互转化 mutual transformation
    阴平阳秘 relative equilibrium of yin-yang
    阴阳转化 mutual convertibility of yin and yang
    阴阳学说 yin-yang theory
    经络现象 meridian/channel phenomenon
    先天之气 congenital qi
    后天之气 acquired qi
    水液代谢 water metabolism
    血液循行 blood circulation
    相互消长 mutual waning and waxing
    相互制约 mutual inhibition
    相互依存 interdependence
    相反相成 contrary and supplementary to each other
    五行学说 five phases theory/theory of five elements
    亢害承制 restraining excessiveness to acquire harmony
    相乘相侮 subjugation and counter-restriction
    土虚木乘 wood subjugate earth, bringing on the insufficiency of earth
    母子相及 mother and child affecting each other
    木喜条达 wood is characterized by growing freely and peripherally
    木曰曲直 wood characterized by bending and straightening
    火曰炎上 fire characterized by flaring up

土爱稼穑 earth characterized by sowing and reaping
金曰从革 metal characterized by clearing and changing
水曰润下 water characterized by moistening and descending
精气学说 essential qi theory
先天之精 congenital essence
后天之精 acquired essence
经络之气 meridian qi
津血同源 homogeny of clear fluid and blood
精血同源 homogeny of essence and blood
藏象学说 visceral manifestation theory
五脏六腑 five zang viscera and six fu viscera
奇恒之腑 extraordinary fu-viscera
元神之府 the residence of mind/house of mind
精明之府 the residence of intelligence/house of intelligence
贮痰之器 reservoir of phlegm
水上之源 upper source of water
通调水道 regulation of water passages
先天之本 congenital origin
膀胱气化 bladder qi transformation
心肾相交 heart-kidney interaction
肝肾同源 homogeny of liver and kidney
经络学说 meridian and collateral theory
奇经八脉 eight extra meridians
十二经别 twelve meridian divergences
十二经筋 twelve meridian sinews
十二皮部 twelve cutaneous regions
十五络脉 fifteen collateral vessels
邪正关系 relationship between pathogenic factors and healthy qi/relationship between healthy qi and evil qi
心主血脉 heart governing blood and vessels
肾主纳气 kidney governing inspiration
肾主水液 kidney governing water metabolism
脾主运化 spleen governing transportation and transformation
肝主疏泄 liver controlling conveyance and dispersion
脾主四肢 spleen governing limbs
上焦如雾 upper jiao/energizer being organ of fogging
中焦如沤 middle jiao/energizer being organ of soaking
下焦如渎 lower jiao/energizer being organ of draining

2. 诊断学类

司外揣内 governing exterior to infer interior/operating the external to surmise the internal

四诊合参 comprehensive analysis of data gained by four diagnostic methods

面色苍白 pale complexion

面色萎黄 sallow complexion

舌苔脱落 peeling fur

舌下络脉 sublingual collateral vessels

咳逆上气 cough with dyspnea

发热恶寒 aversion to cold with fever

手足烦热 vexing heat in the extremities

寒热交作 alternating chills and fever

痛无定处 migratory pain

头重脚轻 heavy head and light feet

咽喉不利 discomfort in the throat

吞食梗塞 blockage in deglutition

心下支结 feeling obstructed in epigastrium

小腹不仁 lower abdominal numbness

泻下不爽 non-smooth diarrhea

小便不利 dysuria

小便失禁 incontinence of urine

脉象主病 disease correspondences of the pulse

三部九候 three body parts and nine pulse taking sites

寸口诊法 wrist pulse-taking method

3. 临床各科

半身不遂 hemiplegia

月经不调 menstrual disorders

月经先期 advanced menstruation

月经后期 delayed menstruation

月经过少 hypomenorrhea

月经过多 menorrhagia

经期延长 menostaxis

经行腹痛 dysmenorrhea

妊娠腹痛 abdominal pain during pregnancy

妊娠恶阻 hyperemesis gravidarum

胎动不安 threatened abortion

妊娠肿胀 gestational anasarca

过期不产 prolonged pregnancy

胞衣不下 retention of placenta
乳汁不通 agalactia
小儿咳喘 infantile cough
舌下痰包 phlegmatic mass in tongue, sublingual gland cyst
口眼歪斜 facial paralysis
突起睛高 sudden protrusion of the eyeball
异物入目 foreign body in eye
高风内障 retinopathy pigmentosa
胎患内障 congenital cataract
赤膜下垂 dropping pannus
天行赤眼 epidemic conjunctivitis
上胞下垂 blepharoptosis

4. 药物及治疗类

升降出入 ascending, descending, exiting and entering
升降浮沉 ascending and descending, floating and sinking
四气五味 four properties and five tastes
发汗解表 promoting sweat to release the exterior
疏风泄热 dispersing wind and discharging heat
宣肺止咳 diffusing the lung to suppress cough
清热生津 clearing heat and promoting fluid production
调和气血 harmonizing qi and blood
调和脾胃 harmonizing the spleen and stomach
散寒祛湿 dissipating cold and dispelling dampness
芳香化浊 eliminating turbid pathogen with aromatics
苦温燥湿 dispelling dampness with bitter and warm-natured drugs
利水消肿 inducing diuresis for removing edema
清热利湿 clearing heat and promoting diuresis
滋阴补肾 nourishing yin and tonifying kidney
补气提神 tonifying qi and boosting spirit
补脾益肺 invigorating spleen for benefiting lung
理气健脾 regulating qi-flowing for streng thening spleen
疏肝泄火 soothing the liver and purging fire
降逆下气 directing qi downward
活血止痛 activating blood to relieve pain
活血化瘀 activating blood and resolving stasis
解毒消肿 removing toxicity for detumescence
行血补血 promoting and replenishing blood
补精益髓 enriching essence for benefiting marrow

散湿祛风 introducing diaphoresis and dispelling wind
温中散寒 warming spleen and stomach for dispelling cold
温经止痛 warming the meridian to relieve pain
回阳救逆 restoring yang and rescuing patient from collapse
平肝潜阳 suppressing hyperactive liver and subsiding yang
熄风止痉 extinguishing wind to arrest convulsions
滋阴潜阳 nourishing yin for suppressing hyperactive yang
潜阳熄风 subduing yang and extinguishing wind
补肾益气 tonifying the kidney and replenishing qi
养血柔肝 nourishing the blood and emolliating the liver
引火下行 conducting fire back to its origin
固崩止带 arresting leucorrhea and metrorrhagia
养心安神 nourishing the heart to tranquilize mind
芳香开窍 resuscitation with aromatics
祛瘀生新 removing blood stasis for promoting tissue regeneration
补气生血 tonify qi and engender blood
温补命门 warmly invigorating the life gate
调肝补肾 regulating the liver and supplementing the kidney
补其不足 supplementing the insufficiency
祛风散寒 dispelling wind and dispersing cold
温补脾胃 warmly invigorating spleen and stomach
温养脏腑 nourishing the viscera
敛汗固表 stopping excessive perspiration and strengthening the superficies

5. **病因病机类**

风胜则动 predominate wind causing motion
阴虚风动 stirring wind due to yin deficiency
肝阳化风 hyperactive liver yang causing wind
热极生风 extreme heat causing wind
血虚生风 blood deficiency causing wind
血燥生风 blood dryness causing wind
痰瘀生风 phlegm stasis causing wind
时行戾气 epidemic pathogen
五志过极 excess among the five minds
五志化火 five minds transforming into fire
五味偏嗜 flavor predilection
水土不服 non-acctimatization
禀赋不足 insufficiency of natural endowment
不内外因 non-endo-non-exogenous cause/non-exoendogenous pathogenic factors

病机学说 theory of pathogenesis
正邪相争 struggle between vital qi and pathogen
邪正消长 exuberance and debilitation of the healthy qi and pathogenic qi
阴阳失调 yin-yang disharmony
阴损及阳 yin deficiency involving yang
阳损及阴 yang deficiency involving yin
阴虚阳亢 hyperactivity of yang due to yin deficiency
阴阳两虚 deficiency of both yin and yang
阴阳偏盛 excess of either yin or yang
阴阳偏衰 deficiency of either yin or yang
阴盛格阳 exuberant yin repelling yang
阳盛格阴 exuberant yang repelling yin
阳损及阴 yang deficiency involving yin
虚火上炎 flaring up of deficient fire
相火妄动 hyperactivity of ministerial fire
内闭外脱 inner block causing collapse
表寒里热 superficies cold with interior heat
表虚里实 exterior deficiency and interior excess
表里俱寒 cold in both superficies and interior
表里同病 simultaneous superficies and interior/syndromes
表气不固 insecurity of exterior qi
表邪内陷 inward invasion of exterior pathogen
热邪传表 pathogenic heat passing into the interior
热结下焦 heat binding in the lower jiao/energizer
下焦湿热 dampness-heat in lower jiao/energizer
热盛伤津 syndrome of consumption of fluid due to intense heat
寒热错杂 intermingled cold and heat
上热下寒 upper heat and lower cold
寒热格拒 expulsion of cold and heat
寒极生热 extreme cold turning into heat
虚实夹杂 intermingled deficiency and excess
气不摄血 qi failing to control blood
气虚中满 flatulence caused by qi deficiency
气虚血瘀 blood stasis due to qi deficiency
气机不利 disorder of qi movement
中气下陷 middle qi collapse
寒凝气滞 qi stagnation due to cold congealing
气血失调 disorder of qi and blood

心火上炎 flaring up of heart fire
心火亢盛 exuberance of heart fire
肝气上逆 adverse rising liver qi
肝气犯胃 liver qi invading stomach
燥胜则干 predominant dryness causing withering
燥气伤肺 dry qi impairing lung
燥干清窍 dryness affecting clear orifices
热胜则肿 predominant heat causing swelling
炅则气泄 overheat causing qi leakage
五志化火 five minds transforming into fire
心阴不足 insufficiency of heart yin
心阳不振 devitalization of heart yang
心血失养 malnutrition of heart blood
心血瘀阻 stagnant blockade of heart blood
热伤神明 heat affecting spirit
痰火扰心 phlegm-fire disturbing heart
痰蒙心窍 heart spirit confused by phlegm
风热犯肺 wind-heat invading lung
风寒袭肺 wind-cold attacking lung
肺气不宣 failure of lung qi in dispersion
肺失清肃 impaired depurative descending of lung qi
肺络损伤 damage of collaterals in lung
痰浊阻肺 turbid phlegm obstructing lung
燥热伤肺 dry-heat impairing lung
金破不鸣 damaged lung not functioning normally
金实不鸣 obstructed lung not functioning normally
脾虚湿困 dampness stagnancy due to spleen deficiency
脾虚生风 spleen deficiency causing wind
脾不统血 spleen failing to manage blood
湿热蕴脾 dampness-heat stagnating in spleen
脾失健运 dysfunction of spleen in transportation
脾虚生痰 spleen deficiency generating phlegm
寒湿困脾 cold-dampness disturbing spleen
肝阳上亢 upper hyperactivity of liver yang
肝气郁结 stagnation of liver qi
肝气横逆 transverse dysfunction of liver qi
肝火上炎 liver fire flaring up
肝经风热 wind-heat of liver channel

肝经郁热 stagnated heat of liver channel
肝经湿热 dampness-heat of liver channel
肾不纳气 deficiency of kidney qi failing to control respiring qi
肾虚水泛 water diffusion due to kidney deficiency
命门火衰 decline of vital gate fire
肾精不足 insufficiency of kidney essence
胆经郁热 stagnated heat of gallbladder channel
胆郁痰扰 stagnated gallbladder qi with disturbing phlegm
胆虚气怯 insufficiency of gallbladder qi causing timidity
胃气不降 failure of stomach qi to descend
胃气上逆 adverse rising of stomach qi
胃热消谷 stomach heat accelerating digestion
胃火炽盛 exuberance of stomach fire
胃纳呆滞 anorexia
小肠虚寒 deficient cold of small intestine
小肠实热 excessive heat of small intestine
大肠虚寒 deficient cold of large intestine
大肠液亏 fluid insufficiency of large intestine
大肠热结 heat accumulation of large intestine
大肠湿热 dampness-heat of large intestine
大肠寒结 cold accumulation of large intestine
热迫大肠 heat invading large intestine
膀胱湿热 dampness-heat of bladder
热结膀胱 heat accumulation of bladder
膀胱虚寒 deficient cold of bladder
热入血室 heat invading blood chamber
热伏冲任 heat lodging in Chong and Conception Channels
冲任不调 disharmony of Chong and Conception Channels
冲任不固 unconsolidation of Chong and Conception Channels
心肺气虚 qi deficiency of heart and lung
心脾两虚 deficiency of both heart and spleen
心肝血虚 blood deficiency of heart and liver
心肝火旺 hyperactivity of heart-liver fire
心肾不交 disharmony between heart and kidney
水气凌心 water pathogen insulting heart
水寒射肺 water-cold attacking lung
心虚胆怯 timidity due to deficiency of heart qi
心胃火燔 exuberant fire of heart and stomach

肺脾两虚 deficiency of both lung and spleen
肺肾阴虚 yin deficiency of lung and kidney
肺肾气虚 qi deficiency of lung and kidney
脾胃虚弱 deficiency of spleen and stomach
脾胃阴虚 yin deficiency of spleen and stomach
脾胃虚寒 deficient cold of spleen and stomach
脾胃湿热 dampness-heat of spleen and stomach
脾肾阳虚 yang deficiency of spleen and kidney
肝肾阴虚 yin deficiency of liver and kidney
肝火犯肺 liver fire invading lung
水不涵木 water failing to nourish wood; kidney failing to nourish liver
肝气犯脾 liver qi invading spleen
肝气犯胃 liver qi invading stomach
肝郁脾虚 stagnation of liver qi and spleen deficiency
肝胆湿热 dampness-heat of liver and gallbladder
肝胆实热 excessive heat of liver and gallbladder
营卫不和 disharmony between nutrient qi and defensive qi
阳明燥热 Yangming dryness-heat
阳明腑实 Yangming fu-viscera excess
阳明虚寒 Yangming deficient cold
邪郁少阳 stagnant pathogen of Shaoyang
半表半里 half-superficies and half-interior
太阴寒湿 Taiyin cold-dampness
太阴虚寒 Taiyin deficient cold
少阴寒化 cold transformation of Shaoyin disease
少阴热化 heat transformation of Shaoyin disease
厥热胜复 alternate cold and heat
卫阳被遏 defensive yang being obstructed
热炽津伤 injury of fluid due to exuberant heat
热入心包 invasion of pericardium by heat
心营过耗 over consumption of heart nutrient
营阴损伤 nutrient qi and yin fluid being damaged
热入血分 heat invading xuefen
血分瘀热 stagnated heat in xuefen
血分热毒 heat-toxicity in xuefen
上焦湿热 dampness-heat in upper jiao/energizer
中焦湿热 dampness-heat in middle jiao/energizer
逆传心包 reversed transmission to pericardium

表邪入里 superficies pathogens involving interior
里病出表 interior disease involving superficies
阳病入阴 yang disease involving yin
阴病出阳 yin disease involving yang
上损及下 deficiency transmitted from upper body to lower body
下损及上 deficiency transmitted from lower body to upper body
气病及血 qi disease involving blood
血病及气 blood disease involving qi
脏病及腑 zang-viscera disease involving fu-viscera
腑病及脏 fu-viscera disease involving zang-viscera
卫气同病 disease involving weifen and qifen
卫营同病 disease involving weifen and yingfen
气营两燔 flaring heat in qifen and yingfen
气血两燔 flaring heat in qifen and xuefen
从阴化寒 cold transformed from yin
从阳化热 heat transformed from yang
因虚致实 excess resulted from deficiency
由实转虚 deficiency transformed from excess
实则阳明 excessive disease located in Yangming
虚则太阴 deficient disease located in Taiyin
肾气不固 non-consolidation of kidney qi
风热头痛 headache with wind-heat syndrome
肾虚不孕 nephrasthenic sterility
阳盛则热 exuberant yang generating heat
恐则气下 fear leading to qi sinking
真寒假热 true cold disease with false heat manifestation
真热假寒 true heat disease with false cold manifestation